A TIME
TO MOURN

For Bob –
In gratitude for
all those long
afternoons in Zulauf
talking Lit. crit!
Thanks for all your
support –
Becky

A TIME
TO MOURN

Rebecca Rice

NAL BOOKS
NEW AMERICAN LIBRARY

A DIVISION OF PENGUIN BOOKS USA INC., NEW YORK
PUBLISHED IN CANADA BY
PENGUIN BOOKS CANADA LIMITED, MARKHAM, ONTARIO

Emily Dickinson. Excerpts from THE COMPLETE POEMS OF EMILY DICKINSON, edited by Thomas H. Johnson, copyright 1929 by Martha Dickinson Bianchi; © renewed 1957 by Mary L. Hampson. By permission of Little, Brown and Company. Also reprinted by permission of the publishers and Trustees of Amherst College from THE POEMS OF EMILY DICKINSON, Thomas H. Johnson, ed., Cambridge, Mass.: The Belknap Press of Harvard University Press, Copyright 1951, © 1955, 1979, 1983 by the President and Fellows of Harvard College.

Excerpts from "Four Quartets" in COLLECTED POEMS (1909–1962), by T. S. Eliot, copyright 1936 by Harcourt Brace Jovanovich, Inc., copyright © 1964, 1963 by T. S. Eliot. Published by Harcourt Brace Jovanovich, Inc., New York, and Faber and Faber Limited, London. Reprinted by permission of the publishers.

Dylan Thomas. From POEMS OF DYLAN THOMAS. Copyright 1945 by the Trustees of the copyrights of Dylan Thomas, 1952 by Dylan Thomas. Reprinted by permission of New Directions Publishing Corporation and David Higham Associates, Ltd.

W. B. Yeats. Excerpt from "Sailing to Byzantium," reprinted with permission of Macmillan Publishing Company from THE POEMS OF W. B. YEATS: A NEW EDITION, edited by Richard J. Finneran. Copyright 1928 by Macmillan Publishing Company, renewed 1956 by Georgie Yeats.

NAL TRADEMARK REG. U.S. PAT OFF. AND FOREIGN COUNTRIES
REGISTERED TRADEMARK—MARCA REGISTRADA
HENCHO EN DRESDEN, TN, U.S.A.

SIGNET, SIGNET CLASSIC, MENTOR, ONYX, PLUME, MERIDIAN and NAL BOOKS are published *in the United States* by New American Library, a division of Penguin Books USA Inc., 1633 Broadway, New York, New York 10019, *in Canada* by Penguin Books Canada Limited, 2801 John Street, Markham, Ontario L3R 1B4

Rice, Rebecca.
    A time to mourn / by Rebecca Rice.
        p.   cm.
    ISBN 0-453-00717-1
    1. Widowhood—United States—Psychological aspects.   2. Rice, Rebecca.
3. Widows—United States—Biography.   I. Title.
HQ1058.5.U5R53   1990   89-39256
305.489654'0973—dc20   CIP

Designed by Nissa Knuth

First Printing, March, 1990

1 2 3 4 5 6 7 8 9

PRINTED IN THE UNITED STATES OF AMERICA

To the memory of Len
and
To Sean

Acknowledgments

I would like to thank my father, mother, and sister for bravely agreeing to appear in this book. My portraits of them are not flattering, especially in the days immediately after my husband died, when I was consumed with rage and struck out at everyone, particularly those I loved. Bereavement does not always ennoble people; some of the most bitter fights between fathers and daughters, sisters and brothers, occur in the shadows of a spouse's or parent's death. At the same time, a crisis of loss can provoke families to talk more authentically with one another. Toward the end of my mourning, I drew closer to my father, mother, and sister, a closeness that grows even as I write. I am grateful to them—especially to my father, who taught me to prize integrity and plain-speaking—for supporting my attempt to re-create my experience honestly and unsentimentally.

My friends in my writing group in Connecticut—Lesley Garis, Christine Lehner, Lilla Pennant, Mary-Ann Tirone Smith—were moved by my articles on grieving in *The New York Times* and urged me to turn them into a book. Sarah Clayton, Ippy Patterson, and Eliza Walton read the first three chapters and gave me the confidence to continue. Steven Kern generously let me use his office in the history department of Northern Illinois University. The atmosphere was perfect—the buzzing confusion of faculty, students, and secretaries provided a happy diversion from my lonely, often anguished work. I am indebted to Jan Vander Meer and

Acknowledgments

John G. Bowen for their proofreading, and my friends in Connecticut and Illinois—Rosalyn Amenta, Diane Bywaters, Susan Heller, Carolyn Perla, Nancy Webb, Jeanne Weiland, and Xie Lihong—for much moral cheerleading.

My editor, Alexia Dorszynski, urged me to revise large sections of *A Time to Mourn*. I am grateful to her for demanding my best. My agent, Anne Borchardt, read each chapter of the manuscript, matched me with a superb editor, and sent many letters of encouragement from New York to Illinois. All writers should be so blessed.

Writing this book would have been far more difficult without the unflagging support of my treasured friend, Sean Shesgreen, who shares, along with my late husband, the book's dedication. For three years, Sean acted as midwife to *A Time to Mourn*—reading each page, usually in two or three versions, offering comments and suggestions, sometimes simply urging me not to abandon it. That the book focuses upon my late husband, whom I discussed at length and of whom Sean, naturally, grew weary, is testimony to Sean's generosity of spirit. I am deeply grateful to him.

Lastly, I thank Len, my beloved late husband, whose memory never fails to inspire and cheer me. Wherever he is, I know he'd be proud.

Preface

I was 23 when I met my future husband, who was then 55.
A doctor of medicine, a doctor of philosophy, a tenured
professor in a New York university, a practicing psychiatrist, and author of three philosophy books, Len was everything that I, a would-be writer teaching high school English,
aspired to, everything that Brian, the man with whom I'd
lived for the past three years, was not. Brian, one of Len's
graduate students, who battled an eating and drinking problem as well as manic depression, had said to me, "You've
got to meet Len Feldstein," as a devout Catholic might say,
"You must go to Lourdes." If an astrologer had warned
Brian that his girl friend would run off with his professor,
he would have laughed. Len was nearly old enough to be
my grandfather.

When Brian and I rang the bell at Apartment 20C on East
End Avenue in Manhattan on the evening of March 5, 1978,
we were greeted by a thin, stooped, ashen-faced man wearing bedroom slippers and a filthy sweater with holes at the
elbows. Brian had said Len was nursing a broken heart from
a woman who had recently left him. Still, I was shocked: I
imagined genius to be muscular and prepossessing, something like Michelangelo's God descending from the whirlwind in the Sistine Chapel. Surely, this disheveled creature
could not be the man who had been analyzed
by Erich Fromm and whose work had been compared to
Whitehead's.

Len cheered up as he showed us around his small, book-lined apartment, which was pleasantly appointed with Rembrandt reproductions and various trinkets culled from his European travels. Fussing over us like a kindly uncle, he set out bowls of macadamia nuts and served us Amaretto in alabaster liqueur glasses he had brought back from Greece. I settled into the shabby, comfortable gold sofa in his living room, expecting to be treated to an informal seminar on the mind-body problem.

We discussed bodies all right, but very different ones from the kinds philosophers conjure up. For almost the entire evening Len regaled us with tales of the women he had been involved with, from the blind date with the secretary from Queens who didn't like trees, to the movie star from Sarah Lawrence who left him for the leading man in a daytime soap, to his last inamorata, a Viennese Jewish-princess photographer who insisted on taking pictures of their love-making. Len told these stories with a self-deprecating, Woody Allenish humor that made Brian and me squeal with laughter.

I don't know if I fell in love with Len that evening or the following Saturday when Len, Brian, and I walked in Carl Schurz Park by the East River and Len became so absorbed in talking about Heidegger that he accidentally stepped in dog shit, or the next week when the three of us had dinner at a West Side café and Len asked the young woman at the next table for her phone number. All I know is that I was increasingly drawn to this homely, excitable little man, who was as brilliant as Albert Einstein and as ridiculous as Alfred E. Neuman.

I left a message with Len's answering service, saying that I needed to meet with him. He thought I wanted to discuss my relationship with Brian or my trials teaching *Othello* to recalcitrant 14-year-olds at Newark Academy. He was shocked, pleased, and a little scared when I told him I was attracted to him. Not only was I the girl friend of his prize student, I was also younger than the Viennese-Jewish photographer who had just dumped him. He had sworn never to date anyone under 30 again. But for me he was willing to make an exception.

We began to see one another, first once or twice a week, then every day. We met secretly at crosstown bus stops, on the steps of the Metropolitan Museum, on the jogging trail in Central Park. We held hands in Greek coffee shops, read poetry on park benches, kissed in East Village bookshops. I had never seen the forsythia so yellow or the cherry blossoms so pink or the sunset skies streaming with so many tropical colors as I did that spring.

I confided my dream of being a writer, and Len told me about his projected seven-volume work in philosophy. In my imagination, I fashioned a life for us: I would leave Brian, and Len and I would marry and live in a cottage in the country, in Connecticut or Vermont. We would rise early, labor all day at our writing, and then come together in the evening to read Shakespeare or listen to Beethoven. We would be like Alfred Stieglitz and Georgia O'Keeffe, like Jean-Paul Sartre and Simone de Beauvoir. We would each dedicate ourselves to the other's creativity. That Len was 32 years older than I was irrelevant; we were soulmates, born in the same generation of the spirit.

We were together six and a half years. During that time, we were apart perhaps one week. We did everything together—went to concerts, plays, and museums, took weekend trips to country inns in Vermont, played chess, read the novels of Henry James, lived in Belgium and Switzerland for a year. I critiqued the manuscript of his fourth book; he edited my first novel. When Len went to the university or saw patients in New York, he phoned me twice a day. If he couldn't sleep because he was upset about failing to receive a merit increase or because he'd been gouged by a dishonest dentist, he'd wake me to discuss it. When I was depressed about my writing and convinced I would turn out like my mother, a gifted but failed artist, Len listened patiently to me for hours.

Len made me happy—happier than I had ever been in my

life. Not only because he was the kindest, funniest, brightest man I had ever met—after all, there are plenty of kind, funny, bright men, and one doesn't necessarily marry them, particularly if they are more than twice one's age—but because he loved me, gave himself to me unconditionally.

The kind of love we shared—a boundaryless, symbiotic tie where Len dissolved into me and I into him, and there was no real distinction between us—might have suffocated some women.

It healed me.

To an outsider, my childhood would have looked like a scene from a Ralph Lauren ad. I came from a well-to-do, upper-middle-class family in western Massachusetts. My father owned a thriving threads mill founded two generations ago. We lived in a rambling eighteen-room home on six acres and belonged to the local country club. My sister and I were given music lessons, tennis lessons, skiing lessons, and riding lessons. We were sent to private schools—to Berkshire Country Day and Miss Hall's. In summer, we vacationed at my maternal grandparents' cottage on an island in Georgian Bay. In winter, we skied in Utah.

But my parents were unhappy with one another, and their unhappiness spread like radon gas through our pretty life until all of us were sick. When I was seven, my mother accused my father of having an affair. He denied it. She did not believe him. When he was at work, she talked on the phone for hours to her Christian Science practitioners, praying to correct his evil behavior. When she hung up, she rifled my father's desk looking for canceled checks, hotel receipts—anything to confirm her raging suspicions.

When I was 12, my father became involved with my mother's Christian Science practitioner. My mother had what I now recognize as a nervous breakdown. She retreated to her bed for months, getting up only to stuff herself with ice cream and cereal. Within a year, she had gained 40 pounds. I can remember coming into her room after school. All the blinds would be pulled tight, and she would be huddled beneath mountains of blankets with black blinders across her eyes and a pyramid of used tissues beside her. Often she would pay me a dollar to rub her back. I would knead the moist, rippling flesh sometimes for an hour. And she would sigh, over and over, like someone who was dying.

I retreated from her, and from my father and sister and from school. I grew to despise my family and my origins; I rebelled against everything. Like my mother, I began to stuff myself with food. I gained 30 pounds. I also took drugs—marijuana, LSD, and phenobarbital. I became promiscuous. I slept with a ski instructor who dropped acid regularly, with an electric guitarist in a rock band who was always stoned on pot, with a speed freak who once went after his mother with a gun, with a guy named Menace who rode in a motorcycle gang and took me to a gang rape.

By the time I met Brian, I had moved away from home, stopped sleeping around and taking drugs, and was doing passably well at Bard College, then at Sarah Lawrence College. (I did not have the grades to get into Williams, where my father and grandfather had gone.) After graduating from Sarah Lawrence, I won a Woodrow Wilson Fellowship to pursue graduate work at Fairleigh-Dickinson University and got a job teaching English at Newark Academy. I didn't particularly want to be a teacher; I wanted to be a writer, but I had no confidence in my talent. I continued to eat compulsively and was overweight. I was still full of rage at my mother and father. When I looked into the mirror, I wanted to smash what I saw.

Enter Len. Who was brilliant, accomplished, and successful, but also neurotic and needy, like me. Well past the middle of his life, Len had been married and divorced, had dated countless women, but had never found his soulmate. He used to tell me I was the girl he had dreamed about when he was five years old and had been searching for all his life. Having lived so long without love, Len could give it all the more freely. His love made me feel special and treasured in a way I'd never felt before. Slowly, this love began to work like an antibiotic upon me, destroying the infection of my rage at my mother and father, helping me to heal myself.

Perhaps because of our great age difference, we escaped the ordinary tensions that afflict most couples. We were neither jealous of nor competitive with one another. We did not engage in power struggles; we did not fight over money or sex or how we would spend our vacations or who would clean the bathroom. Paradoxically, the only thing we struggled over was our age difference. I often felt that strangers and even acquaintances did not accept us because Len was too old or I was too young. Len would say I was paranoid, or get angry because I cared so much about other people's opinions.

When a woman marries a much older man, she knows her widow's weeds menace beneath her bridal veil. Although Len hated talking about death, he would try to assuage my fears by joking about what I would do after he "got dead." He couldn't bear the idea of my loving another man, but if it had to be, he would prefer to select his successor. Len used to speculate that it would be better if he died when I was in my 30s or 40s because then I'd still be pretty enough to land a second husband. But if he were to live to be 90, as he assured me he would, then maybe I'd be an established writer and it wouldn't matter.

These discussions would usually take place at night driving back to Connecticut from New York. As we sped up the long, unlit stretches of Highway 684, we would spin out my fantasy widowhood. I would sell the house in Connecticut, move to Boston, Washington, or even London. The savings and cars were in my name and Len would leave me his pension, so I would not be destitute. It would be better if I could count on a little income from a job or from my writing. On this point we were both vague; my first novel had been rejected, and I was growing increasingly discontent with my latest job as a staff writer in the corporate communications department of a multinational insurance company.

I was not prepared for Len's death. Not when I married him, not when his brain cancer was diagnosed, not even when the neurologist told me in hushed tones that I ought to think about putting Len in a nursing home because he would live for only two or three months.

"After the first death," the poet Dylan Thomas wrote, "there is no other." Len's death was my first death. Oh, I had known others—all four of my grandparents had died of old age, and a friend's mother had been killed in a plane crash. But these deaths were like cork bullets from toy guns. I heard the popping sound they made, even saw them graze a tree or startle a dog, but they hardly seemed dangerous. They did not alarm, hurt, or even astonish me; sometimes, they went off so quietly I barely noticed them.

It is well known among those in the helping professions that the death of a spouse is the most stressful event a human being can experience—more stressful than birth or divorce or moving or losing a job. For a full five years after her husband's death, the widow runs a high risk of committing suicide. And if the bereaved doesn't actually throw herself on the funeral pyre of her beloved, her grief may weaken her immune system, making her more susceptible to illness and disease. Young widows are not necessarily better off than older ones; widows under the age of 45 whose husbands die suddenly are among those considered at greatest risk.

Four months after Len's death, I read an article about the double suicides of Cynthia and Arthur Koestler. Koestler, 77, had been suffering from leukemia and Parkinson's disease. Since he was Vice-president of the Voluntary Euthanasia Society, Arthur Koestler's decision to end his life was not surprising. His wife's suicide was more troubling. Cynthia Koestler, 55 and in good health, "was not known to have any grave ailment." A friend described her marriage to her older husband as "almost impossibly close." In her suicide note, she explained: "I cannot live without Arthur, despite certain inner resources."

My hands were sweaty and trembling when I finished the article. Like Cynthia Koestler, I was decades younger than an older and more gifted husband. Like her, I had been nurtured by my husband's vivid, larger-than-life presence and had achieved little on my own account. Like Cynthia Koestler, I had been so close to my husband that I hardly knew where he ended and I began. I too possessed "certain inner resources," but I did not know if they would sustain me. Like this pathetic woman, I sometimes imagined that suicide would be preferable to enduring the bleak hours of widowhood.

In a desperate moment, I might have taken a lethal dose of barbiturates, as Cynthia Koestler had. Instead, I began the arduous, often manic, work of making a life without Len. I began to see my psychotherapist twice a week. I advertised in my local newspaper for a roommate. I prepared my first tax return. I quit my job. I outlined this book. I traveled to Europe, my first trip abroad without Len. I returned to America and packed up my dog, books, files, and computer and moved halfway across the country. In one year I took more risks than I had taken in my entire life. At times, my perambulations felt reckless, and I wished I could have heeded the sensible counsel that books like *Widow* and *Beginnings* offer: "Do not make any major changes for a year. Take your time." But I was fighting for nothing less than survival. I was also discovering something I never knew about myself: I possessed not only abundant inner resources, but a fierce will to live. I would come through.

Although I have changed the names of some of the people who appear in this book to protect their privacy, every event I recount is true. Nothing has been fictionalized, nothing invented. When I write about vacationing in England seven months after Len's death and waking one morning with my arms around a strange man and noticing the tiny sapphires in my wedding ring glinting like dead bird's eyes against the hairless skin of this man's back, I am not fashioning some literary motif. I am narrating what happened, as honestly as I can. When I explain that I also felt, sleeping with this stranger whom I'd met on an Oxford street, not only guilt but excitement and a lust for love-making unlike anything I'd ever known, my aim is not to shock but to communicate grief's complexity.

Had Cynthia Koestler lived, she would have discovered that mourning, like every other human experience, has its seasons: it is born, grows, sometimes to monstrous proportions, and eventually dies. In the full noonday sun of grief, which for me was about three months after my husband died, I imagined it would never change. Remembering anything about Len, even that he liked ladyfinger cookies, would make me weep. I would drive ten miles out of my way to avoid going past the cemetery where he was buried. Meeting someone casually who didn't know he had died and having to answer the breezy question, "Where are you keeping your husband these days?" was like being punched in the stomach. For almost a year I did not enter a favorite pastry shop in Ridgefield because I was afraid that the owner, who might not have read the obituary, would inquire about Len.

This kind of pain does pass. Time, which takes everything we treasure, takes our grief, too. Now, six years later, I can observe the hands of a clock at 4:15 in the afternoon and not think, *This was the hour of Len's death.* I can wake up on a warm, redolent April day, and my brain will not reflexively record that this was the month when Len's seizures began. I can tell anecdotes about Len to people who never knew him and not feel angry they don't want to hear more. I can follow the Iran-contra hearings on TV and think, not with sadness but with delight, *Len would be watching gavel to gavel.*

"We die with the dying," wrote T. S. Eliot. "See, they depart, and we go with them./ We are born with the dead:/ See, they return, and bring us with them." In permitting myself to let go of my grief, as Len let go of his life, a resurrection begins. Len returns. Not as a man I might recognize but as the mystery I can never know. The mystery no longer of himself alone, which was and is remarkable enough, but of the universe—of all the dead, all the living, and all the unborn. And I return to myself. Not to the one I was before my grieving, but to a wholly other person. To one who has sat, unwillingly, at death's feet and learned how to fear life a little less and embrace the world a little more, learned how to dance as well as how to mourn.

This is the Hour of Lead
Remembered, if outlived,
As Freezing persons, recollect the Snow—
First—Chill—then Stupor—then the letting go—

—Emily Dickinson

December 27, 1984

"He'll probably go tonight," the visiting nurse whispers to me in the kitchen. "His temperature is 104. His pulse is very fast. He can't last much longer."

Vera Dawson wraps her dark, fleshy hand around mine. I begin to cry, and she draws me close in her competent, sturdy embrace. From the bridge of her arm, I look at the window for the first time that day. It is beginning to snow, very lightly, and the darkness is swallowing, very slowly, the last white flashes of afternoon light. The bare branches on the maple tree are skeletal in the oncoming blueness.

"What should I do when it happens?" I ask, counting out my words as I had once counted out Len's anti-seizure pills.

I am scared.

More scared than I had been last April when a friend called me in New York to say that Len had blacked out for 10 seconds on the phone and that I should take the train to Connecticut immediately. More scared than when the doctors led me into the windowless room in the hospital and explained that there was a tumor the size of a lemon in the left frontal lobe of my husband's brain and that, with radiation and medication, he might live two to five years. More scared than on that brilliant fall afternoon when Len and I were walking on a country road in North Salem and Len turned to tell me something and I saw his eyes rolling around in his head like marbles and his knees began to buckle and he tumbled to the ground.

3

Here is death. Which I've tried to prepare for during these nine months. Which I've imagined while waiting for the results of arteriograms, CAT scans, NMR scans, and the five-hour craniotomy. Which has hidden behind the pictures in the magazines I've leafed through in doctors' offices. Death, which is as close to me now as Vera Dawson's wedding band, as the coffee-stained cups in the sink. And yet remote as the darkening sky from which the snow keeps falling and falling.

Vera Dawson and I sit down on the couch in the living room. She gives me her felt-tip pen and a Patient Information Report, which I turn over to its clean side and upon which I write out, in large block letters, the name and number of the doctor I should call to sign the death certificate and the funeral home I should contact afterward to take the body away.

"They're pretty good at that Georgetown Funeral Home," she reassures me. "Their prices aren't bad, and they don't try to rook you. Just make sure you get everything in writing first."

I have heard about crooked funeral directors and their conniving attempts to get you to buy, in the midst of your grief, the most expensive casket, with a velvet interior and ornate gold handles. *They aren't going to use their slimy tactics on me,* I think angrily.

Outside, it is getting darker and the snow is beginning to cover the brown rings around the trees. The snow is heavier now, and it makes everything very still. I can no longer hear the steady tock, tock of the icicles dripping into the mud trough beneath the window. Vera's face grows smaller in the room, and suddenly I feel unutterably alone and my mouth is suffocating with dryness, like the dryness of an old Christmas tree waiting in the trash to be taken away.

"I'm really not supposed to," Vera Dawson says, "but I want to give you my home phone number just in case you need to call me."

I hug her and try not to cry again.

"There, there," she soothes. "Nothing anyone can do for him now. Why don't you go back into that room and sit by him and hold his hand and talk to him some. He's pretty far along, but I always say, as long as the good Lord sees fit to keep the breath in their bones, they still kind of know what's going on.

"You go ahead while I finish up these forms—no matter what you do, they gotta have their forms—and I'll check with you before I go."

I creep, a little guiltily, into the downstairs bedroom to begin the long vigil. How little time I've spent in this room over the last few weeks, when Len's condition began to worsen and it was harder and harder for him to get out of bed and he was incontinent and the bedsores were multiplying, like chicken pox, across his body. I had found it agonizing to sit beside his bed, his breath rasping and heavy, his eyes either closed or partially open and staring past me, at some spot of light on a far wall. I couldn't bear to look into that face, which was no longer the spirited, mobile-featured face of my husband who had argued about modern art, who had clapped and danced to Beethoven's Ninth Symphony; now it was hollowed, narrowed, and half eaten away by death, like a relic of a saint preserved, for centuries, in the crypt of a medieval cathedral.

And so it happened that I gave over most of my dying husband's care to Gail, a young woman from New Zealand whom I had hired two months ago to live with us and help me look after Len. In the beginning, she took care of him only while I worked at my job in New York three days a week. But in these last weeks she took over more and more of the daily nursing. It was Gail, not me, who passed in and out of that room a dozen or more times a day, Gail who washed him, dressed him, sat him on the commode, fed him, and when he could no longer eat, held the child's cup to his trembling lips so he could suck the few sips of apple juice or bouillon. Over the last few days, his body had gotten so heavy and stiff that she could no longer lift him herself. She called me in to help. Together we positioned him on the commode or carried him, she with her elbows linked under his shoulders, I with his legs and arms, into the living room when his children and friends came to visit. But afterward, pleading work that needed to be done or phone calls that must be made, I retreated upstairs to my study to read novels. In the last week I had finished *The Prime of Miss Jean Brodie* and *The Voyage Out.*

God knows I felt guilty, although my therapist, Dr. Heller, whom I had started seeing six months ago when I realized I couldn't cope with Len's illness, explained that my reaction was not unusual. After all, Len was leaving me, she said. Not willingly or willfully—but the heart didn't make these kinds of intellectual distinctions. The man who had loved me for the past six years, who had married me and promised to share his life with me, was abandoning me. I would be superhuman if I didn't feel betrayed. Because the relationship had been so close, I was losing more than a husband. I was losing my best friend, my mentor, my family. It must have felt, she said, as if I were being robbed of huge chunks of myself. Withdrawing from him was my way of preparing for his death, of beginning the long process of letting go. It didn't mean that I was a bad person. Or that I didn't love him.

Dr. Heller's words seemed eminently sensible in her soundproof office on West 84th Street among her stick-figured sculptures and modular bookcases, but when I returned late at night to Connecticut and stuck my head in Len's room only to see whether he was still breathing and then snuck away, I despised myself. If only I could have wheeled a cot into his room and slept beside him, as his mother had done when he was seven and gravely ill with a mastoid infection. If only I might have read to him—poetry or the Bible or even a novel—as I had done only a few months ago when he was in the hospital.

Last night, in an act of penance, I forced myself to sit with him in bed while I watched TV. It was a special about van Gogh, about his years in Arles before he'd gone mad. Len had loved this brilliant, troubled artist; in Amsterdam, we had spent an entire afternoon at the van Gogh museum, moved by the poverty-stricken peasants in *The Potato Eaters,* by the sad, lost inhabitants of *Night Cafe.* Last year for Valentine's Day, Len had given me a two-volume, gift-boxed edition of Vincent's letters to his brother, Theo. If anyone could move Len back into consciousness, this artist, who had felt suffering and joy so acutely, could. With my arm around Len, I tried to talk to him about the feverish swirls of sunflowers and gnarled trees, about the stars and crows that sizzled across the small Sony screen. But Len's comatose body continued to lie inert against me, and his breathing, so rattling and uneven, terrified me. After 20 minutes, I turned the TV off and flew up to bed.

This morning I vowed to spend more time with him. But it was Gail who ended up holding him for nearly two hours while I lay upstairs on the love seat in my study talking on the phone to Dr. Heller about how angry I was that I had to stay home from work, how I just wanted it to be over.

I'll make it up to him now, I vow as I move the wheelchair out of the hallway and tiptoe across the threshold of the room. I shall pull up the faded armchair close to the bed, and I shall sit by his side and hold his hand and let him know that I love him. I shall wait with him for the whole night and into the morning, and he will leave this earth, this last red light of Christmas and the winter solstice, with me, loyal and loving, beside him. This, I know, is what he hopes for. This is why I have kept him, against the doctors' recommendations, at home until the end.

"I want you with me when I die, Beck," Len said to me once before we were married as we walked along a beach on Martha's Vineyard. We rented a house that summer in Gay Head, and every afternoon, after we spent the morning writing, we walked to Zach's Cliffs, where nude sunbathers dived into the waves like sea nymphs. It was fine and windy, that day, with the clouds massed above us like horses and

7

the waves high and white-capped and crashing against the rocks near the shore. The hard sand beneath our feet wriggled with living things—kelp and mussels and translucent beetles that burrowed in and out of bubbling tunnels. As the tide took away our footprints, we talked of the patterns of shells and the fissures in the clay cliffs and the lines in our hands. Len said that humans and the teeming world around us could not have been created randomly, that there was, though we might never understand him or her or it, a God. As we rested on the warm sand and watched the gulls diving for fish, Len blurted out that he wanted me with him when he died. I remember thinking, yes, this would come to pass, even though we had known each other only four months, even though we hardly knew whether we'd last beyond the summer. For to tell another human being that you want her to share your last moments on the earth, to wait with you as you begin your last journey, creates a blood-bond more intimate than sex, more indissoluble than marriage.

These final hours of December 27, 1984, would be my last chance to ride the long ebb and flow between that day six years ago and this one, my last chance to make of Len's death something sacred and profound. I would not fail him.

But when I draw close to the bed, I know immediately something has changed. Len's body has ceased its feverish shaking. A strange stillness suffuses the room. He is turned on his side away from me, and his mouth is slightly open as if he were about to speak. His eyes are also open and very clear, clearer than I have ever seen them during these long months of sickness. As I place my hands upon his narrow shoulders, I hear one last, very quiet, almost grateful sigh, like a sigh from someone who is no longer exhausted but just a little tired. Then silence. And the snow outside the window. And the dark room. And my own breathing, now the loudest sound in the room.

The next few hours pass in a strange twilight, at once ordinary in the way that all human time, filled with phone calls and plans, is ordinary, and yet so disturbing that there are moments when I fear my entire body—head, heart, nerves, veins—will break the sound barrier with its terror.

Vera Dawson confirms what I already know: Len is dead.

I go upstairs to tell Gail, who has a cold and has been sleeping for most of the afternoon. In her red flannel night-shirt she runs downstairs barefoot and rushes into the room. She cries uncontrollably when she sees him. She sits on the bed and strokes Len's forehead and, still sobbing, says how peaceful he looks, how much more peaceful than just a few hours ago. Then she takes him in her arms and holds him and weeps into his chest. I am a little taken aback by her reaction: I didn't know she cared so much. As I watch her help Vera prop him up against the pillows and fold his hands neatly upon his chest, I wonder how it is that I, who have known him when he was well and have laughed, argued, and made love to him, I wonder how it is that I can feel nothing.

"I know you'll want to be alone with him now," Vera whispers, "so we'll just leave you two, and I'll go and call the doctor."

Gail closes the door softly behind her.

I stand in the center of the room, tentative before this inert form stretched out on the bed. Vera has tucked a rolled towel under Len's chin so that his mouth will not continue to gape open. I remove it. Then, when I see how the mouth jerks open again, I put it back.

I have only once seen a corpse, when a friend took me into the dissecting room of his anatomy class. It was ten minutes before class, and the students were gathering in twos about lumpy tables covered with white sheets. Toes and fingers stuck out from the sheets, and some of the toes were ringed with copper tags. My friend rolled back the sheet of his "specimen," and I saw a grayish, slightly shiny body, now recognizable as a human body, as a man in his early 50s with a bloated face and heavy jaw and an eye that protruded starkly from his jowly face. My friend told me how the other med students named their "people" Hilda or Jerome, after their most hated professors. He said they often got rowdy and played catch with body parts—ears, fingers, toes, eyes. I rushed out the door. For weeks afterward I met that protruding eye in my dreams, and I felt shamed and frightened, as if I had watched a man being raped.

But this dead body, I think with horror as I creep toward the bed, does not belong to some stranger who has lain, with no living relatives, in a plastic body bag in a morgue. This dead body belongs to Len, my husband who held me when I woke up with nightmares about the dissecting room. These hands, now heavy as hammers, once cupped my breasts. These fingers, now rigid as screwdrivers, once played upon my scapula. This tongue circled the tiny tip of my clitoris and made it hard and full. This body, now stiff with rigor mortis, once arched up and down against mine, harder and harder, until the living eyes glittered, faster and faster, until the mouth trembled and the skin shook, until Len cried a hoarse, "Yes," and heaved down upon me like a cliff of sand falling into the ocean.

I sit on the edge of the bed and take Len's narrow shoulders in my arms. I hug him and am startled when his shoulders feel even narrower than I remember. His upper body was always slight and underdeveloped as befitted an intellectual, but his shoulders have never felt this bony, his whole torso so frail I can fold it like a pillowcase in my hands. Has it been so long since I've hugged him that I haven't noticed how frail he'd grown during the illness? I hold him tighter and lace my ten fingers around his cold back.

"Lennie," I whisper.

No response. Just a limp, skinny flapping of limbs. He is like an old Raggedy Ann doll in my arms. A Raggedy Ann doll whose stuffing has come out and whose eyes have popped out of their sockets, whose owner has grown up and gone away.

Then suddenly I feel as if I have ripped the stuffing out of the doll and twisted the eyes from their sockets, as if I have killed him. Had I cared for him more, his face would be full of color again, his eyes motile and shining, his arms and shoulders no longer narrow and bony but strong and muscular because they would be embracing me.

I start to cry, a limp little whimper that catches in my throat.

No, I tell myself. It isn't your fault. He had cancer. Brain cancer. A malignant tumor. An astrocytoma. The cells were multiplying like weeds in his skull. First in the left frontal lobe. Then in the right. Multiplying faster and faster until the weeds had choked out all the flowers, all the shrubbery, all the walkways, up toward the door and into the door and through the kitchen and living room until the entire house began to crumble and weeds sprouted through the floorboards. Until all words, thoughts, feelings, and touch succumbed to the riotous growth of decay. Until there was only this. A dead body. A house from which the owners have moved away. A garden from which the gardener has fled.

I kneel down and take the heavy hands and place them on my head. I close my eyes tightly and try to pray—"Our Father, which art in heaven, Hallowed be thy name." The Lord's Prayer, which I whispered to Len only a week ago in this very room. Which we recited before the operation in Room 705 in Lenox Hill Hospital, while 82-year-old Herbie, dying from cancer of the colon, moaned on the other side of the green curtain. Which we said after the operation in the TV room of the neurology ward while the off-duty nurses watched "The Guiding Light." Which Len said at four o'clock in the morning with one of the black orderlies in the intensive care unit, their voices drowned in the clanking of respirators and cries of the dying.

"For thine is the kingdom, and the power, and the glory, forever. Amen," Len had loved this last part, and when he had come to the word "glory," he had drawn out the "o" until it sounded like "awe" and the word expanded like a trumpet in his mouth: "glawe-awe-awe-ry."

I place my own hands over his and press them down

harder upon my head. But it is no good. I feel only the gravity of my own tendons straining against my skull. I feel only the inertness of bloodless flesh beginning its swift metamorphosis into bone.

I rise heavily to my feet and stumble out of the room.

"It will be at least an hour before the doctor comes," I hear Vera say as I slump down on the couch. "The snow is coming down pretty heavy, and he's down in Stamford finishing rounds. He wanted directions here, but I told him there was no way I could give them to him with all those turns and windy roads. I said you'd call back in 15 minutes.

"I'll stay with you until he comes, and then I really have to get home. My kids'll be wanting their dinner." She pats me on the head as if I am a sick child.

I should tell her that she doesn't have to stay, that Gail is here and I won't be alone, but I don't have the energy.

"Would you like some coffee, Bicky?" It is Gail's cheery voice calling from the kitchen. With her broad New Zealand accent, my name always comes out sounding like "Bicky," instead of "Becky." "Len" became "Linn." Since she arrived in October her funny pronunciations and expressions have provided much entertainment for Len and me—a sweater was a "jumper," a blanket a "rug." In the evening, when she would step out to one of the local bars, she said she was getting "all tarted up."

"That would be lovely," I say. *Luvlee* is one of her expressions. I wish I could ask her to recite every funny word we ever laughed at. I feel those months vanishing like the evergreen branches outside being consumed by the snow.

"Do you want me to call the funeral home?" Vera asks.

"Oh, yes. But well, no. Not yet."

"You shouldn't wait too long, you know," she warns. "They get to looking pretty bad. With the rigor mortis and all. I don't think he'd want you to see him like that."

"You're probably right," I agree, knowing that Len would be appalled to have me hovering about his corpse, remembering how he always quoted Spinoza: "The wise man thinks on life, not on death."

"But I just can't bear the idea of having them take him away. Not yet. I think I'd like to keep him through the night and then maybe I could call the funeral home in the morning? It wouldn't matter to them, would it?"

"Makes no difference. You do whatever you need to do." Her voice is gentle, infinitely soothing.

"In New Zealand, the Maori keep the bodies of their dead for 48 hours before they bury them," Gail ventures. "All the family gathers around a big fire and they pray to the spirits of their ancestors and they sing songs . . ."

"Well, that's all very fine," Vera says, "but you probably ought to wash the body if you're going do that. The smell can get pretty bad."

"Gail and I can do that, can't we?" I have images of Mary and Martha washing the body of Jesus before they laid him in the tomb.

"No law against it," Vera says.

"If that's what you want, Bicky."

Gail is nodding, but her voice is tentative. I remember that I am only paying her $125 a week and that it isn't fair, after she washed Len when he was alive, to ask her to wash him now that he is dead.

"You don't have to decide anything now," Vera says. "Why don't you see how you feel after the doctor comes?"

I nod and realize that, from now on, I will have to take every moment one step at a time. Not even every day one step at a time, which was the way it had been during the illness, when I never knew if Len would live beyond the next week or the next month. Or if tomorrow there would be some new and unforeseen debilitation, such as the incontinence.

During the illness, when I asked Len a question and a long pause followed as he tried to answer and he stared at me with his mouth slightly open and, after an eternal silence, stammered only, "B-e-c-k-y," I would think: It can never get any worse than this—Len's prodigious intellect reduced to rubble and both of us powerless to rebuild it. "Cruel cerebration mocking human imagination," as he put it in a poem he wrote in the hospital before the craniotomy. And in the months after the operation, the continuing "fogginess," as he called it, which robbed him of such rote skills as driving a car or writing his own name. But the deterioration of his mind seemed minor in comparison with the deterioration of his body. There was the paralysis of his right side, the loss of sphincter muscle control, and finally, his inability to swallow solid food—each new trial pushing our limits of endurance, each new harbinger of death more grisly than the last.

And now, here is death, in which there is no echo of Len, in which there are only macabre rituals. The rotting flesh that must be washed like spoiled cantaloupe. The nightwatch beside the rigid body that will continue its journey into the underworld.

I can only bear it, I know, if I concentrate, as if I were fording river rapids, on each step, one foot inching slowly ahead of the other, my knees pressing against the current. If I imagine what it will be like when I reach the giant rock in the middle of the river or what I will feel as I draw close to the overhanging branches along the shore, I know I will lose the ground I fight for, my thighs twisting away from me until, all at once, I am swept in a gush of white water hurling downriver.

"Do you want me to call Judi and Mark, Bicky?"

"No, no, I should call them myself. They'd want to hear it from me, I think."

I settle into the folding beach chair beside the telephone in the kitchen. First Judi, Len's daughter, just a year younger than I. She takes the news matter-of-factly. She says she can't make the drive from New Jersey to Connecticut tonight because Steven, her husband, is working late. There is no need, I tell her. In the morning I'll let her know about the funeral arrangements. Then I ask her to call her Aunt

Anne, Len's sister, with whom he had barely spoken for the last seven years.

Before we hang up, Judi asks, in a faint, little-girl voice, if he went peacefully. I assure her he did. She says she will say a Baha'i prayer for him.

I am not able to reach Mark, Len's 26-year-old son. He works at a home for delinquent boys and is off that evening. I might reach him at his mother's, but somehow I just can't face talking with Vivian, Len's ex-wife, whom I've never met. I leave a message for Mark to call me as soon as possible.

Then I call my friend Susan, first in Connecticut, then in her office in New York.

"This is Dr. Susan Simon, speaking to you on tape. I can't get to the phone right now, but if you'll kindly leave your name, number, and the time of your call . . ." Her voice is even, professional, clinically concerned. A psychotherapist, she is perhaps, at that moment, listening to some tale of impotence or adultery. I sigh as I wait for the tone. This is Thursday. She often doesn't finish until nine in the evening. I can't ask her to drive up tonight to stay with me. And I can't utter those strange words, "Len is dead," into an answering machine. I end up leaving a vague message, asking her to call when she gets a chance.

I wait for the dial tone, then call Anna, who lives in New Haven. I lean back in the chair gratefully when I hear her voice. In the background, her two-month-old baby, Clare, is crying.

"What's wrong, Becka?" she says, sensing the tension in my voice. "Is Lennie much worse?"

When I tell her, she weeps.

"Oh, Becka, Becka, how can he be gone?" she sobs. Anna, one of Len's prize students, became friends with both of us over the last few years. She adored Len and had always been a little in love with him. While that created awkwardness between us before the illness, it brought us closer over

15

these last months. To know that she loved him somehow made me feel less isolated.

We talk for a while. I tell her how wonderful Vera Dawson has been. "Thank God it happened while she was there," Anna says fervently. Then the baby begins to cry, and Anna says she has to go but she and Robert will come to Redding tomorrow morning. She tells me to get some rest, and that she loves me.

The receiver is warm in my hands, but there is one more call to make—the Parinis, Len's oldest and closest friends, who live in Bennington, Vermont. They drove down for Christmas only two days ago. It is unlikely they will want to turn around and make the three-hour trip through the snowstorm tonight. Still, when I hear Phil's deep, warm "hello," I hope against hope.

Phil calls Pam to the phone, and her cheery, resolute voice calms me. They confer for a moment. Pam says they'll leave now and will be there by nine. More conferring. An inexplicable scratching on the line, and Pam says Phil is worried about the snow. Do I mind very much if they don't leave until the morning?

"N-n-no, no," I falter.

There is one person who will come day or night, through rain or snow if I ask him, and that is my father, who lives in Massachusetts. Quickly, I dial "1" and then the "413" area code. Then I jab my index finger on the receiver button. I can't face him. The blustering. The bravado. The unsentimental mien of the businessman, the Dale Carnegie teacher, the inveterate jogger and tennis player, who approaches death as if it were failing stock, something to be sold off as soon as possible and then dismissed. The barely concealed relief he would feel now that Len, "the old man," as my grandmother used to call him, is gone and I, his younger daughter whom he adores, can stop playing nurse and get on with my life.

I'll have to let my father know sometime. He'll be furious

if he thinks he is the last to get the news. I'll call him in a few hours, when I am more composed.

Vera Dawson says she can't wait any longer for the doctor. She hugs Gail and me. I tell her she's a saint.

"Just doing my job. Can't do any more than that, can we?"

It is dark as Vera turns her Chevette around in the driveway. The snow is coming down so hard it immediately fills in the furrows dug by her tires. I can no longer make out the yellow searchlight on my neighbor's house a few hundred yards away. My own porch light, which reflects the slivers of swirling snow, shines faint and watery, like a candle in a mine.

Dr. Goodwin, filling in for Dr. Lesser, is an hour late.

"Your directions were way off," he says petulantly as he shakes his woolen ski cap out in the kitchen, scattering tiny pellets of ice everywhere like gunfire. One grazes my bare forearm. "You told me three and a half miles from Route 102 in Branchville, and it was only two and a half miles. I must have wandered around on these back roads for more than forty-five minutes. How long have you lived here anyway?"

I am taken aback by the question, but answer it nonetheless. "Um, a little over three years."

"Well, you ought to know by now that it's not three and a half miles from 102.

"Where's the body?" he barks.

I lead him into the hallway and point, then retreat to the living room. I shudder at the thought of him resting his head against Len's chest or rolling up an eyelid and shining his doctor's flashlight into the motionless pupil.

After five minutes, his squat, suede-coated form reappears.

"How long has he been dead?"

I look anxiously at Gail. I'm sure it was after 3:00, because that was when Vera had come. And I know it was after 4:00, because the room was almost dark. But whether it was 4:15 or 4:30 or 4:45 I couldn't have said. How could I have been so careless not to look at a clock? The time of one's birth is always recorded. Is the time of death not equally important? I scold myself and reflect that this is just one more way I have failed Len.

"It happened about 4:30, Bicky, because I remember looking at the clock by my bed when you came up."

Dr. Goodwin scribbles the information on a form attached to a clipboard.

"How old was he?"

"Sixty-two. He had just turned 62," I answer quickly, then realize how irrelevant that phrase "just turned" is now that Len is dead. And the use, I think abstractedly, of the past perfect tense, "had turned," the use for the rest of my life of "was—how old was he?" rather than "is—how old is he?" How will I accustom myself to these changes, changes that are, in one sense, relentlessly simple in the way that a syllogism is simple: Len was; Len is no longer; Len will not be again—yet so profound as to alter my identity for as long as I live? I, who was Len's wife and am now his widow, who must find a way to be tomorrow and tomorrow even though half of me is over, half of me "was" and will never be again.

"Occupation?"

"Ah, he was a philosophy professor at Fordham. Oh, and also a doctor."

"You mean he had a Ph.D.," he corrects me.

"No. He had an M.D. and a Ph.D."

"What kind of doctor was he?" Dr. Goodwin's tone shifts from one of busy contempt to mild curiosity. It is all very well to palpitate the corpses of ordinary mortals, but when the deceased is an M.D., a member of a brotherhood of gods, it is a different matter. A doctor has died. For doctors, who fancy themselves guardians of life and death, the statement is a kind of medical impossibility, like a man with four intestines.

"A psychiatrist."

"Oh." Dr. Goodwin looks relieved. Psychiatrists, who never took blood or did EKGs, weren't really doctors. The facade of professional immunity snaps back.

"Diagnosis?"

"Brain cancer. Astrocytoma, grade two." I have picked up a smattering of medical jargon during the nine months of Len's illness, and I hurl it back at the doctor. Suddenly I find myself getting furious at Goodwin and Cohen and Rosen and Jackson and all the other doctors I have dealt with, pompous know-it-alls who assured me Len would live and yet couldn't, in the end, save him.

"You know something," I blurt out as Goodwin scribbles away at his clipboard, "if my husband hadn't gone to you people, maybe he'd still be alive today."

"And what evidence do you have for that?"

"The radiation treatments probably increased the tumor's growth instead of retarding it!" I yell. "He was worse after the treatments than before!"

"And if he'd never had them," Goodwin barks, "he would have been dead six months ago."

In the dimly lit room, we argue about dosages of radiation and refractory tumors, about whether the craniotomy was necessary. He infuriates me, this "healer" who has about as much compassion as a Nazi concentration camp guard, this arrogant fool who argues, so cogently, the case for modern medicine when the proof of its failure, Len's disease-ridden corpse, lies in the next room.

The argument fizzles when Dr. Goodwin reminds me, as the neurologist had explained five months ago, that there was a 60 percent chance that a low-grade astrocytoma could advance to a higher grade and that if this happened, nothing could be done. I know my argument is untenable. Len had great faith in his doctors. At the time, the course we had chosen seemed right. Whether he'd still be alive if we abandoned modern medicine and pumped him with Laetrile or put him on an herbal diet or taken him to Lourdes and prayed for a miracle was a question no one could answer.

When Dr. Goodwin leaves, Gail and I open a cheap Yugoslavian wine and sit in the living room drinking. The wine feels cool and soothing as it sloshes down my throat. Gulping it, I understand the Irish Catholic custom of getting drunk at wakes. Death, which mocks all human enterprise, is too gruesome to be faced directly. One needs to turn away, to numb the mind, to envelop oneself in the haze of alcoholic oblivion. I pour us another round, and Gail and I talk about everything except what has happened, about the year Len and I went to Europe and where we traveled and what we liked best. Bruges, I tell her, with its canals and tree-lined squares, its Beguinhofs and red-and-white brick houses with the triangular-paned windows straight out of Flemish paintings of the fifteenth century. And after that, Cambridge in England, with its ivy-covered colleges and "Backs" on the tiny river Cam. Cambridge with its tearooms and bescarfed undergraduates riding bicycles through cobbled quads.

I laugh and tell her about how we took the train up to Cambridge from London and how the first thing I had done when we got there, which mortified Len, was go to a hairdresser. We only had a day, and Len looked at me like I was a Neanderthal, choosing "Hair Bizz" over Trinity, Pembroke, and St. John's, the colleges of Newton, Spenser, and Wordsworth. Len was an idealist, I tell Gail, that's what I loved about him. He was disappointed that I cared more about the cleanliness of my hair than the aesthetics of Kings College Chapel. As it turned out, the hairdresser was great fun. She gave me tea and biscuits and told me about her adventures in LA, where a so-called movie director had tried to pick her up at the Hungry Tiger.

We laugh and twirl our glasses in our hands.

"It's so quiet in the house, don't you think, Bicky?" Gail says after a brief silence.

I nod. It's as quiet, though neither of us say so, as a tomb.

"I'm so aware Linn's not here now. I know he was still

20

here right after it happened because his face was so peaceful, but I know he's gone now. I can feel he's gone.''

We return to the problem of whether I will keep the body through the night. Gail says I should do what I want, but she won't be able to sleep with a corpse in the house. It will make her nervous. Not that she believes in ghosts or anything, but it just gives her "the willies."

I say I'll go into the room and see how I feel.

When I open the bedroom door, I realize immediately that time has already begun to turn Len's body into some horrible and unrecognizable entity. Dr. Goodwin has closed his eyes and removed Vera Dawson's towel from under his chin. His hands and forehead are the color of granite. His mouth gapes open and the teeth are bared in a grin, making him look like a figure from hell. I swallow hard and hurry out of the room.

I dial the funeral home and get the director, a man named, most improbably, Mr. Wakeman, who says he'll be over within the hour.

Mr. Wakeman is a tall, unassuming, middle-aged man who stoops when he enters the kitchen and places his hands square on his knees as he recites the prices of his services. Not exactly the fat, unctuous shyster I have expected. He talks quietly of caskets and outer burial containers, of graveside and funeral services. I have no intention of spending any more than is absolutely necessary, I announce. He says that's fine, he'll do whatever I wish. I ask him in a firm, businesslike manner that makes me inwardly cringe—how can I be so calculating on the night of Len's death?—how much I can expect to pay for the whole business, embalming, casket, burial, et cetera.

Mr. Wakeman says he believes I can do all of it for about twenty-five hundred dollars.

I heave a sigh of relief. For all I know, he could have said fifty-five hundred dollars.

"And now, if you don't mind, Mrs. Feldstein," he says softly, "I'll bring in my assistant and we'll take the body.

It would be better if you went to another part of the house and didn't watch.''

I nod and gulp. They are going to take Len away, away in the black, snow-covered hearse, away to lie in the darkness of a basement room in a funeral home, then in a pillowed casket and then in a steel-encased grave. Suddenly I feel this awful panic wave through me like a thousand rads of radiation. I want to run and shout, ''Mr. Wakeman, no. Please. Come back in the morning, or in a week or a month, or never. I want to keep him with me always in the bed, in the room, in the house. I don't care if his body rots and smells and turns purple or the flesh falls from his bones like peeling paint. I can't give him up. Not yet.''

But it is too late. From the hallway, I watch Mr. Wakeman and his assistant carry the narrow canvas stretcher past the table in the dining room. I hear their winter boots on the tiles in the hallway, then the muffled voices in the bedroom, then the squeaking of bedsprings. In minutes, they appear through the doorway: Mr. Wakeman, grim and determined at the front, and the assistant, hunched over and barely visible at the back. Then, an image that will be framed in my head for the rest of my life: Len's narrow, ghostly face protruding from the mud-colored army blanket, nodding to the rhythm of the men's steps.

I stand at the window and watch them march down the steps toward the hearse, waiting with its motor running. They open up the back, slide the stretcher in, then slam the doors shut. Mr. Wakeman climbs in the driver's seat and his assistant into the passenger seat. They back up in the turnaround, the same turnaround where Len had parked our own cars so many times when returning from Fordham or chores in town. Then slowly, noiselessly, through the falling snow, they drive away.

I do not move from the window. I imagine the hearse passing the bird sanctuary, rounding the curve of Chestnut Woods Road, crossing the railroad tracks, mounting the hill by the old cider mill, waiting at the light to turn left on

Route 7. Gail brings me a glass of water and one of Len's sleeping pills and tells me to take it. I obey. The emerald-colored pill slips easily down my throat, and as I mount the stairs to bed, I can feel my limbs growing heavier and all the events of the day turning to snow in my head as the milligrams of chloral hydrate dissolve in my veins.

The Bustle in a House
The Morning after Death
Is solemnest of industries
Enacted upon Earth—

The Sweeping up the Heart
And putting Love away
We shall not want to use again
Until Eternity.

—Emily Dickinson

December 28–December 31, 1984

*T*he days immediately following a death are strangely carnival-like, a drugged masquerade of flowers and feasting and funeral-making. The house of death, once so still with the absence of breath, is ringing with voices, doorbells, footsteps, and phone calls. Where once there was only the slow pulse of waiting, now there is the fast, numbing flurry of arriving. Of list-making. To do: Call funeral home, newspaper, priest, organist, caterers, pallbearers, relatives, friends, neighbors. Give times, dates, directions to the church, to the house. Decide: What clothes to give to the undertaker; how to word the obituary; whether to serve coffee or wine, sandwiches or cakes; whether to wear black and which coat to carry if it's cold at the cemetery; whom to seat next to whom at the church; which verses to read from the Bible; what music to play at the end; what to say when people, balancing drinks and hors d'oeuvres in their hands, ask, "And what will you do now?"

All this activity, this hurrying back into life, is supposed to be necessary, even therapeutic. For if, in your shock, you were to stop, to lie down in your pool of grief and float downstream into the death of your beloved dead, you might never come back.

On the second day of Len's death, I awake to fog. Fog and rain everywhere soaking up last night's snow and turning the spidery trees brown. My first impulse: to run downstairs and check Len, to prop him up against the pillows and perhaps turn him if he's uncomfortable, to see if he'll take a few sips of apple juice. Then the shock of memory: Len is lying in a funeral home five miles away in a village called Georgetown. Yesterday I could have entered his room with its wheelchair and commode. I would have found him alive with his breathing heavy but his chest still moving, his forehead moist with fever. Today the sheets are pulled back, the blankets knotted at the base of the bed. The wheelchair faces the wall.

Only Gail, padding across the hallway and closing the bathroom door, breaks the silence.

Then I remember that Mr. Wakeman has asked me to call him before 10. I have promised myself I'll call my father, mother, and sister. The Parinis will arrive in an hour. Somehow I will have to get myself together to plan a funeral and bury my husband.

None of my family is to help with "the arrangements." My father has offered. This morning, he says he wants to help me in whatever way I need. I tell him I appreciate his offer, but I think, with the Parinis here, I'll have things under control. I know this hurts him: that I would choose the Parinis, whom I don't know well, to help me get through this crisis. But I couldn't bear it if he started cracking the kind of jokes he made at his own mother's funeral: "Screw 'em all but six and save them for pallbearers." I couldn't bear it if I were to break down and he were to say something that would make me bawl all the harder like, "We're all going to meet our maker someday, so keep your tail up, kid." Or if he insisted on playing tennis before the funeral, whacking overhead smashes harder and harder as he thrashed out his own confused emotions. Rage at his dead son-in-law for making his younger daughter a widow at 30. Relief that that son-in-law, just three years his junior, himself, didn't linger on for months or even years. Fear about what will become of me, his little girl who may not be tough enough to cope with her widowhood.

It would be better if I could speak about these things directly, if I could say, "I know you mean well, Dad, but I don't like the way you deal with death and, let's face it, you weren't exactly wild about my marrying Len and I can't tolerate your ambivalence toward him right now.'' If only I could say these things! But we Rices, biting our stalwart lips for generations among bitter New England winters, have always preferred to repress our deepest feelings. My father never said to me, "Don't marry Len. He's too old for you.'' In fact, he never asked Len's age, and I never told him. But he found other ways of communicating his dissatisfaction, usually through jokes or mockery. When Len's daughter, Judi, had her first child, my father clapped me on the back and quipped, "How's the little grandmother doing?'' This remark, made in the presence of my own grandmother, who barely spoke two consecutive sentences to Len when she first met him, only increased my humiliation.

It could have been worse, of course. My father could have disowned me, as Eugene O'Neill did when his daughter, Oona, married Charlie Chaplin, 36 years her senior. To his credit, my father managed to put aside his mixed feelings for his elderly son-in-law once Len and I married. He and my grandmother threw an elegant post-wedding reception at my grandmother's estate in Massachusetts. My father and Jane, the woman he lived with, urged Len and me to attend their cocktail parties in Pittsfield, even though my father was annoyed by Len's disheveled mien. ("Leonard needs a barber and a tailor,'' he'd bark.) Despite my father's disdain for philosophers who spent too much time "contemplating their navels,'' he attempted to read Len's books and even sat through one of Len's papers at the American Philosophical Association meeting.

But while my father tolerated his elderly son-in-law, he never developed much affection for him. This became painfully evident when Len got sick. The last visit, when my father had driven down from Massachusetts with a carload of Christmas presents, had been grim. During the entire evening he ignored Len, who sat slumped and drooling in his wheelchair, so sick that he could barely hold his head up to eat the food I spooned into his mouth. My father conducted the evening as if nothing were wrong, helping himself to seconds and thirds of Gail's moussaka and booming away at one of Len's former students about the curriculum at St. John's University.

I never told my father how upset I was. When we said good-bye, I gave him the obligatory peck on the cheek and thanked him for coming. He mentioned that he hadn't known what to give Len for Christmas and had decided on a six-month membership in "Harry & David's Fruit of the Month Club." The first shipment of pears would be arriving from Oregon that week. I said I thought it was a good choice; fruit was something that Len could still enjoy. I didn't tell him Len wouldn't be alive in six months, nor did I mention how I too had struggled over what to buy him for Christmas, how I couldn't decide on a gold crucifix or a giant stuffed dog. I didn't tell my father how I had wept that afternoon in the crowded, snowy parking lot in Ridgefield among the decorated trees and rosy-cheeked shoppers, wept because Len was dying and no gift, no matter how carefully chosen, would make him well.

That night, my father squeezed my hand and said, a little wistfully, "I wish there was something I could do."

"There's nothing anyone can do," I said grimly, withdrawing my hand from his.

In the end, I suppose I'm more my father's daughter than I would care to admit. Like him, I hide my emotions, rarely expressing anger or affection. Like him, I affect a tough I-don't-need-you exterior. Like him, I would crush that weak, fragile part of myself that just wants to be comforted, especially by my father.

When I call my sister to tell her that she need not arrive until Monday for the funeral, I can tell by her clipped, businesslike manner that she is annoyed at how I am handling things. Family happiness constitutes a religion for Harriet; by rejecting her attempts to console me, I am failing to promote that religion. If I asked her, Harriet would descend upon me in a flash, her Volvo wagon loaded up with frozen cheese soufflé casseroles, banana breads wrapped in tin foil, chocolate chip cookies packed in layers of wax paper. In addition to which, Harriet would handle, efficiently and un-complainingly, all details of the funeral: Mr. Wakeman, the cemetery warden, Len's children; she'd probably even tell me what dress to wear at the service. Harriet would dispatch Len into the underworld with all the dedication of Eisen-hower preparing for D-Day.

But I don't want my big sister's help. She was no fan of Len's either. One Christmas shortly after Len and I met, she took me aside to tell me that with all I had "going for me," my youth, looks, talent, and intelligence, I didn't have to "settle" for an old man. She once confessed that she preferred my former boyfriend, Brian, to Len. Brian "just seemed to fit in," as Harriet put it. He wasn't averse to putting away a few "Buds" with Harriet's husband, George, or parking himself in front of the tube on Thanksgiving for a football game, or dressing up in some American Revolu-tionary militiaman costume for a volunteer fire department parade. Len, on the other hand, was anti-social, Jewish, and old. Harriet once asked me, in all seriousness, whether Jews celebrated Thanksgiving. Len didn't drink, didn't tell dirty jokes. He hated sports. And he usually disappeared into the upstairs bathroom with Immanuel Kant during Christmas dinners.

Like my father, Harriet grew reconciled to Len after we were married. She presented us with a silver-framed, in-scribed photo she'd taken at our wedding, and George made a beautiful, hand-carved pine table for a wedding present. During family gatherings in Pittsfield or Hanover, she tried to engage Len in psychiatric conversations, soliciting his professional opinions on some of our more neurotic rela-tives. Harriet's code of family togetherness necessitated that she not reject her brother-in-law, that she always add a guilty "Love to Len!" when we talked on the telephone, and yet she could never repress her uneasiness with him. She blamed Len for our spending Thanksgivings alone on Martha's Vineyard instead of in Pittsfield. It was Len's fault that I had given up skiing and tennis and refused to accompany the family on vacations to John Gardiner's Tennis Ranch in Arizona. Len had turned me into this alienated, bookish creature who couldn't bear small talk and who took herself too seriously. On my birthday last year, when she called to joke about my getting "over the hill," and I confessed that Len's cancer overshadowed any feelings I had about turning 30, she said, somewhat huffily, that I didn't have to lose my sense of humor.

There's no law that says a sister has to grieve for her brother-in-law, but now that he's dead, I'm angry that she didn't like him and I'm punishing her. And she is angry at me because she always spent lots of money on Christmas presents for him and, when he was sick, sent flowers and get well cards. From her point of view, she has behaved irreproachably and should be treated accordingly. And because family harmony ranks higher than individual happiness on her scale, I should not care whether Len was loved or spurned and should now permit her and my father to rally round me. She doesn't say this. I am, after all, her little sister who is now in mourning. She also says nothing because she is, on this day after her brother-in-law's death, even angrier at my mother. For my mother is about to commit a greater sin: She refuses to even come to the funeral.

Well, *refuse* is perhaps too strong a word. My mother simply says that she can't come. The reason she gives is the weather. She lives in Florida and cannot take the cold. Her own health being precarious, she needs to stay where it's warm. Actually, she's bloomingly healthy and will probably live into her 90s as her mother and grandmother did. The real reason, and she finally admits this before we hang up, is that she cannot face my father.

"It might put me back in bed for six months if I saw John," she says. "Or Jane. I couldn't stand it if I had to speak to that woman.'' My father became involved with Jane 15 years ago; 10 years have passed since the divorce.

My mother says she hopes I will understand, says she can't imagine Leonard would hold it against her. And after all, she saw him a few months ago when he was alive. She wants to remember him alive, not dead.

I am silent as I remember the last time my mother saw Len. It was in October, and she was on her way south from her summer home in Canada down to Delray Beach, Florida. It had been a year since she had seen Len—she had not visited him in the hospital when she'd come through five months ago—and she wasn't prepared for his deteriorated condition. Panic crossed her chubby, girlish features when she spotted him in a lawn chair in the backyard with a blanket over his knees: His head was completely bald from the radiation, his eyes were blurry and unfocused, and, already slightly paralyzed, he was listing to the left. He greeted my mother with a whisper and a faint smile, but he could only nod to her cheery remarks about how lucky he was to be outside and how balmy the weather was for October.

After an hour, my mother said she and Ginny, her student, who was driving her down to Florida, had to be on their way—they were staying at a hotel that night and hadn't had their dinner. She didn't ask whether Len was in pain or whether he knew he was dying or how much longer he would live. She only wanted to know whether I had a *Science and Health*—if I didn't she'd send it. Her maternal advice was to ''pray over it,'' to read ''The Scientific Statement of Being.'' When I walked her to her car, she whimpered about how awful it was to see him ''just fade away right before your eyes.''

Ironically, my mother liked Len more than anyone in the family. In the beginning, she was alarmed by his Jewishness and his homely looks. She said she wished I could have found someone ''handsomer.'' She claimed that children of ''mixed'' parentage had a hard time. But these reservations vanished once she realized how much Len adored me. She used to compare Len's and my marriage to that of Georgia O'Keeffe and Alfred Stieglitz; she thought Len would "encourage" me in my artistic career, as Stieglitz had helped O'Keeffe. She was also impressed by how few disagreements she witnessed between Len and me; she said our marriage was as happy as her own parents'. And to Len, who patiently lent his psychiatric ear as she poured out her troubles about the divorce, she once confessed how grateful she was that he was able to love me in a way she herself hadn't been capable of because of her "difficulties."

"Leonard wouldn't want me to do anything I wasn't up to, would he, dearie?" my mother asks, as if I am the parent and she is the child.

When my mother and I hang up, she gets a call from George, my sister's husband, who tells her bitterly that he'll have to die in Florida because that would be the only way she would come to *his* funeral. This is designed to make Mother feel guilty and wretched. Which it does. She calls me back and says she feels terrible about not coming. She loves me very much. She loved Leonard and always supported our marriage.

"You won't hold it against me that I can't be there, will you?" she says, as if she is only breaking a dinner engagement.

I tell her I will miss her, but that I understand. Len would, too. Because he was patient and forgiving. I start to cry when I hear myself say his name.

"Now, Becky dearie, buck up. Buck up. Leonard wouldn't want you to be upset. You've got to think about the happy times, the good years, the beautiful life you had together. You've got so much to be *grateful* for!"

As we say good-bye, I realize that, in addition to dreading an encounter with my father and Jane, she may also fear me—her youngest child alone and grieving, craving the mother she rarely had.

I am crushed that she won't come.

I would curl up on my bed, bury my head in my pillow,

34

and sob. Sob for her and for my father and for my sister and for the pathetic, broken family that we are. Sob for me. Because I have lost Len, the one person who could comfort me now. Len, who was all the family I ever needed, mother and father and brother and sister.

But sobbing will have to wait.

When the Parinis arrive, they embrace me, not without a trace of awkwardness and formality. I am young enough to be their daughter, and yet I am also the widow of their closest friend. They have spent only a handful of evenings with me, accompanied always by Len. Our talk centered around art or literature—Pam is an elementary school educator; Phil teaches psychology—rarely of intimate things. They are fond of me, I know. They would not be taking a week out of their lives to help me bury my husband if they were not.

And yet, as I help carry their bags upstairs, I feel the oddness of our association, our mission, together. We barely know one another, and yet we are planning a funeral. I wonder whether we will cry together. I sense we will not.

Before we go to the funeral home, we must choose the clothes that Len will be buried in. This seems macabre, and I am almost nauseated as we open the double doors into Len's closet. Before us is a crowded row of heavy wooden hangers bearing shirts, jackets, and trousers. Most are encased in long, puffy dry cleaner's bags and have not been worn in months. They stir slightly in the darkness as Pam flicks through them until she stops at the blue Harris tweed jacket Len was fond of and used to wear to Fordham. "I think this would somehow be best, don't you Becky?" Pam says with an efficient cheeriness.

To my horror, I hear myself snap, "No. It's much too good," and insist we take a rumpled brown corduroy suit that never fit Len properly and that he rarely wore.

Pam and Phil exchange surprised glances, but say noth-

35

ing. Pam folds the corduroy suit tenderly in a brown paper bag.

We pile into the Parinis' blue Honda Accord. As Phil asks me to direct him to the highway, I feel intense confusion and shame. Why do I want Len to be buried in something shabby? Who am I saving that blue jacket for anyway? How could I be so damned cheap? I tell myself that I chose the corduroy suit because I don't want to part with something that is so much Len. But it also feels as if I'm depriving Len of something, as if I'm punishing him for leaving me. Another voice says, *What difference can it make what he's buried in? He's gone.* But the guilt persists, like a radio jingle that won't go away. I want to tell Phil to turn the car around and go back to the house and get the Harris tweed jacket. But I don't.

Pam asks if I've called Len's sister yet. I explain that Judi promised to contact her. Phil asks what it was like when Anne came to see Len a few weeks ago. Awkward, I say. She was irritated at having to make the long drive from Philadelphia. When I gave her directions over the phone, she asked me whose idea the visit was—Len's or mine. When she arrived, she seemed unable to grasp how sick Len was. She kept firing questions about Judi and Mark and got annoyed when Len couldn't respond. She chattered on about how much money her children were making and the new condo she and her husband had bought in Atlantic City. When she said good-bye, she shook Len's hand. I wished she'd stayed away.

"That fits everything Len ever said about her," Phil sighs. "I doubt she'll come to the funeral; maybe it's just as well."

We ride in silence through light traffic down Route 7. I think how strange families are—my family, Len's family— the bitterness and rage that people of the same blood can feel for one another, the grievances that brothers and sisters, husbands and wives, parents and children carry across

36

a lifetime, and how even death, which should change everything, changes nothing.

As Phil parks the car in the empty lot and opens the doors, first for Pam and then for me, I feel suddenly thankful for their calm, steady presences. They are not family. Between us there are not a thousand hurts carefully stored in the heart, like canning jars in a kitchen cupboard. I take their arms gratefully as we walk up the long flight of steps to the funeral home.

The Bouton Funeral Home is a rambling, wedding-cake Victorian mansion with a wraparound porch. Mr. Wakeman explains that it has been in operation since 1889, that Mark Twain, who died in Redding in 1910, was "taken care of" here. The academic Parinis are pleased with this bit of literary trivia. Pam says, earnestly and warmly, "I think Len would *like* that, don't you Becky?"

Mr. Wakeman takes our coats and hangs them carefully on a long, empty coat rack in the hallway. He leads us into a large, light-filled front room and motions for us to be seated in three folding metal chairs lined in a single row on the far side of the room.

Addressing his questions to me, he asks whether I want an open casket. I say no, I have always thought that morbid and I don't think Len would want it either. The Parinis look relieved and nod. He asks about calling hours. Again, no. He asks where the service will be and if I will want an organist. He wonders whether I'll require a limousine to follow the hearse to the cemetery, because that, of course, will be extra. He says the word "extra" under his breath and almost apologetically. Suddenly, I feel sorry for him. He seems like such a decent man, and yet what grim business it must be to deal with dead people all day and, even worse, to convince their survivors that you're not trying to screw them.

More questions. Len's date of birth. October 23, 1922. Place of birth. Philadelphia, Pennsylvania. Father's name. Maurice Feldstein. Mother's maiden name. Frieda Smellow. He asks about the spelling of Frieda. Whether it's *ei* or *ie*. Phil thinks *ei*, because of the rule "i" before "e" except after "c." Pam says Frieda is a German name, but it could also be spelled *Freda*. I have no idea. Len's parents were dead when we met, and he never referred to her by name, only as "my mother." At least five minutes is given to this problem; we are all finding it a relief to discuss grammar rather than death.

"About the casket, Mrs. Feldstein. You want something fairly simple, is that correct?"

I nod but glance for confirmation to Pam and Phil. They nod. Phil asks Mr. Wakeman to show us something in a medium price range.

Mr. Wakeman directs us into another room whose walls are covered in a rose-colored, quilted material. Matching rose-colored shades are pulled tight against the windows. The room is crammed with coffins. Mr. Wakeman stops in front of one in shining dark pine with an interior of red pleated silk and a matching pillow bolster. Its gold-handled top is ajar. From a certain angle, it looks like a baby grand piano. Phil says, "Yes, that'll do fine," and for one split second before we turn away, I see Len's pale, elongated dead face resting on that plump, red bolster. I see his long, slight frame creasing the red pleated silk, decaying in the opulent darkness. I shut my eyes and bolt out of the room.

At Hillside Cemetery, the earth is soft and porous beneath our feet. Yesterday's snow lies in soggy patches, and a light rain has been falling most of the afternoon. As we walk, we sink deeper into the swampy ground, the mud and puddles releasing us reluctantly with a noisy sucking, the clumps of soggy, brown grass clinging to our boot toes.

"In Bennington," Phil says, "you'd have to wait until spring before you could bury him."

I shudder, imagining the frozen, snowy earth impervious to pick or shovel.

"What about over here, Becky, beside this beautiful pine?" Pam says. "You know how Len loved trees."

A Time to Mourn

The tree, a large Norwegian pine, stands in thick, large-branched splendor in the middle of the small cemetery. Its snow-dotted branches shoot up into the foggy sky across the sloping gray field. There are ten dark granite gravestones, of varying sizes, beneath it.

Mrs. Shipman, the old hunchbacked cemetery warden who trudges ahead of us peering at her charts of squares and numbers, says she's sorry, but that particular grave only comes in a "single" rather than a "double."

Husbands and wives, she says, her eyes meeting mine through the thick fog of her bifocals, usually buy their graves together, which would be the double. Mrs. Shipman says she has plenty of "real good doubles" over there and points to a treeless slope about one hundred feet away.

I shudder at her terminology. "Real good doubles," as if graves were like beds, like top-of-the-line Sealy Posturepedic mattresses, which come in all sizes, colors, and degrees of firmness.

Pam points out that I could always get both now and sell the other later. Mrs. Shipman urges me to buy now. "These here graves have been goin' like hotcakes."

The Parinis and I laugh nervously, unsure of how to respond to this black humor.

Phil says he sympathizes with my reluctance. He and Pam have not bought their graves, although he supposes they ought to start thinking about it. I study Phil for a moment: gray, thinning hair, heavy-lined face, slightly paunched belly. At 63, he is only a year older than Len. How strange it must be for him to be trudging across a Connecticut cemetery, choosing the spot of earth where his friend of 30 years will lie for eternity. He must wonder why he is alive, casting footprints across a muddy field, and Len is dead.

It's getting late and the gray sky is growing dark with streaks of fuchsia. Mrs. Shipman's pen is poised at her clipboard. She needs to know. The single or the double?

As a widow, I am expected to get the double, to seal my dying with the dying of my husband, to sleep with him in

39

death as I have slept with him in life. The idea is not without a certain romantic appeal: to know that all my future journeys across this planet will end here, in a rectangle of moist earth beside the bones of my husband, who has loved me more than any other human being. Despite Len's abhorrence of cemeteries, despite his telling me he didn't care where I buried him, he would want my body to lie beside his, my name to be inscribed beneath his on the tombstone, the carbon of our bones to commingle.

But I cannot do it. I cannot buy my own grave. Suddenly, I feel the blood come charging into my face. My arms begin to quiver, my calves start to flex, and my heels dig craters into the mud. I want to run, run down the slope, past the tiny American flags, past the bouquets of flowers at the gravestones, out through the high stone gates.

Instead, I tell Mrs. Shipman I'll get a single for now, but one that has plenty of space around it so I can change my mind and get the double later. She takes us to a plot halfway down the slope, far from the other gravestones but close to a pussy willow tree. If you look south, you can see a thick brush of evergreens sloping down the valley toward the highway. And if you look north and slightly to the east, you can see a row of leafless maples beside a stone wall and beyond it an open field that climbs upward until all you can see is sky.

As we are about to leave, Pam cries, "Oh, look," and we raise our heads to meet a flock of Canada geese swooping in a firm V westward across the ink-colored sky. Even Mrs. Shipman, who is rubbing her boots against the paved pathway to remove the mud, stops to follow their course across the treetops. The strong, full notes of their calling echo long after they have passed.

I awake the next morning to soft, unseasonably warm weather with the snow all melted in yesterday's rain. I awake to new surroundings: to the small green room that has been Gail's room—she has gone to stay at her boyfriend's house—

and where I will sleep until the Parinis leave next Friday. On the bureau I notice Gail's collection of papier-mâché animals and the heart-shaped jewelry box filled with necklaces. Downstairs I hear the friendly clatter of breakfast dishes, the muted voices of Pam and Phil in the dining room beneath me.

This morning is a little easier than yesterday morning, and perhaps tomorrow morning will be easier than today. And yet, I dread when the funeral is over and the Parinis have gone and I am left alone in the house with the silence and the photographs. I am conscious, too, of wanting these days before the burial to stretch out eternally, for once Len is locked up in the earth, I will never have him back.

Last night, little sleep, only a turning and turning of images. Len five days before he died, stroking my arm over and over again and saying my name, "Becky, Becky," as he sat on the toilet in the bathroom while Gail and I shaved off his beard. Len on Christmas Day, eyeballs swirling, saliva dribbling, knees shaking in the wheelchair beside the Christmas tree and the bright-colored packages. Len's fingers wrapped tight around the fingers of each of us—Judi, Mark, me, the Parinis—who took turns beside him. Len two hours dead, his penis purpled and shrunken like a dead bird.

All I can remember of Len is his dying and his death. Will there ever come a time when the living, healthy Len will be more alive than the dead one?

But memory is submerged in the writing of the obituary—an activity that claims much of the day.

The Parinis and I want the obituary to appear in the *The New York Times*. The problem is that we must convince the "obit" editor that Len was a person of consequence, that his death was a newsworthy "item." Since *The New York Times* obit editors are as haughty as concierges in posh French hotels—you cannot enter the hallowed newsprint unless you have won a slew of prizes or tried to assassinate a president—our task is not easy. If we are not successful, we will have to resort to the tactics of the hoi polloi: taking out a paid notice in tiny print in the bottom half of the obituary page. This feels like defeat, as if we have failed to give Len his due. And so, all our anxiety, all our grief, all our denial of Len's passing is poured into the bizarre activity of packaging and selling his reputation.

Len's achievements are great. A B.S. in physics from Penn State in 1943. An M.D. from Jefferson Medical University in 1947. A Ph.D. in philosophy from Columbia in 1957. Graduate of the White Institute of New York with a certificate in psychoanalytic psychiatry. Professor of philosophy at Fordham University, practicing psychoanalyst in Manhattan, author of three books on the philosophy of the person.

But the obit editor is not impressed. "This is *The New York Times,* Mrs. Feldstein," he says gravely. "Your husband's achievements are noteworthy, but not newsworthy."

More phone calls. To various colleagues of Len's at Fordham. To a big gun in religious studies at Stony Brook who reviewed Len's first two books. It is difficult to get through, since all are attending the American Philosophical Association's annual meeting in Manhattan. Messages are left. Calls are returned. The president of the APA promises to "do what he can." The Parinis and I run from phone to phone in feverish excitement. Phil sits at my typewriter pecking out a few paragraphs to read to the *Times* metropolitan editor if he calls. Phil thinks it will strengthen our "case" if we have something already composed.

Three hours later, the phone rings. It's Clifford Markman from the *Times.* After a perfunctory, "My sympathies, Mrs. Feldstein," he takes down the information, then reads it back to me, checking spellings, dates, locations, the proper hyphenation of Hastings-on-Hudson, where Mark lives. He cannot tell us definitely if the obituary will appear or when. Still, when I hang up the phone we are happy, even triumphant. Phil raises his two fingers in the victory salute. I pound my desk and say, "We did it!" Whether the obituary will be printed is, at this point, irrelevant. We have, in

Len's name, done battle with the forces that would forget him. We have written his name across the sky. For a moment, it's almost as if we have brought him back.

Sunday is a slow day. There are more calls to make. Most people are coming from out of town, and we must give them directions to the church. Like a refrain in a nursery rhyme, I tell them: Go 10 miles north on Route 7, right on Route 57, left on Church Street, then follow the signs.

The food for the gathering at the house is organized. Gold's Deli in Westport is putting together a large tray of cheeses, cold cuts, and breads, which Susan will pick up tomorrow morning. My father is to bring the wine, and he has called twice today to ask what kind he should get, how many bottles, and whether there should be more white than red. My sister will bring a tray of Christmas cookies she baked last week but has kept in her freezer. Both of them seem grateful that I am letting them help me, if only in these minor ways.

There is a problem in getting a cantor to sing at the service. The men Susan has contacted are offended by Len's conversion to Roman Catholicism. All of them express dismay at entering a Catholic church, much less singing there. Maybe I am perverse to insist on the Jewish presence at Len's funeral, but I think he would want it. Although Len felt that Christianity, with its God of love, was an advance over Judaism, with its God of vengeance, he had mixed feelings about cutting himself off from his Jewish roots. When he checked into Lenox Hill Hospital, he gave his religion as "Jew" rather than "Catholic." He joked that if his doctors, all of whom were Jewish, knew the truth it might ruin their bedside manner and why should he risk that? But I think somewhere he was saying, "I want to go out of the world as I came into it, as a Jew."

Susan finally finds a cantor willing to sing. He will cancel his class at the Union Theological Seminary and arrive at the church by 10 to meet with the organist.

I am elated. I think, as I often have over these three days, *Len would be proud of me.*

Gail comes over for most of the afternoon and helps with the cleaning. The living and dining rooms must be vacuumed, chairs rearranged, tabletops shined with lemon oil. Gail works energetically with her usual good humor, though she interrupts herself a few times to call her boyfriend, Tom, to talk about their plans for the evening. Neither of us mention what she will do after tomorrow. A part of me wishes she could stay, that I could keep her on to take care of me. But that would be crazy. After all, it's not as if I'm bedridden or can't feed myself. I'm 30 years old, just 5 years older than she is, in good health and of sound mind, at least for today.

We leave the Christmas tree and its ornaments standing near the fireplace, though Gail thinks it's wrong to leave the two stuffed brown monkeys hugging at the top of the tree.

"Funerals," she says with uncharacteristic gravity, "are supposed to be *serious,* Bicky. Some people might really be *offinded.*"

"If people don't like it," I laugh, "that's their problem."

And besides, I tell her, those monkeys have a lot of sentimental associations. Len and I saw them in Rumpelmayer's window in New York a few years ago. We loved how they were always hugging and how you had to pull against the Velcro on their fingers to draw them apart.

That night, Tom arrives to take Gail to dinner. He's taking her to the Three Bears in Westport, then to *The Return of the Jedi.* Gail is still upstairs, "tarting up," and so we invite him in for a drink. I get out some brie and crackers, leftovers from Christmas, and we sit leisurely in the living room chatting. Tom says he'd like to take Gail to see other parts of the country: Washington, D.C., the Rockies, maybe even California. He is obviously attached to her, and when she sweeps into the room, he beams. We "ooh" and "aah" at her costume: high heels and tight black skirt, plunging electric blue sweater, her frizzy blond hair wrapped in the colorful scarf I gave her for Christmas. Pleased by the attention, she does a little tap dance before the fireplace and says she hopes Tom will spend lots of money on her.

"Behave yourself," I kid as she and Tom sashay out the door.

"Well, I'll do my bist not to, Bicky," she cackles.

Then they are gone, Tom guiding Gail over a sheet of ice in the driveway, Gail's laughter merging with the call of an owl through the dark woods.

The morning of the funeral is chaos. We must meet with the priest by 10:15. My father, sister, and brother-in-law are due at the house at 10 and will follow us to the church. Susan will deliver the food about 10:30, and Gail volunteers to stay behind to help set up on the tables in the dining room. Gail worries that people may not be able to find the house, since the driveway is not properly marked. I make one large sign from an old packing box so it reads "FELD-STEIN" in bold, red, magic-markered letters. I race down to the end of the driveway in my bathrobe to nail it to a tree near the mailbox.

Coming back, I notice a pale, watery sun struggling to emerge through the trees. The air is soft and warm against my bare legs. In the turnaround I meet Phil, who has just returned from getting his car washed. He says temperatures are expected to rise into the high sixties and we're lucky to have such good weather. I think, *yes, thank God for soft air and warm ground; it's better for Len to be buried today than in a blinding snowstorm.*

I am frantic about what to wear. I don't want to wear black. I would like to find something bright, in pink or purple with a long, flowing skirt. To give me courage. For an insane moment, I consider my wedding dress, a long, high-necked Victorian gown of dusty rose. Then I realize how grisly this might appear, as if I were almost celebrating Len's death. When I think about people observing me in the church, when I imagine them pointing and saying, "There's his young wife," I feel self-conscious. I decide on black after all: a conservative merino wool suit with a straight, knee-length skirt and boxed jacket.

I spend an hour reviewing my poems and the passages from Len's book that I will read at the service. Pam is amazed I can have the composure to stand up at my husband's funeral and say anything. She couldn't. I suddenly worry that I won't be able to do it. What if the words crack in my throat? What if I break down?

Harriet, George, and my father arrive punctually at 10. My father carries a copy of *The New York Times* under his arm. He grins and says, "Looks like you twisted a few arms!" The newspaper is open to the obituary page. In the upper right corner in small typeface I spot the caption: "DR. LEONARD C. FELDSTEIN DIES; TAUGHT PHILOSO-PHY OF SCIENCE." I'm startled to see Len's full name in headlines beside the odd word: DIES. It seems only hours ago that we were breakfasting on the porch with the Sunday paper, reading about other people, far away from the coffee in our Wedgwood cups, who had died. What was Len doing there now beside "THEODORE M. NEWCOMB: PIO-NEER IN SOCIAL PSYCHOLOGY" and "HEDLEY WOODHOUSE: WAS LEADING JOCKEY," near a small ad displaying a cut-out telephone and offering home delivery of *The New York Times?*

The Parinis are angry about how little space they gave to Len and how much to "Theodore M. Newcomb," who got bigger, bolder typeface and perhaps ten column inches, against Len's four. Pam is miffed that Newcomb gets "Pi-oneer" and Len only "Taught Philosophy of Science." She wonders why they didn't put anything about Len's books in the headlines.

My father hands me the *Berkshire Eagle,* his local news-paper, which carries a longer notice that my father called in himself, similar to what Phil wrote for the *Times.*

I hug my father and whisper, "Thank you." I remind

46

myself that he is trying to help. I shouldn't be so quick to find fault with him.

Harriet is looking through the kitchen cupboards for a tray for her cookies. She wants to leave them on the counter to let them thaw. She worries that Hector, my little mutt, will get at them. I assure her he won't. Harriet is pregnant and wearing a bright, multi-colored wool jumper. My father, who is nervous and doesn't know what to do with himself, suddenly blurts out, "Now don't everyone say that Harriet looks like a goddamn walking checkerboard in that dress." He laughs so hard his cheeks shake. He peers mischievously around the kitchen to see if anyone else is laughing. Silence. Harriet looks as if she might burst into tears. I want to tell him that it's not funny and why does he always have to say such stupid, hurtful things? But, as usual, I let it go. And seethe.

Harriet wants us to ride in her Volvo wagon to the church. She says there's more than enough room if one of us sits on someone else's lap. I envision us crowded together with more hurtful barbs from my father, this time directed at me. I announce that I need the quiet to go over what I'm going to say at the service. A lie. But useful, since we split up into two cars, the Parinis and I in their Honda Accord; Harriet, George, and my father in the Volvo. Harriet is furious at this new breach of etiquette. She glares at me from behind her blue-tinted aviator glasses.

At the church, people have already arrived, even though the service doesn't start until 11. Many are wandering listlessly in the parking lot. I recognize Len's former students, friends who've driven up from New York, colleagues from Fordham. Their faces are pinched and somber; some have been crying. As Pam, Phil, and I hurry past them, one or two wave. Most turn away. I realize that they don't know what to say, that they are frightened of me—I who have slept with death.

I feel a tap on my shoulder and turn around to find Judi and Mark behind me and with them an older, much heavier woman wearing oversized purple eyeglasses and dressed in a fake fur coat.

"This is my mom," Judi says softly.

I tremble slightly as I shake her hand. Vivian, Len's first wife, whom I've heard so much about, all of it from Len and all of it bad. Len felt such rancor toward her that when he got sick, he begged me not to let her visit him. Last week, close to the end, she phoned me in near hysteria, saying she couldn't bear to have Len go without saying good-bye. She promised she'd only stay 15 minutes. I could not refuse her. She had planned to come on the Friday after Christmas. Too late, as it turned out.

She takes my hand limply and whispers, "Thank you for everything you've done." She has tears in her eyes, and I feel a surge of pity for her; whatever she has done, to Len, to Judi or Mark, is ancient history now. On this of all days, her sins should be forgiven.

We settle in our separate pews, and Mark leans over to ask if I would like him to sit beside me. I am touched by this gesture. I have never been close to Mark. During the illness, we were often thrown together—in Len's hospital room or in conferences with the doctors—but he has always been awkward with me, occasionally even spiteful. A month ago, when he visited Len and stayed for a lasagna dinner that Gail cooked, Mark commented sarcastically on how I had never served anything so edible and how my mother must think I've really "arrived" to have a "maid."

But Mark wants to forget past animosities. He wants to sit next to me. Before I can say yes, Vivian is whispering to Judi and Judi is whispering to Mark and Mark finally says he guesses he'd better not because his mother wants him with her.

At 10:45, the church doors fly open. The measured, somber chords of the organ come louder now, filling up the spaces of the small chapel. Slowly, the pallbearers march down the aisle with the casket. There are six: my father and brother-in-law and Gail's friend, Tom, on one side, three of

Len's former students on the other. All of them are sweating as they strain to keep the long, gleaming box aloft. They set it down on a metal bier at the head of the church, before the altar. Mr. Wakeman emerges briefly to cover it with a long, white linen pall. The white cloth trails down a few feet before the front pews. The effect is so artful that it almost disguises the object and its contents. It might contain valuable tapestries, paintings, antique musical instruments.

My rib cage feels like it is being stretched on a medieval torture rack when I realize Len's body is in there.

In an emotionless monotone, the priest intones, "I will extol thee, O Lord, for thou hast lifted me up . . . O Lord my God, I cried unto thee . . ."

His voice echoes in and out of me like a wave slapping through interstices in a rock. I wish I could be comforted by his words, believe, as one of the priests whispered to me earlier, that "Len is not with us. His soul is soaring, far away." But I am numb; heaven, God, even death itself are abstractions. All I can register is simple, animal sensation: the way the light falls in colored prisms through a stained glass window, the slow, atonal wail of the cantor keening, "YER-U-SHA-LY-EM," my sweaty palm curled like a child's marble in Pam's hand.

The eulogy is brief and impersonal. The priest, one of Len's colleagues at Fordham, speaks of Len's having become a Catholic, how it wasn't a conversion but rather a natural, logical progression from one tradition, older and more limited, to another, more progressive and inclusive. The priest mentions the cantor and how his presence seems fitting, for Len believed that Christianity's intellectual and spiritual roots were in Judaism, that the two traditions were one.

I find myself bored by the eulogy. It's as if all Len did with his life was join the Catholic church. Len converted a year before we met, and although he spoke of the baptism as "mystical," he rarely went to church. In the last few years, he'd grown suspect of the church's backward views on everything from abortion to socialism. In any case, there is nothing of the *man* Len, his passion for teaching, his skill as a therapist—among the mourners there are three former patients, at least five former students. Nothing about his sense of humor or love of nature. Nothing of the man I loved.

Judi rises and walks to the lectern to the left of the altar. She is wearing a wool dress of black and white patterned circles. She is remarkably serene. My anger about the eulogy dissolves when I realize that after she finishes, I must follow her. Around the covered casket, up the red-covered steps, to the tall lectern with hand-carved scrolls on each side.

Judi's voice, though soft, travels evenly and clearly through the small church. She speaks of how her father always told her from the time she was small that every person, no matter how uneducated, humble, or poor, could teach her something, that every human being was gifted. She says she has tried to practice this philosophy in her own life and that she will pass it on to her daughter, Paula.

As she returns to her seat, I reach for her hand. This may be the first time I have touched her spontaneously.

It's time. Pam and Phil give my elbow a squeeze. I rise and begin the long journey from my front pew. It seems an hour before I place my folder of papers on the lectern's oak shelf. I look straight ahead into a blurry quilt of faces. I do not allow my eyes to veer off to the left where the casket is. There is silence. They are waiting for me. I begin: a halting, scattered mess of phrases—this part I have not rehearsed—about the legacy of Len's books.

People cough. Wood creaks as some shift uneasily in the pews. My words crash about me like wrong chords banging on an organ. I should step down before I make a fool of myself.

Frantically, I begin to read from *The Dance of Being,* slurring the words: " 'Man is endlessly fascinated by shapes and patterns, by forces and powers. Strolling along the sea-

A Time to Mourn

shore, he notices the sea in its varied strands of color—gray
to pale blue, deep blue to turquoise of many hues—and the
sky with its complementary spectra. Stopping, he is capti-
vated by the pebbles along the shore . . .' ''

Then something miraculous happens. The words come
flowing through my body like a drug, like marijuana, like
vodka, soothing me, quieting me. My arms stop quivering.
My voice grows stronger. I am wrapped in the reverie of
afternoons on Martha's Vineyard, on the beaches of Zach's
Cliffs and Lucy Vincent Beach, afternoons when Len and I
swam in the hot sun and collected shells and talked about
how lucky we were to be alive.

As I continue, it is as if Len's voice has sung out from
the dark of the casket and flown into my voice, into my
mouth, into the taut muscles of my vocal cords. I can do
anything, live through Len's death, survive his funeral, survive even the thousands of days I must pass without him.
Because he does not, at this moment, feel dead. He lives.
In every hue of the sea, in every granule of sand, in all the
vowels and consonants on these pages. '' 'Each day,
he watches as crabs and fish are washed ashore; he notes
the quivering of a dying body, the decay, the contraction,
the dissolution. . . . The force which disintegrates objects
fragile disintegrates objects sturdy. Both are swept away by
the same inexorable might.' ''

The same inexorable might. Which gave me Len for a
few delirious summer days. Which inspired me to write
these six sonnets I now read. Which has taken, in the winter
of his sixty-third year, Len's body and spirit. The same inexorable might.

As I float back to my seat, I'm aware that this union with
Len may be momentary, may be like what he felt at his
baptism into Christianity—the hour of mystic joy followed
by years of questioning. But whatever this sensation is that
makes my steps so light, my heart so hopeful, for now it's
enough.

The burial is quick. A few dozen people gather around

51

the shallow trench, the mounds of earth covered with a green, grass-like blanket, the tiny metal plate protruding from the earth that reads: "Leonard C. Feldstein, 1922–1984."

The priest reads the lines from the Book of John about the grain of wheat falling into the ground. Judi recites a Baha'i prayer. As the shiny pine casket is lowered by pulleys into the dark earth, I hear someone crying.

My father is beside me at the grave. He takes my hand and squeezes it. I return the pressure. I feel my own tears building inside me, realizing that it's time to make my peace with him, time to stop blaming him for all the hurts, real or imagined, he has inflicted upon me. One day, I will stand before such a narrow trench and watch the coffin containing his body being lowered by pulleys into the ground. For the first time, I know with certainty that this will happen. And for the first time in my young but now so-old life, there is something I know that I wish I could forget.

As we drive out the high, scrolled iron gates, I tell myself I never want to come back here again.

Cars are lined up in the driveway when we arrive at the house. There are cars parked between the trees on the lawn and cars backed up to the bushes at the edge of the property. Inside, the table in the dining room is covered with my grandmother's best blue linen tablecloth and loaded down with serving dishes, paper plates, plastic glasses, and forks. There is pound cake, raspberry pie, salami, ham, olives, tomatoes, carrots, pickles, and mustard. Cream and sugar for the coffee, wine by the caseful.

People hover near the food, as they do at cocktail parties. And, as at cocktail parties, there is the same noisy frivolity. People who haven't seen one another for months or even years: What have you been doing these days and where are your kids and are you going to move and did Robert get tenure and did Quentin get his book published and will you be going to Paris this summer? There are people who've never met, and round they go extending their hands saying, "I'm Miles Gustafson, from Boston. I knew Len at the White Institute."

Among them I circulate, the tireless hostess, smiling and passing trays of cut-up vegetables or cookies, asking them whether they'd like another drink, thanking them for coming. I am glad they have come, these 30 or 40 people who've driven from places as far away as Virginia, Maryland, and Vermont. They didn't have to, after all. Today is December 31. In a few hours, it will be New Year's Eve. They'll have to battle traffic as they drive back to their parties with friends or gatherings in restaurants. At midnight, when they toast the new year, the memory of Len's funeral will make them melancholy.

I am glad they have come. Still, I wish the faces would not be so flushed, the laughter so loud. I wish that Len's "meshuga" cousin from Brooklyn, who will not remove his hat or eat any of the food because it's not kosher, would stop bending my ear about moving Len to an all-Jewish cemetery in Philadelphia. I wish my father would stop booming to Gail about heli-skiing in British Columbia, stop joking about my "screw-up" reading my lines at the service. I'm annoyed at the priest swilling Jack Daniel's and pontificating about who will be the next APA president. I resent my sister's chatter about the Hanover Historical Society or how crazy life will be when her second child is born. I am appalled when I hear a friend's husband, introducing her with a leer as "my first wife."

Before they leave, some of these people take me aside and ask questions that I do not know the answers to: When will you go back to work? Will you sell the house in the spring? Move back to New York? Get away somewhere? Have a little change? These questions, I realize, are a way of touching upon but not broaching the more obvious ones: How will you survive? How will you keep yourself from diving into the grave?

They offer help of various kinds: A meal if I'm hungry,

a phone call if I'm lonely, time that I might need to talk. One friend from my writer's group even offers me a room in her home, to write in or stay in, for as long as I want. I know they mean well, these friends in the midst of their happier, easier lives. But I know that people can say things like "Call me anytime," and yet if I were to wake them at 3:00 A.M. moaning, "I can't bear the silence, the images of Len locked up in the earth," I would burden them.

I do not tell them I am afraid of this grief. What will happen when they leave and I am alone? Alone early in the morning and late at night. Alone riding in the car. Wandering the aisles of supermarkets. Sitting in a movie theater, spooked by the vacant seat beside me. Alone climbing the stairs past the closed door of the room where he died. Alone on Valentine's Day and the Fourth of July and my birthday and our anniversary. I do not tell them that living without Len will be the hardest thing I have ever done—harder than watching him collapse from a seizure in Grand Central on an August afternoon and seeing the terror rip across his face as crowds gathered around us while we waited for an ambulance. Harder than hearing Gail tell me he'd been looking for me in the refrigerator while I was at work. Harder than hearing him whisper, on a rainy November night while I was changing his soiled bedsheets, "Don't forget me, Beck."

But you wouldn't guess I am afraid now. I am wearing a white blouse with a Peter Pan bow and a string of pearls at my neck. My hair is combed; there are two sapphire studs in my ears; my lips are thinly coated with "Softshell Pink" lipstick. I am hurrying, in my low Bandolino heels, into the kitchen to bring out more trays of broccoli flowerets; I am dashing out to the porch to open more wine. I am fetching coats from the couch in Len's study; I am walking people out to their cars. My hand, when people take it to say goodbye, is steady; my voice, chatting about how we'll have to get together when I come into the city, is casual.

When you look into my face, you do not see death.

Pain—has an Element of Blank—
It cannot recollect
When it begun—or if there were
A time when it was not—

—Emily Dickinson

January 1985

I sleepwalk through these weeks after Len's death. I get up in the night calling his name aloud. I go downstairs to sit on the sofa with my arms curled around my knees and watch the moon floating above the trees. I listen to branches scratching against the windows. I observe the wind tossing bits of snow from the rooftops, see the snow sailing in tiny squalls to the ground. And I wonder, *Is the gusting wind Len's voice; is the waxing moon Len; is the snow Len?* And there is no answer. Only more wind and silence. The humming of the refrigerator in the kitchen, the grinding of the furnace in the cellar.

I walk through the bird sanctuary near our house. I watch the sun set across the coppery red bushes and the snow-patched, matted grasses. I wrap my arms around one of the skinny, leafless dogwoods. The tree feels as narrow as Len's shoulder, as skinny as his body.

I canvass every inch of the house looking for him. I take down books from the bookcase in the living room and my study to look for his flourishing inscriptions on the flyleaf— "To my beloved Rebecca on her birthday, 1981, from your adoring Leonard." I look especially for the books we bought after we were married, the paperback or hard-bound volumes he signed with that same exuberant hand, "Leonard and Rebecca Rice-Feldstein." His handwriting has become precious, a bit of his spirit still encoded in this material world. I look everywhere for it: in the back pages of old phone directories where he scribbled "800" numbers for airlines, numbers for dentists in Danbury, department stores in Stamford. In my purse, I carry his tiny black leather address book. I open it daily to the front page where he has written "Becky office: (212) 660-6049."

At night, I hole up in bed with the box of his letters to me. There are bright, gaudy Valentine's Day cards inscribed: "To my Sweetheart," fanciful birthday cards with kissing unicorns on the cover, love notes on heavy vellum paper folded and folded until they are almost as small as postage stamps. But the note I go back to again and again is the one written most recently, the last note he ever gave me, on my thirtieth birthday. Unlike the others, it is written on a thin scrap of paper ripped out from the back of a soft-cover book. The handwriting is recognizably his, the small, fine print with the flourishes in the *y*'s and *g*'s. And yet it is not his. It is tiny and cramped; it pitches unevenly across the page. I imagine his struggle forming the letters. He speaks of his love for me and how it gives him courage to face this illness. But in the last paragraph, it's as if he knows that he won't survive, that I will have to go on without him. Obliquely, he speaks of what is to come: *My own Rebecca, you are on the threshold—for this I yearn, above all and with all my heart—of a rich and wonderful life. Along the way, God grant you joy and peace. Fill yourself, my beloved, with hope and conviction. Your admiring and adoring, your overwhelmingly loving husband, Leonard.*

That letter is for me what insulin is for a diabetic.

Mornings are hell. I awake in sweaty amnesia to a bright sun through frosted windows and find my body spread diagonally across the double bed. I grope into empty space. Then I remember: Len is not sleeping beside me because he is lying in a single grave in Hillside Cemetery. I will never hear his voice, never hold him, never drive him to the doctor, never sit with him over breakfast again. There will be no more conversations with Anna and Robert about modern art, no more watching for his car to pull in the driveway, no more novels to read together, no more planning to go to

Majorca, no more discussions about what's for dinner. All gone. I will not have Len back. Sick or well. Not for a day, not for an hour, not even for one-thousandth of a second.

Although Phil and Pam have encouraged me to go back to work right away, I'm taking three weeks off. Frances, my boss, was not pleased when I told her I wanted to use up my vacation and not come back until the end of January. I had already taken off a lot of unpaid time when Len was sick, even worked part-time during the final months. Frances was sympathetic then, drawing me into her office, asking what the doctors were telling me, what Len's chances were. But now that Len's dead and the funeral's over, it's business as usual again. At IWN, the multinational insurance company, you get three days off after the death of a close family member. With Len dying over the Christmas holidays, I got slightly more. The department also sent me a dozen red roses paid for out of the petty cash fund and tagged with a black-bordered card reading: "With deepest sympathies, from your friends on the third floor."

"Life does go on, Rebecca," Frances says over the phone, her voice cold and reprimanding. Then she puts on her manager's hat and launches into my "future with IWN." She sees two directions for me: the first continuing with the writing and editing I've been doing, perhaps going eventually as an independent consultant, the second moving more into company matters, taking training courses, working my way along "the career track."

It's clear that things will go hard with me if I don't take plan number two. It's even clearer that if my grieving takes priority over the needs of "the department," I'll be out on my ear.

Returning to work depresses me. I have never particularly liked my job of writing light, frothy profiles on underwriters and actuaries and putting together a glossy four-color magazine called *Premium,* for middle managers. But I continued in my position as staff editor at IWN because I wasn't sure what else I wanted to do, especially after I could not get my first novel published and because, when Len got sick, writing my feature articles about business etiquette did take my mind off worrying about the latest CAT scan.

But to go back to 29 Wall Street, to sit at the IBM Displaywriter in one of the windowless cubicles gushing my bright, cheery prose about how Joseph Zablocki just loves his new job as head of the New York region, to worry over whether I'll offend the CEO by using the phrase "lean and mean" to describe the company's corporate culture, to fuss, in long meetings with designers, over whether the spring issue of *Premium* should have a roller coaster or wheel of fortune on its cover . . . to go back as if Len were alive and nothing had changed seems mad. A betrayal of myself—and Len.

I do not reveal any of this to Frances. I can barely explain it to myself. All I know is that I must have time to grieve.

Frances does tell me, in a moment of maternal solicitude, that I shouldn't "rattle around the house." She's right, of course, much as I might not like to admit she could be right about anything in my life.

My mother wants me to come to Florida, my father to Massachusetts, my sister to New Hampshire. The Parinis have offered to let me stay in Phil's office in Bennington. But I decide, instead, to take up my friends Linda and Jean-Guy Carrier on their invitation to come to Ottawa. Canada in the middle of winter? Six hundred miles north of here with four feet of snow and temperatures below zero? Crazy from a strictly meteorological perspective, yes. But not when you consider that Len, three years before meeting me, escaped to Ottawa for a week in the middle of winter after yet another woman left him. He was so devastated, he told me, that he had to get out of the country. For eight days he skated on the Ottawa canals, went to dinner with Linda and Jean-Guy, even bought an elegant winter coat trimmed with arctic fox. When he returned to New York, his grief had diminished.

I am not superstitious, but flying to Canada in the dead of winter is a superstitious act. If I can hold Len's past in my hand like a rabbit's foot, if I can retrace his steps, I will be all right. If Ottawa healed Len, Ottawa can heal me.

Making the arrangements is difficult. First I must pick out the dates, then call the Carriers, then book my flight, then call the Carriers back. I sit at my desk scribbling numbers, dates, and times on a yellow legal pad: It will be nothing short of a miracle if I can get myself in a cab to Danbury to catch the airport limousine to LaGuardia to board, at 2:20, Air Canada's flight 521 to arrive in Montreal at 4:10, to change flights to Air Canada 334 to arrive at 5:30 in Ottawa, where Linda will be waiting.

My journey almost ends in Montreal when I go through customs. I have not brought my passport, and they threaten to send me back to New York. But a young woman, not much older than I am, takes pity on me. She leads me away into her glass cubicle behind the baggage claim area and asks me, gently, first in French and then in English, where I am from, where I was born, of what country I am a citizen. She asks me whether I am a student. These questions seem surreal to me. I want to tell her I am from no town, no state, no country, that I am a student of the university of mourning, that I am existing, just barely, in the demilitarized zone between the living and the dead.

I manage to sputter that my husband died two weeks ago. She takes pity on me. She stamps my ticket. She waves me on.

Ottawa is having one of its worst winters on record. For days temperatures have not risen above zero. Snow is piled as high as houses in the streets; the canals, usually crowded with skaters, are empty. In the heated car, Linda tries to explain to me the difference between Fahrenheit and Celsius. Something about____and_____. I attempt to concentrate on what she is saying and even test myself by asking:

If it's 30 degrees Fahrenheit, what would the temperature read in Celsius? But it's hopeless. Grief has made me stupid.

Linda is one of those warm, maternal women who gives and gives and gives. I am weeping a little when I enter the house. She takes me in her arms and rocks me like a baby. She shoos away her children waiting on the stairs, then helps me off with my boots and hands me a pair of knitted woolen slippers. She smooths the hair from my forehead and sits me down in a rocking chair in front of the fire. She hands me a glass of red wine. I apologize for crying, and she says gently, ''You don't have to apologize, luv.''

For six days I place myself in the care of *la famille Carrier.* I sleep late in the mornings. When I wake, Linda has set the breakfast table for two with her best dishes and wineglasses full of orange juice. We sit in her cozy, cheerful kitchen eating yogurt with maple syrup and sipping cupful after cupful of mocha coffee. We talk and talk and talk. There is no moment when the symphony of our voices stops, when the chords connecting us are broken.

Linda asks whether Len knew he was dying. I tell her that I believe he did know, although the cancer made it difficult for him to verbalize anything. I remember how he listened for hours to Bach's B-Minor Mass, how he grew a thick, long beard that made him look, with his wide, feverish eyes, like a great mystic. I relive with Linda those long, warm autumn days when Len and I would sit in the deck chairs on the lawn and I would read aloud from the manuscript of his fourth book. When I came to the long section on dying, he would close his eyes and sit very still, as if he were preparing himself, as the book instructed, for the final passage into death.

Linda asks what it was like, to live so intimately with death. She says she never could have done it. I explain that it was hard—sometimes so hard that I yearned for it to be over—but now I would give anything to go back to those days. Because even though Len was sick, he was alive. And as long as he was alive, my life had purpose. I tell Linda about the time I brought Len to the internist in Danbury for what turned out to be his final doctor's appointment. Len was so sick he fell asleep in the waiting room and had to be wheeled into the examining room. After the examination, the doctor, who had a gentle, Marcus Welby manner, called me into his office to say there was nothing he could do other than put Len into a hospital, which wouldn't prolong his life but would make it easier on me. I drew myself up very straight and told him that Len's doctors in New York had already recommended that, but I wanted to keep him at home until the end. Dr. Lesser nodded and told me I knew where to find him if I changed my mind. As I rose to leave, he shook my hand and said, "You're a strong young woman, Mrs. Feldstein. Not many people in your position would take on what you're doing." I didn't contradict him. I knew it was true. I was strong, and I was proud to have him see it.

"But doesn't that give you confidence in yourself now?" Linda asks earnestly.

"It should, shouldn't it? But it was almost as if Len's dying body were the source of my strength. Now that he's gone and there's just me, there's this unbelievable hollowness. Everything seems like such an effort. I get up in the morning and think, Why should I bother to brush my teeth or wash the dishes or clean the house or take out meat from the freezer for dinner? Nothing matters anymore."

"You matter, Becky."

"I want to believe that, but I don't even know who or what I am without Len. Len was always telling me how talented I was, how beautiful, how gifted, what an extraordinary writer, et cetera, et cetera, but I never believed it. I have no idea who this person, Becky or Rebecca, is. Mentally, I feel about twelve years old. No, make that six."

"You've been through a trauma," Linda says gently. "You're still grieving. It's going to take time to heal, maybe a year, maybe longer. It won't be easy. But you're a survivor, luv. You'll survive this, too.''

When Linda teaches her photography class at Carleton University, I look after Elie-Simone, who is two and speaks no English. My French is primitive, but we manage. We play a game where I hold up my hand or point to my mouth and say, ''Qu'est-ce que c'est?'' Elie-Simone, amazed that I don't know what these things are, delightedly replies, ''La main,'' or ''la bouche.'' In this way, I learn the parts of the body. I review them with her, and she squeaks, ''Oui,'' when I'm right and giggles, ''Non,'' when I'm wrong. We invent another game with my long hair where she picks it up and then lets it fall: *lever et tomber, lever et tomber.* I love the feeling of her tiny hands stroking my hair and patting my scalp. I close my eyes and purr. For Elie-Simone there is no death. Only this continuous, sensuous present. Repeated again and again. *Lever et tomber.*

Friends of Linda and Jean-Guy's are invited for dinner on Friday evening. Linda apologizes about their coming. She knows I would probably prefer not to socialize with people I don't know, especially now, so soon after Len's death. She explains that she made the engagement months ago. If she were to change it, she and Jean-Guy would not get to see this couple for another two months, since one of them travels every other week on business. I tell her she shouldn't dream of changing it; it won't kill me to spend a few hours with her friends.

When Natalie and Damian arrive, there is much hugging, kissing, and general bonhomie. I notice a significant age gap between them; Natalie, Linda tells me later, is 53, Damian 31. Because I remember the prejudice Len and I often encountered on account of our age difference, I make an extra effort to be cordial. I ask them about their work, where they are from. Natalie is an economist from Ottawa, Damian a taxi driver from Montreal. They ask me about Connecticut and what I do at IWN.

I am praying they won't ask where my husband is. They don't.

But as the evening wears on and the conversation turns to Brian Mulroney, the new Canadian prime minister, the fall of the Canadian dollar, to acid rain and the plight of the Inuits, I withdraw into silence. I am talking about the plight of the Inuits and Len died two weeks ago. I look at Natalie and Damian holding hands, and suddenly I feel no interest in them, not in their age difference or class difference or whether they prefer Montreal over Ottawa.

They never knew Len. It means nothing to them that he was once alive or is now dead. Len is an abstraction, a city they will never visit, a language they will never learn. That he is not in the world anymore neither subdues their laughter nor lessens Natalie's appetite for fettuccine Alfredo nor shortens Damian's anecdotes about taxi-driving, nor diminishes their excitement about vacationing in Cancun nor even makes them want to leave early. They couldn't give a damn that Len is dead.

At 11:30, I excuse myself and retire to the guest room in the basement. I take my photograph of Len and hold it tight against my nightgown-covered breasts. Quietly, so as not to wake the children or cause embarrassment for Linda and Jean-Guy, I begin to cry.

The next morning, Linda apologizes again for Natalie and Damian. She says, "I know you feel you can't go on without Leonard. But it won't always be this way."

I do not tell her this is what I fear most: the diminishment of my grief. For if it goes, Len will go. Even further away than he is now.

"And someday, Becky," Linda says fervently, "you'll meet someone and be happy again, maybe remarry and even have children. You know Len wouldn't want you to be alone for the rest of your life."

One afternoon, I take Gabriel, who is seven, to lunch and afterward to see the dinosaurs in the Musée de l'Homme.

Or, more accurately, he takes me. I am uneasy exchanging my American money for Canadian when I pay for the meal, feel lost as we stroll past the life-sized skeletons of tyrannosauruses and brontosauruses in the huge, dimly lit theaters of the museum.

"You'll have to look after me, Gabriel," I warn him, taking his hand. "I'm not quite sure where I'm going."

"Look after you?" Gabriel replies, with childish incredulity. "You'll have to look after *me*, Becky."

Len and I loved Gabriel. We told him that we liked him better than any other little boy, that we wanted one just like him and were going to go to "the boy store" to pick one up. Gabriel wasn't quite sure whether we were pulling his leg and would say, "I don't think you could get one just like me, could you?"

Before the seizures, Len and I had talked about having a baby. I had always been against it: I thought children would destroy my independence, interfere with my quest to fulfill myself. And yet, as I neared my thirtieth birthday, I began to reconsider. Something inexplicable happened to me when I was around my friends' young children; I felt such peace when I heard their high-pitched voices, snuggled up with them, and read them stories. I began to think I might be missing out on something; I imagined that not having children could make me yearn for them for the rest of my life.

"If Len and I had had a child . . ." I say to myself over and over as Gabriel asks me why some dinosaurs are herbivorous, others carnivorous. If Len and I had had a child, we would have named him Leonard if he was a boy, Emily if she was a girl. He or she would be smart like Len and would perhaps have Len's blue eyes, Len's gentle disposition. If Len and I had had a child, I would be walking at this moment with the hand of his child, of perhaps three or five, in mine. And this child's veins, this child's skin, this child's words, this child's cry—all of this creature would be stenciled with the mysterious genetic wax that was Len, the mysterious something that would not perish.

As Gabriel and I are sipping Cokes in the museum's cafeteria, I ask him if he ever wonders where Len is.

Gabriel says immediately, "No. I know where he is. He's all around us. He's everywhere."

And then, a few minutes later, in a very wise and grown-up voice: "You don't have to feel sad, Becky, because Leonard's right here with you."

When I return to Connecticut, I find a dozen sympathy cards waiting in my box at the post office. There are notices from Jesuits at Fordham promising to offer masses "for the repose of the soul of Leonard Feldstein." There are typewritten letters from Len's colleagues that speak of Len's gifts as a philosopher and teacher, his loyalty as a friend, how much he will be missed. And cards from Len's patients with drooping flowers on the covers and rhyming verses inside: "Although at times of sorrow/there's so little/words can say/Still may these words of sympathy/help comfort you today."

I had always thought the custom of sending sympathy cards, even writing eulogistic letters, pointless, a contrived bit of funeral etiquette drummed up by greeting card magnates to rake in more cash. After all, it is too late for Len to hear what an extraordinary person he was, and what good does it do me to get corny rhyming verses that confess to their own ineffectualness? But as I drive to the West Redding post office each day, I look forward to the vision of my mailbox window white with these missives. Eagerly I note their return addresses, slash my finger through the back flap, devour the paragraphs or sentences or signatures. I stuff them into my purse and take them home and place them on my desk like trophies. Each day, the pile grows larger. Sometimes I pick up all of them and run them through my fingers as if I were shuffling cards.

I imagine replying to all senders and telling them that if they really wanted to help, they would keep mailing these cards, at the rate of one or two a month. For as long as the cards keep pouring in with the blue or black or green ink proclaiming the precious letters "Len," then he is not really dead. As long as people write that he loved the Grand Canyon or inspired them to become a psychotherapist or made Plato come alive, then his life force still pulses through the world. As long as people say, "We will miss him," I have not lost him.

Gail, who has been staying with Tom while I've been in Canada, calls to ask whether I will write her a recommendation. She has signed up with a nanny agency in Stamford and will be interviewing for a live-in position with a family in New Canaan. She is excited about this new job. The pay is double what she was getting from me; she will be part of a large household staff including cook, maid, and gardener and will accompany the family to their condominiums in Vermont and Florida. Her only responsibilities will be to look after the two children, aged 8 and 10.

"These people are filthy rich, Bicky," Gail enthuses. "It's like right out of 'Dallas.' "

I assure her I'll write something so good that they'll have no choice but to give her the job.

She wants to stop by that afternoon to pick up the letter and to gather the last of her belongings. After the funeral, she moved most of her things to Tom's cabin on Candlewood Lake in Danbury, but she did not take her papiermâché animals or summer blouses. I told her she was welcome to keep her room and stay as long as she wanted, although I couldn't afford to keep paying her. I hoped, selfishly, that her affair with Tom wouldn't work out and she'd be back.

As I sit at my typewriter to compose the recommendation, I realize that, after today, I may not see her again.

She is all bubbly when she arrives, chattering about how she wants to work for maybe three or four months at this new job to save up enough money to go to England in the summer. She'll stay with a friend in London and then "tod-dle" off to Spain for a month.

We sit at the dining room table sipping tea and eating the pumpkin bread that she baked weeks ago and that I discovered in the freezer. We gravitate to our usual places, I at the head, she in the middle. We set our saucers down on the green linen placemats; at the other end of the table rests the third matching placemat where Len would sit. The silver sugar cube caddy, which I had brought out months ago for Gail, stands in its familiar spot on the silver trivet in the center of the table. As the warm, thawing sun pours through the windows and shines upon Gail's round, eager face, it feels as if nothing has changed. Gail and I are buttering the warm, crumbly slabs of pumpkin bread and chatting as we had on dozens of afternoons when Len was resting. Only the closed door to Len's room, the door I haven't opened since the funeral, reminds me that everything is different.

Gail gives me a great bear hug when we say good-bye.

"Take good care of yurself, kid," she says, bestowing a final motherly pat on my shoulder, "and remember to git those three squares a day. Can't have you fading away into a ghost."

She loads her backpack into Tom's car, puts the envelope with my recommendation on the dashboard, and then starts up the engine. As she backs up into the turnaround, she rolls down the window and shouts above a Madonna song blasting on the radio, "And remember, Bicky, if you're ever in New Zealand, ring me up. I'll probably be an old married fart by then, but we'll have a good laugh, I promise you." Then a quick beep-beep, and she is gone.

I stand at the back door watching her. When her car dips away through the tangle of bare winter branches, I let the tears come.

That night, lying in my bed with the electric blanket turned up to "9" and stuffing myself with the remains of the pumpkin bread, I realize that what is so terrible about death is not that it happens once and for all, but that it keeps happening, again and again. Each day, I find fresh evidence of Len's passing: The empty closet in Gail's room. The plastic orange vials of his medicine clinking in the kitchen drawer. The soap dish that he ripped out of the wall last November when he stumbled in the shower. The dark spot on the beige sofa where he "wet himself," as Gail called it. His camel's hair coat hanging in the hall closet, reminding me of life before cancer. I try to assimilate the meaning of these images. I cannot. I'm willing to believe anything— that Len is delivering a paper in California, that Len has gone on vacation, that Len is in Paris—but the truth. I discover more evidence: the typewritten death certificate in its waxy envelope signed and sealed by the Redding Registrar of Vital Statistics. Like a poor student who flunks a test repeatedly, I try again to learn the theorem that refuses to be committed to memory: Len is gone. He won't come back.

At the post office next morning, I find, among the sympathy cards addressed to me and junk mail for Len, one thick legal-sized manila envelope addressed to me. The upper left hand corner bears the stamped insignia of the Teachers Insurance and Annuity Association, 730 Third Avenue, New York, New York 10017. I rip it open anxiously. The cover letter attached by paper clip to the packet of green and white forms informs me that I have been designated the beneficiary of Len's pension from Fordham and that I am to receive approximately $115,000 and would I kindly fill out the attached forms and return them in the enclosed envelope as soon as possible. The letter is signed by Roberta Frank, associate pension administrator of the benefits department of TIAA.

I had, in fact, known about this money before. When Len and I were first married, I remember Len signing beneficiary forms, putting documents together in oversized manila folders marked "IMPORTANT PAPERS," and storing them, along with old tax returns and mortgage papers, in the black filing cabinet in the downstairs closet. At the time,

I paid no attention. Len's death seemed about as likely as a nuclear winter.

Now I stand beside the zip code books in the post office, staring at the typed characters of this letter from the Teacher's Insurance and Annuity Association. Since it is the middle of the day, the post office is nearly empty save for the two postal clerks who make soft, rustling noises as they sort the mail and stuff it into the boxes. On the radio, a weatherman announces that traffic advisories have just been put out for all of southern New England. Outside, I notice a thin layer of snow beginning to cover the windshields of the cars.

I whisper, "Len has left me over one hundred thousand dollars." I would have to work at IWN for over five years to make this kind of money. Now I will receive it in a matter of weeks. I feel like someone who has just won the lottery. I want to throw up all my mail in the air and scream out, "I'm rich! I'm rich!" to the postal clerks.

But then I remember that I am making this "killing" only because Len is dead. And suddenly I feel a whiplash of guilt. This money isn't mine. I didn't earn it. It represents years and years of *Len's* hard work at a job he began years before he met me, a job he trained for before I was born.

Why should I get this money? Why me and not his children, Judi and Mark, or even Vivian, who was married to Len for fifteen years?

I remember the two insurance policies that Judi and Mark are to receive. Each is worth about fifteen thousand dollars. But fifteen thousand dollars is peanuts compared with what I will get. Is it fair that Len's own flesh and blood, who are only a few years younger than I, should inherit less than a fifth of what I receive? Len wanted *me* to have this money, I remind myself defensively. It's not as if I threatened to leave him if he didn't change his will. It's not as if I stood over him demanding that he sign the change of beneficiary forms leaving me the money rather than Judi or Mark. It's true that when Len got sick and I became obsessed with money and terrified that there wouldn't be enough, I did consider, in a desperate moment, asking him to change Judi and Mark's policies to benefit me. But I never got further than thinking about this.

A man enters the post office, stamping his snow-laden boots on the floor. He unlocks his box and takes out a crumpled packet of letters. "Bills, bills, bills," he grumbles. "Nothing but bills."

Suddenly, I remember my own bills waiting for me on my desk beside the pile of sympathy cards. There is an invoice in triplicate from the emergency room of Lenox Hill Hospital demanding immediate remittance of two thousand dollars; a form letter from the Phoenix-Mutual Insurance Company explaining that my health insurance benefits, which I had gotten free as Len's wife, will be cut off in six months; a second itemized bill from Mr. Wakeman with a hand-scrawled note telling me to ignore this if I've already sent my check; a "reminder" from the People's Savings Bank noting that I am delinquent on my mortgage payments and informing me I have fourteen days to pay.

"We're supposed to get about two feet of this stuff," the man grumbles. "Who needs it? That's what I want to know." He pulls his ski hat down over his ears and stamps out the door.

For the first time since Len's death, I realize I'm alone in the world. No husband to support me anymore. No one to attend to all the nasty practical details that I've managed, for most of my adult life, to ignore. If I don't pay my mortgage, the bank will take away my house. If I don't get health insurance, my savings could be wiped out by an illness. If I don't send Mr. Wakeman and the Lenox Hill Hospital emergency room their money, lawyers will haul me to court.

I reread the letter from TIAA. I think, *Not only am I not going to give one penny of that money to Judi or Mark or Vivian, I had better figure out how to get my hands on it as quickly as possible.*

I spend every day of the next week rummaging through

that black filing cabinet in the downstairs closet hunting for documents: Len's social security number, birth certificate, our marriage certificate, copies of two different change of beneficiary forms that Len signed before and after we were married. For entire mornings I am on the phone. With my lawyer. My accountant. Janis Trott in Benefits at Fordham. Roberta Frank at TIAA. I ask them hundreds of questions: What is a fixed annuity? A life annuity? A qualified pension? A non-qualified pension? An IRA rollover? Which should I take? Is the pension taxable? By the federal government? By the state of Connecticut? Is there a percentage that's not? Since Len died in December of 1984, will I be taxed in 1984 or 1985?

Janis Trott refers me to Roberta Frank at TIAA; Roberta Frank to my accountant; my accountant to my lawyer; my lawyer, who is based in Connecticut, back to my accountant, who is based in New York. With each call, my head swirls in the fallout of more acronyms I'd like to blast out of my cranium: CREF, FICA, IRS, IRA. I hang up the phone and cradle my head in my hands and beg for Len to come back and make everything go away, sweep up all these cancerous excretions on my desk and float them back into the drawers of the filing cabinet, and I will shut the closet door forever and the forms will argue, like the cartoon characters they are, among themselves. And I won't have to look at them again.

In my worst moments, I imagine I'm being punished for playing hooky so long from this practical world. Today I receive a computerized letter adressed to "Leonard and Rebecca Feldstein," stating that tax returns from 1983 are currently under investigation and that the above-named respondents will be contacted within ten days by an IRS representative.

I remember how Len raged when he got one of these communications, ripping it open in a fury, screeching, "What in God's name are the bastards hounding me for this time?" I, who had never been investigated by the IRS, who had never even filled out my own tax return, was always slightly confused, even a little amused by these outpourings, particularly when Len's diatribes would spew forth in all their vitriol.

Now I understand Len's anxiety. Driving home with this signatureless letter on my dashboard, this KGB-like communiqué with only a box number and an anonymous town somewhere in New York State for a return address, I imagine nightmarish scenarios. What if the IRS says I owe them fifty thousand dollars in back taxes? What if I can't come up with the money and they put a lien on the house? What if they put me in jail?

I call my accountant in stuttering terror. His secretary, who is sympathetic to my plight, puts me through immediately. Lester Goldberg, who talks very fast and is a Jewish mother at heart, tells me not to worry, assures me he can get a delay, thinks that I might have to pay a few hundred dollars at most. He explains that Len was always being investigated because his deductions for his psychiatric practice exceeded his income—''perfectly legit. But the IRS doesn't like it.'' He tells me to mail him the letter right away, then suggests I drop by to meet with him when I'm in New York.

I make an appointment for the next day.

Lester, whom I'm meeting for the first time, is a sweet, funny, nervous little man with a crew cut of gray hair and a chubby, childlike face. He talks no slower in person than on the phone.

''I always liked Leonard,'' he says. ''Of course, he was very disorganized and always waited till the last minute to file his returns. But we got along. You know a lot of people come in here and complain, and bark and carry on, but Leonard would come in and we'd talk abut Karl Marx. Stuff like that.''

He shakes his head and sighs. ''He's about the tenth person I know who's died of cancer in the last year. It's a damned shame.

"But it's pretty rough for you now? Huh?"

I nod and feel the tears stinging the corners of my eyes.

"I always tell my wife and daughter, 'You'd better learn how to do these things now because someday you're going to have to do them alone.' "

He asks me what I plan to do with the pension money. I tell him I don't know, maybe put it in the Merrill Lynch money market fund Len took out a few years ago.

"You know that you wouldn't have to give a cent of that money to the IRS if you rolled it over into an IRA," Lester says, pronouncing "IRA" like a boy's name and leaping around the office excitedly. Not giving a penny to the IRS clearly appeals to him. "You'd be getting 11 percent on it every year until you're 59½. Of course, it means you can't touch it until then, and you'll still have to pay taxes on it, but you'll probably be in a lower tax bracket by then and you won't pay as much."

I need the money now, I tell him.

"Okay, okay. You're the boss," he says. "Just do me a favor. If you do go with Merrill Lynch, fine. I'll put you in touch with Richard Klausner in the New York office. But if you start to get fancy ideas like playing the stock market, talk to me first. Don't call me up after it's too late and say, 'By the way, I've invested in shopping centers in Puerto Rico.' There are a lot of scams going around, and widows are sitting ducks."

I spend an hour with him. I leave feeling reassured. I will always keep Lester Goldberg for my accountant.

As I walk back to Grand Central, I remember how my father had lectured me to be independent. When I was eight, he had put me on an airplane from Salt Lake City to Hartford with a tag around my neck: "If lost, please contact . . ." When I was 14, he had pushed me to get my first job as a ski instructor, waking me at seven every Saturday and Sunday morning for four winters with a bellowing, "Get the lead out.'' He had gotten me an internship on the *Berkshire Eagle,* calling at my desk each day to make sure I wasn't ''goofing off.'' When I turned 21, he gave me a trust fund of one hundred thousand dollars (which Len and I had used for a down payment on the house), explaining that he never wanted me to be financially dependent, on *him* or any man.

How did I end up so helpless, I wonder, as I pass the movie theater where Len and I had seen *La Traviata* three weeks before he had been hospitalized. Why did I let Len pay the mortgage, keep the checkbook, do the taxes? Why did I prefer to sign my name to his gold MasterCard rather than apply for my own? Unlike my mother and grandmother, I'd grown up in an era in which women were encouraged to be independent, had heard Gloria Steinem declare that women needed men like fish needed bicycles. Unlike my mother and grandmother, I'd gone to graduate school and worked. I'd married a man who wanted me to achieve, who never expected me to cook and clean for him.

No, my helplessness was rooted not in forces outside me, but in psychic needs within me—in that passive, frightened little girl who, like her mother, had no confidence in her ability to negotiate the world, that child who found it so much safer to let her daddy carry her. Then, all at once, I am flooded with memories: early memories of me at age seven or eight, riding the baby rope tow at Bousquet's, scrunched safely between my father's immense legs. I remember when I was 10 waiting for six o'clock, when I would hear his Corvette zooming up the driveway, and how I would run to the window and wait for that delirious moment when he would clump through the back door and I would leap into his arms, gratefully inhaling his outdoor masculine smells of wallets, pens, and suit pockets chinking with quarters—such a relief from the cottony, sickbed smells of my mother among her blankets and tissues. I remember, as an adolescent, taking long walks with him, complaining about how the other ski instructors had called me Rotunda and how lonely I was and how I thought obsessively of death.

My father didn't know how to cope with his miserable teenage daughter and so prescribed the punishing when-the-going-gets-tough-the-tough-get-going regimen that had worked for him. He said I was too "sensitive," too "thin-skinned," too much like my mother. I could control my moods by developing a positive mental attitude. He quoted Shakespeare: "There is nothing either good or bad, but thinking makes it so." He said I could reduce my weight by exercising more and not eating so much; he and my grandmother wanted to enroll me in an Elaine Powers Figure Salon to reduce my derriere. He prescribed "Dale Carnegie" for my shyness, "Outward Bound" for my boyfriend troubles. I never attended "Dale Carnegie," but I did go to a 28-day "Outward Bound" program in the wilderness of northern Minnesota, where, among other character-building trials, I was placed on an uninhabited island for three days with nothing but a book of matches and a fishhook.

I survived "Outward Bound," only to rebel against my father's macho approach to life. I took drugs, became less athletic, grew fatter and more melancholy. I married Len, who was Jewish, unathletic, an "egghead," a "shrink," and twice my age. The irony, of course, was that in marrying a man old enough to be my father I had never relinquished that dependent, daughterly side of myself. Len, I suddenly realize, had guided me through my turbulent young adulthood as my father had guided me through my turbulent childhood and adolescence. Like my father, Len had ministered to my faltering self-esteem—providing unconditional support rather than stern criticism. Like my father, Len had helped me negotiate the outer, masculine world, at once so thrilling and terrifying. Len had mediated my depressions, prescribing psychotherapy and poetry writing instead of "Dale Carnegie" and violent exercise. Len was wiser than I and could advise me—not just about the IRS but about why human beings were coarse or weak or cruel, why my mother was so undone by her troubles with my father that she took to her bed, why she and my father married in the first place, why I bore within my own troubled soul the conflicts between them.

As I write out a check for my return train ticket—one of the new ones with only my name in the upper left hand corner—it occurs to me that now Len can no longer father me and now that I'm too old to return to my own father, I have no choice but to master the art of fathering myself.

At 9:00 the next morning, Janis Trott from Fordham calls. It seems that Vivian has been calling her, sometimes twice a day, to ask whether Len made any "provisions" for her. Janis Trott explained to Vivian that Dr. Feldstein left his pension to me and two fifteen-thousand-dollar insurance policies to his children. That's it. Vivian insists there is some other insurance policy that was to be maintained exclusively for her. Was I aware of such a policy? Janis Trott asks. No, I tell her. Janis Trott is in a state. How should she handle Vivian? She doesn't like being in the middle.

Fifteen minutes later, who should call but Vivian. In a panic. Apparently, the divorce agreement stipulated that Len was supposed to have kept up a ten-thousand-dollar life insurance policy for her. Did Len ever mention it? I explain that the only policies I know about are those for Judi and Mark.

"At least he remembered his own children," she says bitterly. "It wasn't much, but at least he left them *something.*" Then her voice gets very sweet and cajoling and she says she knows it's a lot of trouble, but would I mind looking through Len's papers and seeing if I can find this policy. And if not the policy itself, maybe records of payments. Anything.

I am annoyed that she is pestering me, but I promise to look. I call her back to tell her that I can find nothing in the black filing cabinet or in Len's desk or even in some old papers in the cellar.

"The bastard," she whimpers. "How could he do this to me?"

I tell her that I believe she is due to receive some social security benefits. I give her the phone number of the social security office in Danbury.

"How much can it be?" she whines. "Probably not more than one hundred dollars a month. A lot of good that'll do me."

The next day my lawyer calls to tell me Vivian is suing the estate for ten thousand dollars. He doesn't think she can win, but he has already spoken with her lawyer and there is some technicality in the new probate laws of Connecticut that could go in her favor. What Vivian has got going against her, my lawyer says, is that she's not suing for "big bucks"; if the case can be dragged out, as my lawyer intends to do, Vivian's lawyer could drop her if he thinks there's nothing in it for him.

"Oh, Len," I sigh as I retreat into the bedroom to lie down. "Look at what an awful mess you've made by dying. Vivian and me battling each other in a lawsuit. Me spending half my day weeping and the other half jabbering with lawyers and accountants and pension administrators. None of this would've happened if you'd lived."

I pick up the framed photograph on the nightstand. It's a picture of Len and me, taken six years ago at a cabin in Vermont. Len looks eagerly into the camera, eyes squinting in the sunlight and grinning like a boy. He is wearing the cobalt-blue Irish-knit sweater we had bought that morning in Stowe. He looks 10, maybe 15 years younger than his age of 56. His arm is around me, and my head rests blissfully on his shoulder. My face is sunburned and rounded with a happy chubbiness. My long blond hair, which I have just washed, shines in the sunlight like some advertisement for nutrient-rich shampoo. I look no more than 18, though I have just turned 25.

Rebecca Rice

I study these two people and realize that not just one of them is dead, but both of them are—Len, who told me my love would make him live as long as Picasso, and me, that happy, innocent child who believed him.

The distance that the dead have gone
Does not at first appear;
Their coming back seems possible
For many an ardent year.

—Emily Dickinson

February 4, 1985

I rise in the dark as the alarm goes off.

I jerk my legs out of bed, heave them onto the cold rug, and rush into the bathroom, flicking on the bright makeup lights on either side of the sink. My eyes, still sunk in sleep, blink in the flash of fluorescent light, blink and sting as I splash my face with cold water. I brush my teeth very fast and very hard, so hard that my spittle turns red in the sink. I throw my hair over my head and brush it swiftly a dozen times, then gather and pin it at the base of my skull.

I glance at the glittering red letters of the digital clock. 5:58. Ten minutes. Barely time to work my legs into the cream-colored pantyhose, shimmy the gray wool skirt over my hips, tie the bow of my white silk blouse, and straighten the shoulder pads of my matching gray wool jacket. As I bolt down a glass of orange juice before the open refrigerator, I think, *The last time I stood here with these clothes on, Len was alive.''*

Alive and still asleep in his bed. And before I threw my briefcase in the trunk and scraped the ice from the windshield, I would first slip into his room and lie down beside him and kiss him good-bye and tell him I'd be home tonight and Gail would be there while I was gone and everything would be all right. Although he would never awaken fully, he would murmur something to let me know he knew I was there. Sometimes, before he was really sick, he would smile and whisper, ''Come back soon.''

Even though I knew he was dying, I knew he would not,

83

in all likelihood, die on that particular day. Death, I imagined, was so awesome that it couldn't possibly happen on a Tuesday or Wednesday at 1:00 or 2:00 in the afternoon while I wolfed down a tuna fish sandwich at my desk. As I waited for the car to warm up each morning, I wagered that my chances of coming back in the evening to Len and Gail by the fire with Mozart on the stereo and a casserole in the oven and the table set for three . . . my chances that life—sweet, unremarkable daily life—would prevail were high.

Driving to the station, I would sometimes find myself inexplicably happy with the ice-covered trees or the occasional woodchuck blinking in my headlights or the first silver patches of dawn sky. To my surprise, this happiness stayed with me as I moved through the day. It was there when I bought my apple-cinnamon muffin at the Whistle Stop and grumbled with my fellow commuters about the train delays; it followed me at work when I put my stocking feet on my desk and called Len on my lunch hour; it even got me through my rage at rewriting a profile because Frances said it was too "controversial."

Len was alive. All was still right with the world.

Now, on this morning of my first day back to work, as I wait for Hector, my little mutt, to finish his business in the snow, I feel only cold and winter darkness, a silence like the silence of the deaf.

I listen to Hector's toenails making thin tap-tapping noises on the ice. I watch his mangy, wheat-colored body navigating through the trees. I think guiltily of how I have neglected him during these weeks, how my grief has made me oblivious of everything but myself. I remember how Len loved Hector, nicknamed him "the beast," and fed him tidbits from the table. Animals, I've read somewhere, mourn just the way people do. I wonder if that's why Hector pushes open the door to Len's room every night and curls up on the bed with his head on the pillow.

As I measure out his Kibbles 'N' Bits, I remind myself to turn down the heat, switch off the lights, lock the back door, and pull down the garage door all the way so raccoons won't get into the garbage. When I back the car around, I notice Hector at the window, head cocked and wagging his stub of a tail. I drive away quickly, realizing that I dread coming back.

At the station, the raincoated men are lined up, briefcases in one hand, newspapers in the other, on the far end of the platform. The morning is cold, and some stamp their rubbered feet to keep warm. Others sip coffee from Styrofoam cups and stare languidly into the fog.

No one speaks.

I recognize a few faces: a thin, somewhat scruffy man with a graying beard eating a muffin, an elderly man with a bow-tie and derby-like hat reading the *Wall Street Journal,* a plumpish, heavily made-up woman, one of the few other female commuters, galloping across the parking lot in rhinestone boots. Once last September when two freight trains collided in Stamford and the morning trains were canceled, I rode with all of them in the elderly man's gray Oldsmobile into New York. We sat in traffic on the Merritt for close to an hour, and I learned that the scruffy man wrote television commercials and the plump woman worked three days a week as assistant food editor at *Woman's Day* and the bow-tied man was a vice-president at the Chase Manhattan Bank. After this adventure, we always greeted one another as we waited for the 6:32. Sometimes we asked how the advertising was going or what was new at the Chase, and sometimes we said how glorious the fall days were or that winter was around the corner.

As I line up to board the train, I find myself avoiding the gaze of these three. I dig holes with my boots in the snow; I fix my eyes upon the ramshackle houses above the tracks. If I say hello or even just nod, how do I know they won't ask, casually of course, where I've been the last month? And what will I say? I hurry down the aisle. When I spot an empty two-seater, I grab it. I settle by the window and pile my coat on the seat beside me. I bury myself in my paper.

The newspaper is full of deaths, deaths in Iraq and Iran, deaths in Israel, Lebanon, India, West Germany, and California. When Len was alive, I would read about the murder of a promising young actress on the Upper West Side of Manhattan or the machine-gunning of a French journalist in Beirut and grieve for the human being who had suffered, the "I" quivering inside the dying body, never to see the sky again. Today, as I scan an article about five people in California who were massacred in a McDonald's last year, as I remember their bodies bloodied and draped over one another on the front page of *The New York Times,* I feel neither shock nor pity nor sadness. I think only that Len has died. All other deaths are of no consequence.

In Grand Central, I wait in a long line near the central information kiosk to buy my return ticket. Although the large, circular face of the Newsweek clock reads only 8:20, there are people everywhere—stampeding through the narrow gates on the upper and lower levels, dashing up and down the incline beneath the computerized news flashes, grabbing train schedules, waiting in line for newspapers, stuffing croissants and pastries in their mouths as they race to catch the 4, 5, 6, and 7, the shuttle to Times Square. As they whirl past, like so many bits of human confetti, I scrutinize the faces, which are mainly male faces. There are old faces. Young faces. Tanned faces. Blotched faces. Skin that's slack at the chin. Skin pulled razor tight at the chin. Waved hair. Slicked down hair. Bald pates. Trimmed beards. Ears that stick out. Ears lost in graying sideburns. Blue eyes. Baggy eyes. Bright eyes. Bloodshot eyes.

I stare at all these men, astonished that none of them will ever be Len.

At IWN, my co-workers greet me with the hushed, "I'm-so-sorry-to-hear-about-your-husband," and hurry away. I sit at my desk staring at the stacks of insurance magazines in my "In" box, the pile of correspondence addressed to *Pre-*

mium Editor, and the memoranda from Frances headed with my initials, "RRF." In the hallway I hear Gloria, the secretary, giggling as she tells Jim about some survey in the *Post* that found most people would rather eat out at a good restaurant than have sex. The phone rings and Gloria answers it with an especially hearty and giggly, "Good morning, Corporate Communications," and then bellows out, "Frances, it's Mr. Sternberg. Line one." I stare out the film-streaked window at the limousines and delivery trucks three stories below. I think bitterly, *Life goes on.*

Then, a cautious knock at my door. The knock is unnecessary, since the door is open, but I say, "Come in," and Liza, one of the other editors about my age, pops in, all smiles. "Look," she says, plopping down in a chair on the other side of my desk and smoothing the pleats of her skirt, "I know it feels really weird to be back here, and we're all going to be very busy and you're going to hurt a lot. I just want you to know that if you ever need a shoulder to cry on, I'm here. I know what my mom went through after my dad died, and I know it's not pretty."

"Thank you, Liza," I say, ready to burst into tears. "I really appreciate that."

"Oh, and by the way," she says, still all smiles, handing me a typed memo, "there's a staff meeting at 10:00." Waving her fingers at me as if she were waving a hanky, she tiptoes out.

In the windowless conference room, Frances begins by welcoming me back and then goes around the room in the usual way, asking us what we have "to report." Liza is first, and she describes, with her usual enthusiasm, her last meeting with the risk managers to plan the next issue of *Forum.* Penny lights a cigarette and says that the blues from *Premium* have just come back. Molly brings everyone up to date on her story about rate hardening. Jim says that Sternberg expressed an interest in doing a cover story on the Life Division.

"Sounds like a neat idea." Frances beams. "After all,

60 percent of our profits last year came from the Life Division.''

''Sixty percent of our profits came from the Life Division,'' I mutter to myself; 100 percent of this job is in the Death Division, under the departments of inanity, boredom and absurdity. Len's body is disintegrating in a steel-cased grave, and I'm sitting around a conference table talking about life insurance. How can I stand this place for an hour, let alone a week or a year, or, God help me, the rest of my life? Someday I'm going to lie in a steel-cased grave and what is my tombstone going to say—''She wrote about term life''?

When Frances nods in my direction, I imagine standing up and shouting, ''I'm quitting!'' Instead, I sit up straighter and read from the notes I've scribbled on my legal pad. In a voice that surprises me with its evenness, I announce that I will continue with the stories I was working on before I left: an executive profile on Ted Marks, a news story on insurance in Brazil, an update on the ''Employees Of The Year'' contest.

Jim and Molly relax visibly when I finish. They were probably worried that I'd be out of commission for the next few weeks, which would mean more work for them.

''Well, Rebecca''—Frances beams—''looks like you've got a lot on your plate.''

After asking whether anyone has anything else to add, she says, ''Meeting dismissed.''

I head for the ladies' room, carrying a book of poetry that I keep in my desk. I slip into the last stall, lock it and open the book to a Yeats poem that Len and I used to read together: ''Come away, O human child!/To the waters and the wild/With a faery, hand in hand,/For the world's more full of weeping than you can understand.'' As I close my eyes and release a long, continuous stream of urine, I remember how we lay in bed reading these lines, and how Len sang out the words, ''For the world's more full of weeping,'' and then murmured ''than you can understand.''

Snuggled beneath our Hudson Bay blankets before sleep, arms and legs nesting together, we were that human child and faery flying away from an adult world of widows and astrocytomas. If we held each other tight enough, said the words feelingly enough, we could stay there forever with "the lowing/of the calves on the warm hillside."

I start to cry as I stand up to flush the toilet. At that moment, I hear a key in the door and a series of efficient, ladylike steps. I crouch down to watch the shoes passing into the next stall, and I spot a pair of brass-buckled, patent leather pumps that I recognize as Frances's. My whole body stiffens in dread as I listen to the intimate rustle of her movements, the lifting up of her skirt, the pulling down of her pantyhose. I wait until I hear the final whoosh of the toilet flushing and the door slapping behind her before I venture out.

I return to my office, replace *The Collected Poems of W. B. Yeats* in my bottom desk drawer, and sit at my desk with my hands folded on my beige blotter. I glance at my watch. Only 10:45. Over an hour until I can escape for lunch. I stare at my notes from the staff meeting. Frances wants the Marks profile in two weeks. Damn. I pick up the phone to call his office, telling myself it's unlikely I'll reach him directly. Marks's secretary calls back and says Mr. Marks has a half-hour free now and why don't I come up and see how much I can get done. A second interview can be scheduled when he returns from China. I'm about to say no, I can't possibly do it today. Then I realize that anything's better than sitting here staring at *Insurance Underwriter*.

Before riding the elevator to Marks's office on the fifteenth floor, I inspect myself in the compact mirror in my desk. The whites of my eyes are threaded with blood, and there are black craters beneath my lashes descending all the way to my cheekbones. I should have worn glasses instead of contacts today. The tortoise-shelled wire frames would have provided camouflage; with Hydro-curve contacts, my pale, grief-stained face lies exposed. I take out a small bottle of "Sensitive Eyes," lie back in my chair, and bathe each cornea with two or three drops. I blink, then review myself again. Whatever happens, I must not break down.

Ted Marks, chief financial officer at IWN, is a nervous, hollow-cheeked man in his early 50s who answers most questions "Yes," "No," or "Why are you interested in that?" as he holds himself pen-knife erect in his black leather chair behind his massive desk. At the beginning of the interview, he complains that he doesn't see why he has been chosen for the executive profile; there are other people in the company who are "far more scintillating," as he puts it. Overseeing the company's assets is "pretty dull stuff," except to an investment banker. Furthermore, he commutes two hours each day from Upper Saddle River, New Jersey, works 50 to 60 hours a week, and doesn't have time for the kinds of hobbies that make for "good copy."

A long silence.

I flip through the pages of my steno pad as if I am reviewing my notes. When Len was alive, no matter how badly an interview went, I would go home at the end of the day and give him a blow-by-blow account of it, after which Len would give his psychiatrist's diagnosis of the guy's problems. Then we would amuse ourselves imagining, as if he were a case study or character in a novel, the details of his childhood, relationship with his mother and wife, what he might have become had he been free to pursue his youthful dreams. Under our microscope, even the most boorish of these characters would begin to look interesting. And back I would go to write a fanciful profile in which the guy would appear so intriguing he'd barely recognize himself.

Marks's secretary buzzes him: Mr. Sternberg is on the line. Marks's cheeks get even hollower as he takes the call; clearly, he is terrified of the man who was voted by *Fortune* to be one of the toughest bosses in the country.

Marks mutters something about a pressing matter and scurries up to Sternberg's office on the eighteenth floor; when he returns, he fires all sorts of irrelevant information at me: his ranking at the Harvard Business School, his grade point average at Cornell, the prizes he won in science and math in high school. When I ask him what he wanted to be when he was a boy, he barks, "I have no idea. I can't remember back that far."

Another silence. Marks looks at his watch and scowls.

I have two choices: Either to tell him that Len is dead and I couldn't give a damn about him or his lousy profile, which could lead, at best, to a reprimand from Frances and, at worst, to being fired, or I can maintain the dubious illusion that I am a professional and hunt for something to save the interview from disaster.

Marks says he hopes my other interviews are more productive.

I pretend I haven't heard this and inquire about two black and white photos of snow-clad mountain peaks on a far wall. He tells me one is the Jungfrau and the other is the Matterhorn. He has climbed both. For the last ten years he has taken three weeks off every summer to go on climbing expeditions in the French and Swiss Alps. He has hung from sheer rock faces, rappeled down steep crevasses, missed fatal avalanches by inches.

My relief is palpable as I scribble away to keep up with him. When I ask him what he loves about mountain climbing, he says, "I don't want you to print this, but it's the only time during the year when I forget about IWN."

On the way back to my office, I hear my phone ringing. "That's your phone, Rebecca," Gloria chimes out. As I lunge past her, my only thought is, *Who could it be but Len? Calling to find out what train I'll be on, calling to say it's 12 o'clock and he misses me.*

As I grab the dusty beige receiver, I imagine Len's warm, raspy, "Hi, sweetheart," coming through a background of static as it travels, oh miracle of engineering, across miles and miles of underground cable.

"Hello?" I answer breathlessly, forgoing the usual business of answering the phone with my name.

"Rebecca? Frances. I'd like to meet with you for a few minutes this afternoon, say around 4:30. You usually catch a later train to Connecticut, right?"

The conversation lasts 30 seconds, but when I hang up, I am trembling. I shut the door and collapse in one of the chairs on the other side of my desk. I cradle my head in my hands. For the rest of my life I will answer the phone and Len will never again be on the other end. He won't call to tell me he just got rid of his last patient or gave a "bang-up" lecture on Kant or got a good review in *APQ*. He won't call me from Fordham or Redding or from his room at Lenox Hill. He won't call collect or person-to-person. He won't call to say, as he did a week before he died, "Becky, Becky, Becky."

At that moment, a knock on my door. It's Jim and Molly asking me if I'd like to go to the Seaport for lunch.

"We're really going to pig out," Molly says gaily.

"Come on, it'll do you good," Jim urges.

I thank them, give the false excuse of errands to run, and tell them, "another time."

I've got to get out of here. I peer through my doorway to see who is in the hall. When the coast is clear, I bolt out to the elevator. I've just missed it. I make a dash for the stairs. I race past the bald, sour-faced guard in the lobby, nearly knocking over a deliveryman. I whirl through the revolving door and into the noontime crowds.

I walk east toward the river.

I wander into a crowded bookstore on Water Street. There are rosy-cheeked, baby-boy executives in "Business and Finance," bespectacled, bow-tied young women in "Real Estate," fat-ankled, gum-chewing secretaries in "Romances." I shuffle to the back of the store to "Classics," which is almost deserted. Beside it, there is a small section, of perhaps three shelves, called "Death and Dying." The only reason I know about the "Death and Dying" section is because I stumbled across it one lunch hour last summer while looking for a copy of *Oliver Twist* to read aloud to Len in

92

the hospital. Then I paused beside titles like *Death: The Final Act of Life* and *Living Your Dying.* But I didn't even browse through them. I worried that if Len saw me with one of these books, he'd think there was no hope. And so I'd hurried to the cash register with *Oliver Twist,* vowing to bring back books that assert the thick, roiling presence of the material world, that promise life.

Now I pick up, tentatively, one of the books from the bottom shelf and wipe the dust off its cover with my coat sleeve. It is a slim paperback, maybe half an inch thick, and it is called *Beginnings.* I roll over a metal stool from "Child Care" and squat down, drawing my knees close together like a schoolgirl. I finger the glossy lemon cover with a pale pink butterfly at the top and the subtitles: *A Book for Widows—Wise, Compassionate, and Practical Suggestions for Getting Back on Your Feet.* " In tiny print at the bottom, I read "Ballantine/Epiphany/Inspirational." I think contemptuously: self-help gibberish telling you it's okay to cry.

I am about to return *Beginnings* to its shelf, but then I bend down to the fragrant, new pages, fold back the spine, and open it at random. I read: "Freud said that the bereaved has to withdraw her emotional attachment from the deceased. 'Withdraw the libido,' he said, and, at the same time, begin to 'internalize the lost love object.' That means letting go, letting go of your husband, without losing your memories of him."

I close my eyes and bow my head and try to imagine what those words can mean: letting go. Nothing comes. Except this: a memory of Len, a week before he died.

Nighttime. Gail and I are carrying him from the toilet, where he has been for half an hour, back to his bedroom. He has already "wet himself," as Gail calls it, on the living room couch, and I have left him so long in the bathroom to prevent another accident. But he has sat on the toilet for all that time and nothing has come. When Gail and I take him back, he grins apologetically and says softly, "I tried, Beck; I really did." I stroke the soft hairs of his bald head and

93

say, "It's okay." I don't tell him that I dread peeling off his sopping underwear and socks again and hauling the soiled bedding to the washing machine.

Gail holds his legs and I hook my arms under his arms and we shuffle slowly into the bedroom. As we step across the threshold, he grabs hold of a piece of molding on the doorway. He clutches it very tight, so tight that his fingers become sinewy and white-knuckled with the effort. His hold is amazingly strong for someone so sick. We cannot move forward. Gail says, "Linn, you'll have to let go of that." Finally, I have to pry his fingers one by one from the ridges of the molding.

Letting go. Hard for Len and maybe just as hard for me.

As I wait with the crowds at the crosswalks for the stick figures on the stoplights to flash from red to green, I think, *If I were to dash out into the rush of cars speeding north up Water Street toward Chinatown, dive into that blur of lights and gleaming bumpers, if I were to give myself up to that noisy river of certain death and my arms and legs were tossed up on the hoods of the cars like empty beer cans, what then?*

I would not have to meet Frances at 4:30 or ride the 6:07 back to Connecticut. I would never have to go to IWN again or give away Len's clothes or sell the house or make my own life.

A cacophonous bleeping of horns assaults me as I stand in the middle of the street. Taxi drivers scream at me, and I freeze until all the cars in my path have screeched to a halt. Then, amidst great calm, I walk slowly to the other side. As I mount the sidewalk, I realize that what keeps me in life is the very force that drives me from it: my love for Len. Because much as I rage against this lifetime of sepa-rateness where I will never walk upon a Manhattan street (or any street in the world) feeling his arm through mine again, much as I yearn to follow him into tranquil, easy death, I feel him coaxing me back, into this world. I re-

member him telling me how, even at moments of excruci-
ating loneliness after women left him and he feared he would
grow old without being loved, he never contemplated suicide. Not because he considered it sinful or an act of cow-
ardice—three of his closest friends, including one
psychiatrist, had taken their own lives—but because he had
this unshakable faith in the healing powers of life: in the
passage of time and the coming of spring and the quickening
of his pulse as he listened to Beethoven. Life that was larger
than his own dejection, that carried its invisible, unfath-
omable trajectory and could reverse itself, could change.
And did change. For he had, long past his middle years,
met me. Then I hear him telling me, as I pass a crowd of
people lined up for Lotto tickets, as I gaze into the glass
eye of a bum holding a sign saying "JESUS SAVES," as I
meet the furtive glances of three young businessmen toking
a joint in an alleyway, to be patient, not to give up. My life
will change, too.

I spend most of the afternoon at the computer, attempting
to transcribe my notes from the Marks interview. I take out
a new file titled "marks.not," format it, and type out
"LEAD IDEAS" on the first page. But I can no more pick
out a metaphor connecting Marks's mountain-climbing with
his position at IWN than I can help Molly fix the jammed
printer. All I can think about is Frances. Why does she want
to see me? Did Marks complain to her about the interview?
Unlikely, but I wonder how it can be any secret that I despise IWN. A few months ago, I found an article in my
"In" box with my initials scrawled in Frances's flowery
hand at the top. The article, "Those Petty Embezzlers: Your
Gabbing Employees," was about people talking too much
on the phone at work and how they are, in effect, stealing
money from the company. Time is money, the article said,
and time away from the job is money lost. Frances never
confronted me with my "petty embezzling," but she obvi-

ously wasn't happy with my talking to Len every spare minute I could find.

I imagine Frances giving me an ultimatum: "I want you to know you've seriously jeopardized your position here by the time you've taken off. Molly, Jim, and Liza have had to double their work load to cover for you. I can't afford to keep anyone on who doesn't pull her weight. If you can't get yourself together in the next month, I'll have to find someone else."

As I press the "save" key and there is a slight gurgling and grinding as my words are converted into bits and bytes on the "STORY" disc, I think, *And if Frances got someone else, if I were fired?* I take a deep breath, jabbing my spine against the swivel chair. In the next cubicle I hear Jim complaining to Molly about mortgage rates.

I take out a pen and begin scribbling on the back pages of my steno pad. One hundred and fifteen thousand dollars invested at 10 percent yields $11,500 per year. Plus another three thousand dollars from the Merrill Lynch money. Total: $14,500 per year, only $3,000 less than $17,500, my IWN salary. I could make up that three thousand dollars if I sold the second car, plus another four hundred dollars a month if I took in a boarder. And if I decided to sell the house? It's probably worth $150,000, which means I could clear a $20,000 profit and buy cheaper, invest that money for 10 percent, and bring in another $2,000, which would net me over $20,000 a year.

In the distance, the phone rings. "Good afternoon, Corporate Communications," Gloria chimes out. As I stare at the flashing cursor on the screen before me, it finally dawns on me: I don't *have* to be here.

But what would I do? I remember Len's suits in their plastic dry cleaner's bags in the closet, Hector's quizzical face framed in the window. I imagine myself locked up with Hector in that house, buried alive like pets in a sultan's tomb. I picture myself lying on the couch staring at a row of photographs of Len on the bookshelves. I imagine listening for the sounds of Hector nudging his dog bowl across the kitchen tiles, listening for these noises because they are the only proof of life in the house. And I imagine padding about in my bedroom slippers, watching the sun rise in my bedroom window and set in my study window, watching the hours blur together like snow on a TV screen until there is no distinction between morning and evening, noon and night.

Write a poem, says a voice, which I recognize as Len's.

A month before Len's death. We are sitting on the couch discussing hard things. Where should he be buried? Who should give the eulogy? Len's eyes are feverish and watery with sickness; he comprehends what I am saying, and yet I can tell by that glazed look in his sad eyes that he wishes I would stop, that to speak of his death is to rob him of the hope that keeps him alive—that he can keep death away. As I become more and more panicked about how I will live without him, I blurt out, "Tell me what to do after you're gone." After I have said this, I realize how unfair and self-pitying a question it is. For Len, that little word "gone" carries with it the irrevocable canceling of all love, all hope, all self, while for me it signifies merely extreme anxiety about a lived future.

After a long silence, Len's face creases into an enigmatic smile beneath his thick, gray beard. "Write a poem," he says, so softly I have to ask him to repeat it.

I am taken aback, for I was hoping for more practical advice, such as, "Stay at IWN for a year." "Go back to teaching." "Sell the house." "Move to New York."

"And then what?" I ask, a little exasperated.

"Write another poem."

I glance at my watch: 4:00. The hour of Len's death six weeks ago. Outside, the same slate sky, the same hint of snow. Once 4:00 in the afternoon would have been indistinguishable from 3:00 or 2:00. Now it will take its place with other numbers and dates that will be clocked into my consciousness forever: December 27, the date of Len's death;

October 23, the date of his birth; November 7, the date of
our marriage; March 3, the date we met; six years, the time
we were together; the entire year of 1984, which has no
more associations with futuristic nightmares but only with
Len, with his last months on the earth. Then, all at once, I
imagine myself upstairs in my study hunting for metaphors
not about Ted Marks and his mountain-climbing but about
bearing witness to these hard hours, telling what it's like to
be touched by death.

Write about Len's death, about my grieving? Quit my job
and go home and lock myself in that silence and spend my
days finding words to describe weeping and loneliness? Descend for months and maybe years into the underworld of
mourning and live with the shadow of Len's emaciated,
granite-colored face nodding to the rhythm of the undertaker's steps as they take him away?

This is what you know about, another voice answers. *This
is what your life has brought you. Maybe if you go into that
cave of death, you will be surprised. You'll find something
more than absence and decay. Maybe you will discover,
dancing in the shadows of your loss, light particles of acceptance and understanding. Even hope.*

"Come in, come in, Rebecca," Frances says, beaming,
when I present myself in her office.

"I just want you to know we're glad to have you back on
board." She leans back in her chair and tucks her folded
hands behind her head.

"Thank you." I glance toward the door, hoping that's all
she has to say.

"Rebecca, I realize you'll probably want some time to
think this over, but I had lunch today with Dave Strand and
there's an intensive training seminar coming up in mid-
March. It's rigorous. Five days a week from eight to five for
four weeks. I've already spoken to Jim about it. He thinks
the department can spare you.

"Rebecca," she says, leaning toward me eagerly across

her desk, "this would be a fabulous opportunity for you to learn about insurance.

"I don't expect you to give me an answer today or even next week. I know you've got a lot on your mind." She pauses and knots her brow to simulate the "concerned boss" look.

"But I think I should be frank with you. Although your profiles have met with generally good response, you won't go places in this company without more background in insurance."

I nod and Frances rises to walk me to the door.

"You'll stay in Connecticut?"

"Yes."

"That's sensible. People say you shouldn't make any major changes for at least a year."

She taps me lightly on the shoulder and says she'll see me tomorrow. Bright and early.

On the 6:07, the men have unloosened their ties and there is much gaiety and noisy jostling, especially in the smoke-filled bar car where I wait in line for a screwdriver. Since I don't usually drink on the train coming back, I feel self-conscious among the loud, rumpled men, the half-dozen husky-voiced women who slouch against the ripped vinyl seats and roar at the jokes.

In addition to my drink I order a bag of peanuts and potato chips. With my down coat in one hand and my briefcase in the other, I have difficulty locomoting everything, and I am forced to carry the bag of potato chips between my teeth. As I wait to pass through the double glass doors and into the next car, one sweaty, drunken man comes careening down the aisle and lurches into me, nearly overturning my cup.

"Ah, geez," he says. "I'm awful sorry. I spilled your lil' drink." He takes out a dirty hankerchief and begins patting at my briefcase.

"It's okay," I say, grabbing the swinging door and holding it open with my foot. "You didn't spill it."

"I didn't? Well, that's the best news I've had all day, honey. Say, why don't we celebrate and I'll buy you another one?" He winks at me and sways into a silver post as the train jerks forward.

"No thanks," I answer primly. As the door bangs behind me, I hear him dissolve in gales of laughter.

The train is almost full, but I finally capture an empty seat. I toss my coat and jacket in the crowded luggage rack above me, take off my shoes, and slouch down in my seat. Tucking my knees against the seat back before me, I take a long sip from the colorless cup. The cool, metallic-tasting orange juice slides easily down my throat. It takes immediate effect, and I feel the muscles in my spine grow limp and pliant. I pull open the bag of potato chips, and I stuff them, two at a time, into my mouth, crunching their salty ridges against my gums and mashing them into a warm, runny paste. I lick the tips of my fingers, and when the bag is empty, I run my index finger along the bottom seam to retrieve any stray crumbs. Then I rip open the beer nuts and grind their sugary, carbohydrate-rich plumpness against my upper molars. When I am finished with the peanuts, I take out a half-opened packet of Lorna Doones from my purse and pop them whole into my mouth.

I am aware, by the continuous, irritated snap of my seatmate's head in my direction, that my chomping and gobbling is obscene.

I don't care.

The train wheezes and grinds through the night, with the lights overhead dimming, flickering, and then blazing on again. Now and then I read snatches of the evening paper: "Star Tracks" and "Dear Abby" and my horoscope. As the train speeds farther and farther from Manhattan, past the highways along the tracks in New Rochelle, past the harbor lights at Greenwich, past the spaceship-like sky-scrapers in Stamford, it occurs to me, like a dreamer sensing a dream's end, that tomorrow I'll have to turn around and ride this train back again to New York, ride through a day not much different from this one.

In my half-drunken, gluttonous state, I lapse into referring to myself in the third person, as in: *How is she going to get out of that training course? How could she endure eight hours a day, five days a week of casualty, excess liability, and term life? She'd go stark-raving mad. When will she summon the courage to march into Frances's office and tell her the truth? That she doesn't need the job anymore. That she wants to go home and write about Len's death.*

"Sack her, fire her, terminate her," I murmur sleepily as the conductor calls out, "South Norwalk," then "Kent Road," then "Cannondale." My spine rises and falls to the starts and stops of the train. All I want is for the conductor to sing out "Branch—ville," breaking up the word into two long syllables like Len, a lifetime ago, singing, "Beck—y," to announce that he was home.

And then for the train to wheeze to a halt and the conductor to help me down the high steps. Then to stumble across the icy parking lot, jump in my car, which is turned around to go, speed through the blinking yellow light and down the narrow, dark roads, pull on the emergency brake of the car in the driveway, drag myself into the dark house, hurry past the closed door of Len's room and up the stairs, turn up the electric blanket as far as it will go, bury my head in my pillow, and sleep.

"Hope" is the thing with feathers—
That perches in the soul—
And sings the tune without the words—
And never stops—at all—

—Emily Dickinson

March 1985

I spend hours on the phone with friends. I have also started seeing my therapist, Dr. Heller, twice a week. All of them give me varied and conflicting advice. Dr. Heller warns that I may start to feel anger. Susan, who lost her lover in an automobile crash a few years ago, tells me I am alone and no one can really understand what I am going through. Anna, whose father died a month ago, thinks my pain will get worse before it gets better. One of Len's colleagues, whose mother died last year, explains that my body is "programmed to get better" and that a time will come when I'll feel "guilty for being happy." Len's former patient, who has been calling regularly, says that I am "in my third month," as if widowhood were some retroverted form of pregnancy.

Although I have never been pregnant, this image strikes a resonating chord. In my journal, which I have almost filled since I began it last December, I write of how Len's cancer swelled in his brain for eight and a half months before he died and how the passages into and out of life are not, in the end, so different: Both are organic processes in which the body goes quietly or unquietly about its work of building and breaking down. Both are natural events rooted in a mystery over which we ultimately have no control. What I wonder is this: Where will I be when my nine months of mourning are finished? At the beginning of my life or the end of it?

All I know for certain is that I am moving toward some

new phase. In the "Rent Wanted" section of the *Redding Pilot* I have taken out the following ad: *Professional woman, aged 30, desires neat, quiet, cheerful professional woman to share one-half large country home in beautiful wooded setting.*

Today, on March 2, a balmy Saturday morning with melting icicles drilling tiny holes in the snow, I stand before the closed door of the room where this mysterious professional woman will sleep, the room were Len died. In my arms I carry a bucket of warm water, a roll of paper towels, and a bottle of disinfectant.

Is it fear of ghosts that keeps my fingers suspended on the antique black metal latch? Or guilt that if I disturb the contents of this room, I will scatter Len's spirit forever?

I enter on tiptoe, like a child creeping across the broken boards of an abandoned treehouse. On the bed, which Gail stripped and then covered with a clean sheet before she left, there are two slanting rectangles of sunlight. Stepping deeper into the room, I notice sunlight everywhere—on the seat of the armchair, on the traveling clock on the bedside table, on the gilt mirror on the far wall. Sunlight illuminates even the dust along the bookshelves. Opening the windows and sniffing the warm, end-of-winter air, I sense the room has changed in these months. It is no longer charged with the terrible energy of dying.

I begin. I work backward from the doorway. I vacuum under the chair, beneath the table. I remove the detachable brush and run the nozzle alongside the baseboards. Under the bed I unearth a crumpled copy of *Good-bye, Mr. Chips*. As I dust off the cover, I remember reading the book aloud to Len in the hospital and how Len's roommate, a cantankerous old man in his 80s who had no visitors except the wife whom he despised, would beg me to open the dividing curtain because he too wanted to hear the story of the beloved English schoolmaster. I remember how the old man's wife once came in when we were beginning the part about

Chips falling in love and how she said, ''When I get sick, will you come and read to me like that?''

All gone now. The cantankerous man, his pathetic wife, those slow hours with Len in the hospital, which were oddly vivid and close. I sigh and slip *Good-bye, Mr. Chips* among encyclopedias in the bookcase.

Pam Parini suggested I rearrange the furniture. I move the double bed away from the wall and into the center of the room. I take down both leaves of the nightstand and place it lengthwise beside the bed. I haul the armchair into the opposite corner beside the telephone jack. I roll up the fraying Oriental runner and store it in the hall closet.

Standing on the far side of the bed, I survey my work. The geometry of the room has been altered. Planes of open space now dominate areas once filled with the cubic density of chair and bed. There are bright, unworn patches of gold carpet everywhere. When I run a damp cloth along the now exposed baseboards, they too look brighter, as if they had been freshly painted. Now the entire room looks bigger, airier, almost as it did three years ago when Len and I first moved in and were busy hanging curtains, deciding whether to put the telephone there or there. Now this room readies itself for the future, when new life will domesticate its spaces, life unburdened by memories of the twenty-seventh day of December 1984.

The hardest part of my task—cleaning out the closet—I save for last. Susan offered to help me with this, but I told her I thought I could handle it. I was wrong. When I open the double doors and find the thermal socks that my stepson, Mark, gave to Len for Christmas still in their red box and wrapped in tissue paper with a gold seal, I bite back a flood of tears. When I discover the Nordic ski sweater that I gave Len for his last birthday in October, when I remember how I helped him pull it over his head and how he caressed its pattern of blue and gold snowflakes and said he wished he'd learned to ski, I sink to my knees and sob. I cry because these personal effects endure and Len does not. I cannot give them up, and yet to keep them is to memorialize the part of Len furthest from me.

I fold the sweater and stow it away in the bottom drawer of the bureau in Gail's room. I place the red box in the wicker basket with the rest of Len's socks, which are rolled in neat, woolen balls. I haul the basket upstairs, along with armfuls of shirts and trousers, still on their hangers. I shove everything into the closet. One day, I'll be ready to give the clothes away.

In the afternoon, the phone begins to ring. The first caller is a divorced management consultant with three teenage children and a garage full of furniture. Her children, she tells me, will visit her every other week and during the summer. She wants to come over now and see whether the house suits her. Stunned at the prospect of this pushy woman and her three teenagers installed in my house, I am chastened into silence. "I'm sorry, but the house isn't big enough," I finally mutter.

Next is a psychiatric nurse, also divorced, with only one child. She sounds promising until I explain that I am widowed. "You're too young to be widowed," she clucks in a tone she might have used to tell her daughter she was too young to wear eye shadow. I scribble "no way" next to her number.

To my disbelief, I like the next caller and agree to meet her. Alice Schneider is a commercial illustrator, aged 44 ("A young 44," she says gaily, pronouncing the "44" with a high-pitched Queens accent, so that it comes out "fawty-faw"), single with no dependents. "There's only one problem," she squeaks. "I've got two dogs." I tell her it's not a problem as long as they get along with mine. She assures me they are well-behaved. Two dogs, I reflect, are better than three teenagers.

An hour later, a battered Volkswagen bus with California license plates chugs up my driveway. A tall, slender woman with a graying pageboy steps tentatively out from the driver's seat. She is wearing jeans, a plaid work shirt, and a down vest. *She'll do,* I think, as I watch her clomping through the snow in her red rubber boots. Her face, long and fine-boned, looks intelligent, sensitive. When I greet her at the back door, I notice that her green eyes are large and a little frightened. For a woman of 44 she seems oddly childlike.

"I got lost," she apologizes. "This place is like a needle in a haystack. But I'll bet it's great in a snowstorm, huh?" She smiles an eager, girlish smile.

She loves the room and also Len's study, which she says she could use as her studio. I show her around the rest of the house, which she admires. In my study, she picks up a photograph of Len taken at Mount Desert Island in Maine. He is standing on a rocky ledge with the Atlantic Ocean behind him. He is doing a kind of dance, and his arms are outstretched as if he were embracing the sky. "Your husband?" she asks. I nod. "He looks like quite a guy," she says.

"He was," I tell her. "He was."

We sit on the couch in the living room. She wants to stay for four or five months until she finds a house in Bethel or New Milford. She is looking for a farm, something with a little land where she can have a garden and space for the dogs to run, something like this house. She grins. "Wanna sell?"

"Maybe," I tell her, "but not right now."

"Just kidding," she says.

She has not mentioned money. I am worried that when she hears I'm asking four hundred dollars a month plus one-half utilities plus one month's security she'll say no. But the numbers don't faze her. "When do I move in?" she asks.

"How about this week?" I say.

"The dogs are gonna love it," she says.

We shake hands. Then she says, in her funny, high-pitched Queens accent, "You know, I think it could just work out for the both of us."

As she walks out to her car, she tosses a hunk of snow

against one of the dogwoods. I wonder what she would have done if I told her that Len died in the bed where she will sleep?

I do not adjust well to Alice Schneider and her two dogs, LA and Pucci. Everything they do exasperates me.

It begins the night she arrives. She drives the Volkswagen bus up so close to the garage door that she nearly rams into it. I remind myself that she has to unload her things and can't very well park 50 feet away. Still, I am annoyed by her colonization of my driveway, especially since she continues to park in the same spot every night, forcing me to park in the turnaround.

Even though I consider myself a dog lover, I don't take to LA and Pucci. Pucci, whose name is not spelled *Poochie* but *Pucci,* after the Italian designer, is a plump beagle with a high-pitched, soul-shattering yap that echoes through the woods in the morning when Alice lets her out, inspiring every other dog in the neighborhood to howl in kind. On the first night, Pucci squats on the blue Belgian rug in the living room and pees.

But since Hector has taken a fancy to Pucci, I reserve my wrath for LA. LA, whose name has no clever double-entendre except Los Angeles, where Alice used to live, is a huge, unruly Lab whose chief activity is eating everything in sight. The first week, he inhales a box of unopened muffins on the kitchen counter, overturns the neighbors' garbage cans, and provokes Hector to a dogfight that could go down in history as the canine equivalent of Gallipoli. But these transgressions are minor compared to what LA does one afternoon shortly after he arrives. While I am at work, he chews one of the hand-carved chess pieces on the coffee table. Unfortunately, the piece happens to belong to the expensive Charlemagne-style French set that I bought Len for his fifty-seventh birthday.

That evening, Alice presents me with the white queen, whose head is savaged and whose delicate red mouth and braids are gone. All apologies, she promises to repaint it and to keep LA confined to her bedroom. When I explain, somewhat tearfully, why the set is so special and how Len and I played with it all through Europe, she pats my shoulder and says she'll have it looking like new in no time. Meanwhile, she advises me to put the other pieces away.

I had told her she could use Len's study, but when I see her brushes and pencils lined up in coffee cans on his desk and her cartoon-like sketches of Pucci and LA taped to the bookshelves, I want to weep. I tell myself this is absurd; if she weren't using the room, who would? And wouldn't Len be happy that an artist was working in his study? He worshiped artists. He respected them more than doctors or philosophers. He'd be thrilled to see Alice's large, glossy book on Georgia O'Keeffe on his desk, opened to the painting titled *White Trumpet Flower*. This is what I tell myself, but when I enter the study and espy Alice's gray head bent over her sketch pad, I want to order her out.

Then there's the problem of our different musical sensibilities. She favors "easy listening," the tuneless, background Muzak one hears in elevators and dentists' offices. Every evening when I return from IWN, that Muzak is the first sound to greet me, its mindless, anemic swing as shattering to my eardrums as Led Zeppelin. When I ask her to turn it down, she usually turns it off, explaining that she just likes to have something to "keep her company" when she's alone. I'm not so diplomatic when she objects to my music. Last Sunday, when I was lying on the sofa listening to one of Bach's unaccompanied cello suites, the solemn, funereal Suite no. 2 in D Minor played by Pablo Casals, she asked me, very sweetly, if we couldn't have something else that wasn't so "heavy." Outraged, I turned off the stereo and stomped to bed.

Alice and I go for days without exchanging more than a dozen words. This is not hard to do, since I leave before she is up and return after she has finished supper. We never share meals and always keep our food in separate cupboards and on separate sides of the refrigerator. Most of the time, I take my supper—a bowl of the beef stew that I make in bulk—to my room. By the time I am back in the kitchen for dessert, she is in bed with a dog on either side of her watching TV. Sometimes she invites me in to watch the news, but I claim that I can't stay up.

On weekends I disappear into my study. I am creating a memorial notice to send to everyone who has written me a sympathy card. To my surprise, I find a peculiar satisfaction in this work—picking out selections from Len's books and from poems he loved, figuring out how to arrange them, and discussing the card's design and typeface with the printer.

I spend hours scanning *The Dance of Being, Homo Quaerens,* and *Choros,* underlining passages that best crystallize Len's thought. Hours leafing through the Bible, Shakespeare, and Wordsworth. I call Pam Parini to get her reaction to the lines from a Shakespeare sonnet—"But if the while I think on thee, dear friend,/All losses are restored and sorrows end." We also discuss whether to print Len's picture on the cover. Pam says no, a photo would be morbid, a reifying of the physical part of Len that is gone. Besides, Len was a writer, she says: It's better to remember him in words.

I agree and promise to call back when I have the rest of the card finished. After our conversation, I remember the passage from the New Testament that Len quoted in *Choros:* "In the beginning was the Word, and the Word was with God, and the Word was God." I am no philosopher. I couldn't say if words create the world or if they are God, but I do know that when I read Len's words and the words of poets he loved, I feel a deep kinship with him, a connection more unshakable than anything I've felt during these long months of his absence. When I copy out the passage I've chosen to end the memorial card, a passage about dying that Len wrote four years ago when he was well and sitting at a desk like me, when I write "I must learn . . . to give myself to the earth, to its endless cycles, to its dark, silent, consciousless pulse; to permit myself to be remade in nature's womb, to be reconstituted and metamorphosed, or even transfigured," I hear him telling me to be still. To accept life, accept death. To give myself to the presence of something larger than my grief for him, larger than self or love or death.

One Sunday, when I have been working all day, I hear a soft tap at my door. I am startled. Alice never trespasses on my territory upstairs. What can she want?

"Rebecca? I'm taking the dogs for a walk. I thought you might want to come."

Alice is dressed in her red boots, navy-blue down parka, and blue-and-white snowflake ski hat with a pom-pom on top and matching mittens. But for the few gray hairs protruding out of her hat, she looks about ten years old. I smile. There's something likable about her, despite all my efforts to believe the contrary.

"Thanks, but I've got to get this to the printer's tomorrow."

"You've been cooped up here all day," she squeaks. "It's not good for you. You need fresh air."

"Another time," I tell her.

"Is that a promise?"

"Okay, a promise."

But who is this woman, I sometimes wonder, and what does she live for?

I know from phone messages I have taken for her that she has a brother in Los Angeles, a woman friend in New Jersey, and one or two acquaintances in New York. From a few desultory conversations when she first came, I know she has worked for the past 15 years in commercial design, took off three years to paint in upstate New York and take care of her aging parents, then moved to California after they died. I did ask her at one point whether she had ever been married, and she said no. I wanted to ask her, but did not, whether she had ever been in love.

I would guess she has not. Why? Only because she seems, more than any other woman I have met, so self-contained and self-sufficient. She seems quite content to spend her evenings and weekends alone—drawing in the study, taking Pucci and LA for walks, doing her laundry or washing her car, occasionally roasting a chicken for her Saturday night meal. The remarkable thing about her is that she is not in the least bitter about her solitary lot and even seems to rejoice in it. She loves it when it snows and when it rains and when it's blustery cold. She takes a kid's delight in going to the supermarket and bringing back Hydrox cookies and Bird's-Eye chicken dinners and Früsen-Gladje ice cream. She looks forward to sleeping and waking early and coming home from work. "The best thing about going to work," she says, "is that you've really earned it when you come home."

I gather that she could take or leave her job doing paste-ups and mechanicals for a small graphic arts company. She had a better paying position in California in tabletop design, but gave it up to come east. I think she once said that the work she did to earn money was irrelevant; what she wanted most was to pursue her art. Perhaps like Georgia O'Keeffe, who fled New York to live alone in New Mexico, she dreams of some ideal existence in artistic communion with the earth.

She spends hours sketching. She does the trees outside her window and the small mountain ridge in the distance, but mainly she does pen and ink studies of Pucci and LA, often personifying them as a kind of goofy married couple with Pucci in a frilly tutu carrying a handbag and LA strolling gentlemanly beside her in bow-tie and tails.

The only person with whom she seems to have much contact is her friend in New Jersey. They talk on the phone every other night. Once Alice switched the dial of my answering machine to "record" instead of to "off." When I pressed the "playback" button to get my messages, I heard their conversation. I should not have listened, but I did. It wasn't terribly juicy, mostly Alice telling Kim about her day at work and about a house she had seen in Litchfield. The tone between them was warm, even jocular, more like two adolescent girls—Kim kidding Alice that her beat-up VW bus didn't give her "the Connecticut look" and Alice charging Kim with being a "no-good Yuppie." They also talked about the latest antics of Pucci and LA, at which point I got bored and erased it.

It has occurred to me that Alice and Kim could be lovers. Last Friday night, Kim drove up from New Jersey to stay the night. I told her she was welcome to use Gail's room upstairs, but she and Alice said they'd fix up something downstairs. The next morning, when I came down for breakfast, the two of them emerged in their nightgowns from Alice's room giggling and roughhousing.

Whether Alice is or isn't gay is none of my business, of course. As long as she pays her rent on time and doesn't intrude upon my privacy, she has a right to do what she likes. Though I do find it a little creepy to imagine lesbian play going on in the bed where Len died; on the other hand, I did want new life in that room and I guess I've gotten it. The fact is I'd rather have Alice sleeping with Kim than picking up stray men in bars and bringing them home. At least I know Kim isn't likely to come back and rob the place. Speculating on Alice's sexuality does, however, make me wonder what she makes of me: a woman grieving passionately over the loss of another human being, grieving over a man.

Perhaps I appear to her as she often appears to me: opaque, shadowy, quiet, and inscrutable as a nun.

Our first real conversation takes place on March 20, two weeks after she arrives. It is about 9:30 at night, and I am returning late after staying at IWN to finish a profile. I find Alice seated by a blazing fire sketching Hector, who is sleeping on the sofa. Alice knows I don't like Hector on the sofa, mainly because I don't want to set a precedent for her dogs climbing on the furniture. I'm annoyed at her breezy disregard for "house rules." Still, I'm touched that she is fond enough of Hector to draw him. It suggests a kind of displaced affection for me. When she asks me to sit down, I feel I can't say no.

"You're really on the graveyard shift tonight," she pipes gaily.

She obviously doesn't realize how tasteless her remark is. Nor that she sounds, with her high-pitched Queens accent, like Archie Bunker's wife, Edith, when she utters it. I let it pass.

"Tell me what you do at IWN," she says, holding her sketch pad away from her to scrutinize the drawing. "You get up in the dark and come home in the dark. For all I know, you could be betting on horses all day."

I laugh, grudgingly appreciating her sense of humor.

"I write profiles on people who work in the company."

"Do they let you write whatever you want?"

"Hardly."

"So, like what do you say?"

"Well, the one I was writing, or rather rewriting tonight, was about this young executive from Staten Island who spends his weekends in soup kitchens for the homeless."

"But that's great," she squeals, pointing her pencil in the air to align it with Hector's head. "This guy, what's his name?"

"Bruce Todd."

"Bruce could be out raising premiums. Isn't that what insurance companies do?"

"Among other things."

"And instead he's helping people at the bottom of the barrel. So what happened? Didn't they like what you wrote?"

"No. Bruce Todd happens to be very religious. He's a Moravian. I quoted him as saying some pretty idealistic stuff about being your brother's keeper, and Frances, my boss, said to me, 'Look, this is an insurance company, not a church. The religion's got to go.' "

"So they're not really interested in telling the truth about Bruce Todd. They just want some watered down version of him that won't ruffle anyone's feathers."

"Right."

"How can you write lies, Rebecca?"

For a moment I don't answer. I'm angry at the turn the conversation has taken. Who is this woman with her 15 years in tabletop design to castigate *me* for working at IWN?

"It's what they pay me for."

"But you care about writing, don't you?"

"Of course."

"I mean, your husband was a philosopher, right? I have no idea what philosophers do, but it's about trying to get at truth, isn't it?"

"Yes."

"So how can you do work that is against everything he believed in?"

"Good question," I say, somewhat sarcastically, "and now I'm going to bed."

Although Alice's existence annoys me most of the time, I sometimes admit—not to her, but to friends like Susan and Anna—that I'm lucky she has come into my life. When I wake on a Saturday morning and hear her bustling about, yakking to the dogs, clanging pans, and opening cupboards, I think, *Thank God for Alice, for her life force that brings me back from the dead.*

The house has undergone subtle changes, not all of them objectionable, during her tenure here. You can see it most clearly in the kitchen. Now the counters swell with jars and tins. There is flour that she keeps in a clear glass bubble jar, tea bags in a cookie tin with kilted bagpipers on the cover, a bottle of Irish Cream liqueur towering above a row of spice shakers. Although Alice has left most of her dishes in storage, she did bring a few pans—a new Revere Ware double boiler and a turquoise-blue ceramic teakettle, which she occasionally leaves on the stove. On the refrigerator she has put up colorful fruit-shaped magnets and tacked to them notices of art exhibits and postcards of Connecticut snow scenes.

Alice more than lives up to the requirement for neatness specified in the ad. In fact, she is neater than I am. "The German hausfrau in me," she says when I remark on it and apologize that I hope she doesn't find me too much of a pig. "Only 98 percent of the time," she jokes. The kitchen sink is now dotted with wire-meshed scouring sponges, a heavy-bristled scrub brush, a bottle of lemon-scented Joy, and a can of Comet. Every morning, after Alice washes up her breakfast dishes, she scours the sink until it shines and then hangs her blue-and-white checked dishrag over the faucet to dry.

If I were a painter, I would do a still life of that dishrag draped over the faucet. I would place it in the center of the canvas with the window open just a crack above it and the hint of the maple tree beyond. I would trace out the lines and folds of its colorful, limp shape. For contrast, I would make the gleaming aluminum faucet strong and defined beneath it. I would shade and color the planes around the blue and white squares so that the light from the window would shine upon them. With eye and hand, I would try to say how happy Alice's dishrag makes me feel.

Occasionally, Alice catches me wiping tears from my eyes and turns away awkwardly. I know her response is not unusual. Like others, Alice doesn't know what to say or fears saying the wrong thing and so says nothing. Death is such a stranger to most people's lives—I remember my co-worker Molly informing me she had never known anyone who died—that they simply do not have the language to speak of it.

Perhaps because Alice took care of her dying parents, she is more adept than most. She senses accurately that it is more painful for me not to speak of Len and every so often brings him up in little ways that can't help but endear her to me. When she notices my juicer in the cupboard beneath the sink, she asks, "Did your husband like fresh orange juice in the mornings?" She never refers to him as Len—that would be coming closer than either of us is prepared for. But even in referring to him as "your husband," she acknowledges that there was a time when he walked about casually as we do now, squeezing and drinking fresh orange juice of a morning. She doesn't know that this simple question can elicit a dissertation on the subject of Len and orange juice: How he liked nothing better than guzzling down a large tumbler filled to the brim with the thick, pulpy stuff; how he used to say that FDR demanded fresh orange juice every morning and that if it was good enough for him, it was good enough for Leonard Feldstein; how he often got up early before I caught the train to New York and squeezed me an entire glass of it and how he said, in that funny Jewish-mother way of his, "How can you survive Moishe's joint without your juice?" (Moishe was Len's nickname for M. D. Sternberg, the CEO.) Alice listens patiently to anecdote after anecdote about Len. Perhaps because she lost both her parents, she understands how hard it is for me to let Len go, that I need to resurrect him—the silly Len, the wise Len, the ludicrous Len—whenever I can.

I know it's taxing to listen to tales about the dead, especially the dead whom we never knew. These shadowy figures are twice removed from the world: vague as living people since we never met them, but vague as dead people, too, since we glimpse them only through the memories of their survivors.

I remember once spending an evening with a friend of the Parinis who talked incessantly about his deceased wife: How she loved chocolate but never got fat, how she adored dogs and at one time had four, how her favorite country was Luxembourg. As we drove back to Connecticut I complained to Len how bored I was by it all and wondered why

Bill didn't realize how dull it was to hear about Rose, whom neither of us had ever met and whom he always painted in the most saintly, glowing colors.

I probably talk about Len in the same way. But Alice indulges me and doesn't complain.

One night, however, she does ask me a startling question. And out of the blue, as is her fashion. I am returning late again, this time from Dr. Heller's. When I get back, Alice is at her usual spot beside the fireplace. She is leafing through one of Len's books on van Gogh. She noticed it in the bookcase in her studio and thought I wouldn't mind if she borrowed it. She wonders whether I've had dinner and says I'm welcome to some chicken soup, which she has kept warm on the stove for me.

This is the first time she has offered to share her supper. Some vestigial part of me hesitates before ladling out the runny broth dotted with peas, rice, and shredded chicken. Will eating her food bind me to her in some unforeseen way? But I realize, as I sit down beside her with my soup bowl balanced on my knees, that we are already tied together, that it isn't possible to go back to the days when we passed through the house without meeting.

We exchange pleasantries about the weather. We're due for some snow tonight. Alice is amazed that it can still snow at the end of March. Then she says, in that naive little-girl tone she adopts when dealing with difficult subjects, "I was wondering, did you and your husband ever fight?"

I must look startled, because she then adds, "All you ever talk about is how wonderful it was."

I crumble a piece of pita bread into my soup. I'm not sure I want to confide in her. What can she know about the love between a man and a woman? And yet maybe she is right. Maybe I do romanticize how it really was.

"We fought about our age difference," I slowly admit.

"How could you fight about that? I mean he couldn't change his age."

"Well, with him being so much older I always thought

people were staring at us and thinking we were perverted. A couple of times we were mistaken for father and daughter—it didn't happen often, but when it did, I would get upset and lash out at him. Once it got so bad he called me a bitch and said that if I couldn't affirm our relationship, he'd leave me.

"We always made up. I don't think we ever went to bed angry. But it was hard for him. He loved me very much and couldn't bear to be rejected."

"Was that all? Just the age difference? I mean, it isn't any of my business . . ."

I scrape my bowl, spooning up the last fleck of chicken.

"Our relationship was changing when he got sick," I finally confess. "I was becoming more independent, wanting to do things on my own, stay overnight in New York sometimes. Not to be with anyone else, just to be alone. Discover who I was independently of Len, which I needed to do. He was so brilliant and accomplished and so much older that I felt dwarfed by him. It wasn't anything he did deliberately. It was just who he was and who I was. His life was complete; mine wasn't.

"I think he tried to understand but couldn't really. He hated to be apart from me, even for one night. He needed to take care of me and was threatened when I wanted more space. If he had lived, there would have been hurdles for us. I think we would have survived them, but it wouldn't have been easy."

"Do you ever think that maybe his death wasn't all bad? I mean, not that it was good, but maybe you were meant to do things that you couldn't have done if he had lived?"

"There's a silver lining in every cloud, is that what you mean?" I say, irritated with her sloppy pop psychologizing.

"Yeah, I guess that's what I'm saying," she answers defensively.

"I don't buy it. I could win the Nobel Prize and it wouldn't be worth the price of Len's life. If he'd lived, we would have struggled, yes. But he would have been alive.

And whatever we would have gone through, we would have gone through together. Two living people. He's dead now. Nothing's going to bring him back. And I'm supposed to fold my hands and say, 'Oh, well, it's for the best'?''

"Gee, don't get all worked up," she pleads. "All I'm trying to say is maybe something good will come out of this. You're young. You've got a lot of years ahead. You can't just go on being a widow for the rest of your life. Your husband . . . Len wouldn't want that, would he?''

To learn the Transport by the Pain—
As Blind Men learn the sun!

—*Emily Dickinson*

April 1985

A century ago, when I fell in love with Len, I was strangely intrigued by the idea that he would die before me, that I might witness his metamorphosis from living man into invisible spirit, that I would see, close as my own breath fogging on an October morning, this "distinguished thing" that had inspired poets, baffled philosophers, and eluded scientists. Staring into Len's dying face would be like what the astronauts felt when they stood on the moon and looked down at the tiny earth spinning beneath them. From the perspective of near-eternity, large phenomena would become small. Imponderable questions would telescope into minor ones. Something new would be revealed. Even when Len was dying and I saw how thoroughly undistinguished a process dying was—no moon walk, no romantic "fog in the throat," but simply an attenuation of the desire for moon walks, the passion for fog—I still imagined that death held some secret. I hoped Len would tell me what that was, send me messages from the grave, but even if he did not, I believed I would be wiser after his death than before.

In my fourth month, when my grieving is big inside me, I await these radiant insights that will throw my life into relief. What do I know? That it is spring and everything— the tangled skeins of forsythia bursting along the roadside, the daffodils waving their white and yellow petals—is surging back to life but Len? That even if Len were, as Walt Whitman wrote, under my "bootsoles," I could not converse with him, could not learn the language of grass? That a time will come when all the anguish of this particular consciousness, Rebecca Feldstein, née Rice, who would like to meet her widowed solitude heroically, will inhabit less and less space in the world until she, too, is no more? That, instead of clarity, death brings confusion because now I know from the very hair follicles in my head that I shall die, understand that my life and death are as noisy but insignificant as the migration of Canada geese, and yet, as long as I am alive rather than dead, my spirit cries out that everything I do—stay at IWN or leave, write or not write, accept or protest Len's passing—matters.

I have started going to church, to an old New England Methodist meetinghouse in West Redding about two miles from my home, close enough to bike to. The widows' books I've been reading warn that Sundays are hardest—"white-knuckle days''—and advise keeping as busy as possible. I considered attending mass at the Roman Catholic chapel in Georgetown where the funeral was, but I can't bear to go near any place that reminds me of those days. And despite Len's conversion, I've never been drawn to Catholicism— its authoritarianism, its rigid belief structures, its misogyny. Not that I have any particular passion for Methodism, or any organized religion, for that matter, including Christian Science, the religion in which I was raised. But I like the minister at the Long Ridge Methodist church, a radiant young woman of about my age whose sermons are sprinkled with references to Thoreau and Annie Dillard and whose commitment to her calling inspires me.

Breathlessly I pedal along the narrow, wooded roads, my face stinging in the spring wind, my gloveless hands red as lobsters on the handlebars. Once I'm seated with my program in one of the side pews, my cheeks thawing in the sunlight pouring through the high, arched windows, I'm glad I have come. I like it when the organ begins to pedal softly and Sarah Gunn, splendid in her long, white robes, begins her slow, magisterial walk down the center aisle, nodding to her sparse flock of elderly lady parishioners. I'm always

taken aback when she begins each service with announce-
ments about Bible study classes meeting on Tuesdays rather
than Wednesdays. Or how we must pray for Scott Ledbetter
in Danbury Hospital where he's having his gallstones out. I
want this fair-haired, flawlessly complexioned lady minister
to spirit me away from boredom and sickness, to gather me
up in her long, white robes and take me to her God.

I envy her, proud as Saint Cecilia above the lilies donated
in memory of Sophie Marcum and speaking, in her resonant
soprano, about trusting in Jesus and how only in losing our
life can we find it. I think: If I had her faith, I could believe
that the loss of Len has been given to me to make me
stronger. My grief would be transcendent, part of God's
plan of breaking me down to build me up again. I would
compare my suffering to Jesus' 40 days in the wilderness or
his betrayal at Gethsemane or his anguish on the cross. I
would regard loss not as tragedy but as opportunity, death
not as end but beginning. I would deliver my pain trustingly
into God's greater power, like a child presenting a bloody
knee to her mother.

After the sermon, Sarah Gunn tells us to turn to page _____
in our hymnals and motions for the congregation to rise.
This is the part of the service I like best. Slightly off-key,
with the elderly ladies stretching into creaky sopranos and
the handful of men droning flat as hammers on sheet rock,
we sing. "Every day will be an Easter, da-da-da-da-da-da-
da-da." I don't know if I believe every day will be an Easter. Or even whether there was an Easter, two thousand-odd
years ago when Jesus rolled away the stone of his sepulcher
and appeared, in the risen flesh, to his mother. But while I
am singing, it doesn't matter whether Jesus was or was not
the son of God or whether he did or didn't ascend into the
heavens. I am singing, loud as the Mormon Tabernacle
Choir, for the Easter not of the Methodists or the Catholics,
but for the ancient, pagan festival of spring that will draw
Len's spirit out of the Vermont marble tombstone, make
him one with the sunlight blooming on the bare walls of the

church, one with the sunbursts of white and pink dogwood along the roadsides, one with the daffodils and the forsythia and all living things in this world that refuse to remain dead. And I am singing for me, for the Easter that will free my heart from bitterness and confusion, that will make me whole again.

In the end, however, the person to whom I turn for spiritual guidance is not the Reverend Sarah Gunn but my therapist, Dr. Louise Heller. After work each Monday and Thursday evening, I come to the soundproof quiet of her ground-floor office on West 84th Street with its skinny clay figurines on the end tables and *The Collected Works of Carl Jung* in the modular bookcases. Sometimes, all I can do is throw myself down on her Haitian cotton couch and cry. She sits patiently with me, stopping her note-taking and saying little, but with her round, attentive face inclined toward me in sympathy. At the end of our sessions (they're supposed to be 50 minutes, but she usually lets me run over), she will take me in her arms and hold me for a few moments before leading me out to the waiting room and telling me she'll see me next time.

Dr. Heller says I'm doing two things simultaneously—grieving over Len, which takes me into the past, and making a life without him, which catapults me into the future. That must account for my flightiness: One day, my head is awash in plans for leaving IWN or writing my book about mourning or traveling to Europe or putting the house on the market and I am thinking that striking out on my own might not be so bad, might even be an adventure, while the next, I am reading about widows and widowers contracting the illness of their dead spouse and I'm feeling a fear that begins at my kneecaps and ascends into the hollows beneath my eyes and I don't know how I will have the courage to invent this new life, how I will feel magic or adventure again without Len to mirror these things back to me.

I bring to Dr. Heller armfuls of photos, letters, poems,

and journal entries. We study them together, searching for Len.

I show her snapshots that were taken about a year and a half ago on a brisk September day spent walking in the Weston Nature Preserve in Connecticut, long before I had ever heard of a craniotomy. There is one of Len and me that I have always liked: We're turned slightly away from the camera and mugging to one another, Len sporting that goofy lopsided grin that gives him the incongruous appearance of a five-year-old clamoring to get out of an old man's rumpled body where he doesn't belong and me, much younger, but with my eyes flashing in that same expression of bemused silliness. But this time, when I pass it to Dr. Heller, I notice details I hadn't picked up before. Len banks much closer to me than I to him. His whole body is looser, rounder, and more generous than mine, as if he were at ease in surrendering himself to me. Whereas I am stiffer, tauter, pulling slightly away from him, as if bracing myself against some fierce gale emanating from him. It's subtle. Because there I am smiling with my eyes flashing from behind their tortoise-shell glasses—we were talking about my future as a writer and Len was saying I could write a bang-up exposé of the insurance world and it would be a best-seller and we could retire to Greece on the proceeds—and yet even my smile is cracked too wide, revealing this same recoiling.

Dr. Heller interprets our differences as extrovert and introvert—Len the extrovert who must give himself away to the world, Rebecca the introvert who needs to contain and preserve the inner world from assault. Possibly. And possibly these differences are those between Eastern European Jew and New England WASP—the Jew forever arguing and gesticulating, the WASP restraining and withholding. Still, I am troubled by what I see in the photo: It challenges my idealized vision of Len and me as twins, feeling and thinking in the same way, our love secure in its constancy and reciprocity.

129

I read Dr. Heller excerpts from my journal, all dated before the illness, before I had begun to see Len beatified by loss.

September 20, 1979, Rome, Italy: A disturbing experience booking a hotel room near the Spanish Steps. Len asks for a room with a double bed, and the hotel-keeper, a paunch-bellied, grimy Roman in his 60s, points at me and smirks. "No! No! Signorina too young. Only room with *due letti."* Len gets angry and repeats in his broken Italian, "Excusi, Signor, camera with uno letti." "No!" the hotel-keeper shouts, folding his plump hands across his belly. We storm out. All day I am upset. This stupid altercation brings back the other humiliations we have suffered over our age difference in these two months of traveling. In Vienna, we ask directions to Freud's house of this crazy older woman who offers to take us there. Chattering nonstop in German to Len about Vienna under Anschluss, she ignores me before she finally asks Len, "This must be your little girl. Yes?" In Jerusalem, hiking up the Mount of Olives, I fall into conversation with a French Catholic priest, who points to Len and asks, "Votre Papa?"

Len finds ways of dismissing these experiences—if we were wearing wedding rings (we weren't married then) or we dressed more alike (Len always looks professional in his Harris tweed coat, in contrast to my dirty T-shirts and jeans), it wouldn't happen. Why should I care? Len asks. We love each other and we're happy. True. We are happy and I wouldn't want to be with anyone but Len. But how troubling for our mutual happiness not to be recognized, to be regarded as freaks.

Redding, Connecticut, July 14, 1981: Today, Len and I decide to get married and buy a house together. Len says, "I have something to tell you, something so terrible you may change your mind about marrying me." *Oh my God, Len is dying of cancer,* I think. We take a long walk through the bird sanctuary near Chestnut Woods Road. Len says he will let me go if I want to, even help me move into a place of my own. "For God's sake, what's going on?" I ask. Finally, he blurts out the secret he's been keeping from me these three years. "I lied about my age, Beck. I'm 59, not 52. I would have told you before, but I couldn't. I thought you would leave me if you knew." I throw my arms around him and laugh and laugh. "Silly, crazy old man! The original fool for women. I thought you were going to tell me you had leukemia. Of course I'm not going to leave you."

"Weren't you angry he'd kept his age from you?" Dr. Heller asks.

"A little. I'd written him these poems about our being 25 years apart, how it made our love more precious because we were defying flesh and time. All along, Len was hiding this dark secret about his age. What troubled me most was that Len's real age was dangerously close to my father's. It felt weird, incestuous. You're not supposed to grow up and marry Daddy. That's exactly what I was doing."

"You didn't think of leaving?"

"I loved him too much. It seemed like a ridiculous reason for breaking things off. After we were married, I used to kid him that I was going to find a younger version of him. He'd insist I'd never find such an animal. Which was probably true. A younger man wouldn't have loved me with that total, unselfish love Len had, listening to my problems for hours, always willing to minister to my depressions.

"I can remember every Sunday sinking into these black moods after reading the newspaper. I'd read about some woman writer, my age or younger, who'd written a novel or book of poems, and I'd start to feel I was no good, a failure like my mother. I'd eat too many croissants, which would make it worse, until I was too miserable to move off the couch. Len would drop what he was doing and propose an outing. We'd go for a walk or take the train into New York or see a movie in Westport. He never failed to cheer me up. He was my psychiatric 'sugar daddy,' always willing to buy whatever I needed emotionally. The problem was I never learned to take care of myself."

"Maybe you weren't ready to."

"What do you mean?"

"We seek out the people who will give us what we need at our particular stage in life. When you met Len, you were recovering from a mother who could not be available to you and from a father who loved you but was critical. Len helped you heal those early wounds. As time went on, you outgrew the need for his unconditional love. You were leaving home. Not literally, but you were leaving the child in yourself. It sounds to me as though it was scary for you. For Len, too."

"The irony is that when Len got sick, we had no choice but to reverse the dynamics. I became the parent. I called the doctors, drove him to his radiation treatments, decided whether to go ahead with the spinal tap. I paid the bills— the mortgage, the credit cards, the doctors who insisted on being paid before the insurance companies reimbursed me. I, who had done so little in the relationship, suddenly had to do everything."

"What was that like?"

"Liberating and terrifying. I remember going to the hospital, dressed in one of my IWN business suits, armed for battle. You know how doctors can be—offhand, condescending, talking to you as if you were a child. I was determined not to let them do that; I would force them to treat me with respect, to explain every detail of Len's cancer to me, until I understood it completely and could make my own decisions. I felt strong, empowered. Even Len couldn't believe the change in me. 'I'm so proud of you, Beck,' he'd say to me. 'You're handling everything.'

"There were other times, especially toward the end, when I felt totally helpless. Len and I had always discussed every little problem, now I had to go through the biggest trauma of my life—losing him forever—and he couldn't help me.

"I remember one night last October when Len was still well enough to take the stairs, when we still slept in the same bed. We had come back from making the rounds of doctors in New York. The prognosis was bad. 'Two months if you're lucky,' the radiologist said, turning over the ashen pages of the X rays while Len sat in the waiting room. 'Think about putting him in a nursing home,' the internist said. 'Or back into Lenox Hill,' the neurologist said. 'I want him to die at home,' I said. They warned me it would get worse. What would I do, they asked, when he started swallowing his tongue?

"That night, as we lay in bed, I whispered to Len, 'I'm scared. I feel so alone.' But he was tired from traipsing around from the radiologist to the neurologist to the internist, from getting in and out of the car and standing naked, weak-kneed and trembling, beside stainless steel tables. 'Lennie,' I said, shaking him, 'I'm scared. I feel so alone.' Still no response. Just a labored breathing and an occasional involuntary twitching in his legs. As I continued to shake him, I felt the bed growing warm and soupy around my legs. I yanked the covers down, knowing immediately what had happened. Len had had an 'accident.'

"I was furious. I shot out of bed, pulled off the blankets, and screamed, 'Goddamit, why do you have to do that now when it's late and I just need you to hold me!' By this time, Len was awake and staring at me in terror, like a dog waiting to be spanked. I pulled him out of bed, yanked off his sopping underwear, and washed him fiercely with a towel. When he said, softly, a little sadly, 'Please, Beck, not so rough,' I knelt down before him, buried my head in his trembling knees, and cried. He patted my head and said, 'I've been so much for you.' I heard this as, 'I've been a burden to you.' The tears subsided. The heroine returned: 'I love you. It's not too much. We'll manage.' Again, Len said, 'I've been so much *for* you.' I realized, guiltily, that he meant he had always loved me, supported me. Which was true. Until the cancer."

"We're going to have to stop now," Dr. Heller says.

Widows, I've discovered from the books on mourning piled beside my bed, seem to react to the loss of their husbands in two ways. The experience breaks them and their lives dissolve into alcoholism, suicide, or a pining so intense it makes them sick, or they grow stronger, emerging, phoenix-like, from the ashes of their dead husbands, to become far more vital people than they were while their husbands were alive. After Phillip Graham's suicide, Katherine Graham took over his job as publisher of the *Washington Post* and created one of the leading newspapers in America. Lynn Caine, author of *Widow,* and Betty Jane Wylie, author of *Beginnings,* both became successful writers. Cynthia Koestler and Dora Carrington collapsed under the pressures of grief: Koestler killed herself in a suicide pact with the mortally ill Arthur, while Carrington, two months after the death of her long-time companion, Lytton Strachey, put on his yellow bathrobe and shot herself.

I admire the heroism of women like Katherine Graham, who refused to succumb to adversity, who made, as Betty Jane Wylie called it, "lemonade out of the lemon." But I am haunted by Cynthia Koestler's suicide note. "Despite certain inner resources, I cannot live without Arthur," and Carrington's diary entry before her death: "I feel as if we had collected all our wheat into a barn to make bread and beer for the rest of our lives and now our barn has been burnt down and we stand on a cold winter morning looking at the charred ruins. . . . It is impossible to think that I shall never sit with you again and hear your laugh. *That every day for the rest of my life you will be away.*"

This is what's hardest about death, I think. The finality of it. That ultimate good-bye. The door slammed in the face. Which will not be opened again. Not in this lifetime, anyway. No other loss is so total. Not divorce, which can be healed through remarriage. Not a failed career, which can be rebuilt. Not a lost fortune, which can be remade. Not illness, which can be cured. Not aging, which can be slowed. Death is the hurt for which there is no help.

But Katherine Graham survived and Dora Carrington did not. Why? Dora Carrington had been a member of the

Bloomsbury group and an amateur painter. She had attended the Slade School of Art in London. She had also
been, to judge from the image about the wheat in the barn,
a gifted writer. Her talent was as great as, if not greater
than, Katherine Graham's or Lynn Caine's or Betty Jane
Wylie's. Surely she had as much to live for as they did. And
what about Cynthia Koestler? She had been a writer, too.
She had co-authored the joint autobiography, *Stranger on
the Square,* with her husband. Like Dora Carrington, she
belonged to a vibrant literary community in England. By
her own admission, Cynthia Koestler possessed "inner resources," one of which was the patience to accommodate
her demanding husband, who did not like it if she walked
"out of step" with him along a street. But when it came to
walking those London streets without him, she refused to
try. Her talent, her patience, even her own good health, for
she had not been suffering from any illness when she killed
herself, could not compete with Arthur.

I grieve for Dora and Cynthia, and yet I will marshal all
my "inner resources" not to do what they did.

On the train or at the Displaywriter at IWN, I start making notes and copying down passages from *Widow, The Oxford Book of Death,* and *A Grief Observed.* I note that the
word *widow* comes from the Sanskrit and means "empty."
I copy a passage from Konrad Lorenz about what happens
to the grey goose when it loses its mate: "From the moment
a goose realizes that the partner is missing, it loses all courage and flees even from the youngest and weakest
geese. . . ." From *A Grief Observed,* I underline: ". . . passionate grief does not link us with the dead but cuts us off
from them. It is just at those moments when I feel the least
sorrow—getting into my morning bath is one of them—that
H. rushes upon my mind in her full reality, her otherness.
Not, as in my worst moments, all foreshortened and pa-
theticized and solemnized by miseries, but as she is in her
own right. This is good and tonic." In my journal, I jot
down my reflections on newspaper obituaries—how quickly

the text moves from a description of death, "he died of emphysema," or "she died of cancer," to jump back 20, 30, or 40 years to when he was a boy or when she went to law school—as if there is nothing to be said about death, only about life.

On April 12, I pay a long-overdue visit to my father, driving up to my grandmother's estate in Pittsfield after work on Friday and arriving for a late dinner that night. Although we've spoken by phone, I haven't seen him since the funeral, and there are awkward pauses and false starts in our conversation as I vacillate between wanting to tell him everything, as I used to when I was an adolescent, and needing to keep a certain distance. I still fear, after all these years, his criticisms of me, that he will say something wounding like, "What did you expect? That the 'old man' would live to be a hundred?"

But my father is on his best behavior. He asks about Alice and IWN and even about my dog, Hector, whom he's never been fond of. I tell him all are fine, saying nothing about leaving IWN because I know he will tell me that giving up a good job is a mistake. He will point out that I've failed once with my freelance writing career, that I shouldn't risk failing again. Although he himself had literary aspirations and now busies himself in his retirement by writing book reviews for the *Berkshire Eagle,* he once said that I could write *War and Peace*—but that if it were never published it would be worthless.

He wants to know about Vivian's lawsuit against the estate, says he'll put me in touch with his lawyer if I think it would help. I tell him nothing much is happening now, but my lawyer is optimistic that Vivian has no case. He wonders how my finances are doing; all I have to do is say the word and he'll help me out. He has offered money before when Len was sick, but I've always prided myself on never taking it. After all, my father was the one who impressed on me the virtues of financial independence.

We take our coffee in my late grandfather's library, where, among butterscotch- and rust-colored collections of Thackeray and Dickens, I notice Len's three maroon-spined books on an upper shelf in the built-in bookcase. I'm touched by this gesture, for I know my father dislikes philosophy and has never been able to read Len's works. I should tell him I'm touched, but like him, I am awkward about expressing my feelings. I remain silent.

"I wish I'd known Len better," my father says, as he offers me a piece of Jane's chocolate cake, "but I guess I knew him as well as he wanted me to know him."

"What makes you think he didn't want you to know him?" I decline the cake and sit up straighter in the red leather bank officer's chair that belonged to my grandfather.

"I had the feeling Leonard wanted you all to himself and didn't want anyone else in the family raining on his parade." My father shifts his massive, navy-blue, sweat-suited legs in his matching red leather chair and stuffs a large piece of cake into his mouth. His intense blue eyes, sunk in pouches of skin in his heavy-featured, former-football player's face, challenge me across the coffee table.

"I think he felt you and Ma and Harriet never approved of him. Which you didn't." My eyes meet a photograph of my late grandmother on the mantelpiece above the fireplace, remembering with a shudder how she had trained those fierce, hooded eyes and arrogant jaw on Len when she first met him.

"Ma may have been a little brusque, especially when you were living together; people in her generation didn't do that sort of thing. Harriet probably would have preferred you to marry someone more like George, but I don't think I expressed any hostility to him. Did I? I tried to bring him into the family. We invited him to our cocktail parties and introduced him to the Riggs crowd and other limousine liberals like you two."

My father lays his silver fork against my grandmother's butterfly-patterned china plate and furtively studies my face to see if I am laughing. "Limousine liberals" was what my father, a staunch Republican, called us after we moved to Redding, a town, my father was quick to point out, notable for its absence of blacks. I am laughing, remembering how even Len used to giggle at this clever, alliterative put-down.

"Sure, I thought he was too old for you. But I knew better than to tell you. Besides, it wouldn't have done any good, would it?"

"No," I admit, reflecting that another trait we Rices share is a certain pig-headedness. If my father or anyone had advised me not to marry Len, I would simply have redoubled my resolve to marry him.

"I never thought Len was the risen Christ, but he did a lot for you and I tried to support that."

I wince at my father's use of the term "risen Christ" just three and a half months after Len's death, but the phrase is so typical of my father's blunt way of speaking that I let it pass.

I also realize what must have been obvious to anyone else: My father was jealous of Len. After all, during my childhood, I had worshiped my father. He had taught me to ski and play tennis, to appreciate writing and music and books. For hours we had sat up late at night talking about "the eternal verities," as he dubbed them. My father had been the one in whom I'd confided my anxieties about weight and my melancholy moods—the parent I'd called from college to discuss my term papers. There was a time when I considered *him* the "risen Christ" and believed all would be well if only I could be as smart and strong and decisive as he, if only I could please him.

"What really annoyed me about Leonard," my father continues, warming to this opportunity to release his feelings for his deceased son-in-law, "was how he'd never let you out of his sight when the two of you came up here. Even when we'd play tennis, he'd insist on tagging along. From Leonard's perspective, I was bad for your health."

Fighting with the part of myself that wants to placate him,

138

and knowing that part wants, finally, to confront him, I falter over my answer. "Len knew, that is, he worried about how sensitive I was to your criticisms and he, well, he just wanted to protect me, that's all."

"Protect you? From what?" My father's once-dark eyebrows, now white-blond with age, rise in genuine befuddlement.

"You," I tell him, chidingly, as I realize, perhaps for the first time in my adult life that our roles have shifted, that I'm no longer the daughter gingerly approaching her father as suppliant, but am his equal, with my own intellectual and spiritual powers. "You know how you were always on my case. I was too fat. Too thin-skinned. Too lazy. Too sloppy. Too this. Too that."

"Maybe you needed someone to ride herd over you. Someone's got to tell you when your breath is bad, Becky. Better me than a stranger."

"Take my writing. I always had the feeling you thought I was wasting my time writing a novel. That I should be in some training program at Banker's Trust or something. Like Jane's daughter, Dale."

"I might have said that if you were going to be a writer, you should be published and not let your book gather dust in a closet."

"I'll never forget the time you took me out to lunch at the Top of the Tower and ripped into one of my early short stories. It was too flowery. It had too many adjectives, too many similes. I was devastated."

"Lots of writers, especially beginning ones, write badly, Becky. You didn't want me to lie, did you?"

"No. I guess it just seemed like you never praised me, whether it was my writing or anything else. You never told me I was wonderful. Just for being me."

"I thought you were good. But you could be better."

"Remember the time when I was going to move in with Brian and you called me a whore and told me no one would be able to live with me because I was such a slob?"

139

"I? Called you a whore?" My father's furry eyebrows arch again in surprise. "A slob, maybe. A whore, no."

"You did, Dad. That's not something I'd forget, believe me. Anyway, the point is that I was in terror of you, always worried that I'd do something to incur your wrath and you'd withdraw your love from me."

"But every time I turned around, you were doing something to incur my wrath!" My father grins, and cuts himself a second wedge of cake. "I sometimes thought your marrying Leonard was designed to incur my wrath."

"I probably needed Len," I say, choosing my words carefully and noticing another photograph on the mantelpiece—a snapshot of my father and me on the tennis court fifteen years ago, my father's six-foot frame towering above me, his sweaty, muscular arm clasping me possessively, and I, chubby, frowning face framed in messy braids, struggling to weasel out of his grip. "I probably needed Len to free myself from *you*. You yourself once said we were 'too close' and you treated me like a 'surrogate wife,' burdening me with your troubles with Mother."

We are silent while the grandfather clock in the hallway chimes the quarter hour. I gaze into my father's heavily lined, vein-flecked face, a face no longer capable of evoking such primitive feelings of adulation or terror. I close my eyes and take myself back to those adolescent years when we were "too close." I remember the snowy night we sat in my father's Sting Ray in the circular driveway on East Street for close to an hour and talked about whether my mother should be institutionalized.

My mother hadn't gone out that winter at all, and she had rarely gotten out of bed, except in the middle of the night when I'd come home from a date, drunk or stoned, and she'd be in her nightgown in the kitchen eating ice cream straight from the carton. I remember telling my father that it wasn't normal for her to be living like this and that she needed help. He said he'd tried to get her to see a couple's therapist, but she wouldn't because she thought the therapist was against her, and anyway their troubles were all my father's because he "ran around with other women." As we talked about the possibilities—whether she could be committed or had to sign herself in—I confessed how much I hated her and how I didn't blame him for Jane.

I had some vague intuition that what I was doing was wrong, sitting there in a dark car with my father conspiring against my mother, as if he and I were lovers. Oh, I hated my mother all right. She was so absorbed in her own "difficulties," as she called them, that she was oblivious to the havoc I was wreaking in my own life—losing my virginity at 14, taking drugs, getting bad grades in school, and gaining thirty pounds. But she was still my mother. In joining forces with my father against her, I was betraying not only her but myself. Everyone said I took after her: I had her delicate face, her artistic nature, even her fat rear end. In divorcing myself from her so vehemently, in refusing to empathize with her, I was slicing myself in two, creating a schism in my soul that would take years to bridge.

"No doubt I made some mistakes back then," my father says as he glances at his watch and announces it's past his bedtime. "You know that old saying, 'They fuck you up, your Mum and Dad.' But all that's in the past. What matters is now. We've been estranged for a long time. Whether Leonard did or didn't aggravate it is beside the point. But I don't think we need to be estranged now, do we?"

"No," I sigh, wishing my father didn't insist on barking out "Leonard" like some drill sergeant dressing down a tardy recruit and yet realizing that I can't force him to feel more tenderly toward his son-in-law. "I want to make peace. With you and Harriet and Mother. Most of all, with myself. That's what death teaches you—we're not here for long on this planet, and we'd better not waste our years hating and feuding."

" 'Love one another or die,' W. H. Auden said, if I'm remembering correctly. Anyway, child, you don't mind if I still call you 'child' for old times' sake?"

"I prefer 'limousine liberal,' " I joke, "but I won't disown you for calling me 'child.' "

My father grins impishly, a grin such as I remember from years ago when I was very small and we used to press our faces together and play a game called "owl eyes." Suddenly, I realize that he is as eager for me to tell him that he's been a good father, that all the afternoons we spent playing tennis or skiing or going to concerts at Tanglewood, all the nights we sat up past midnight having our "deep-dish" talks—he is as eager for me to assure him that these long hours of fathering were not spent in vain as I am for him to tell me that I'm not the failure he once predicted I'd become.

"I may not tell you enough, but I *am* proud of you, Beck. What you did for Leonard is what I hope would be done for me. When the time comes."

"That's a long way off, Dad," I say softly.

"We all have to shuffle off this mortal coil sooner or later," he says gruffly, gathering up his night-time reading, *How to Profit from a Money Crisis,* and taking a final swig of cold coffee. "Anyway, Beck, Jane and I are here if you need us. You're a pretty tough cookie. But it helps to know there are people you can fall back on."

"Thanks, Dad," I murmur, feeling my eyes puffing with tears.

"And, Becky, I probably don't tell you enough. Jane says I don't tell her enough. But I love you."

"I love you too, Dad."

Then we both rise from my grandfather's red leather chairs and my father says, "How about a hug?" And I throw my arms around his towering form and I let the tears come, because I know there are a finite number of times left in both our lives when I will be able to embrace this big, blustering, gruff man who is almost 70 now and who has taught me so much about living and loving and even about being angry and in pain, this man who is my father.

* * *

142

Who shall I be without Len? Will I inherit his character-
istics, as I have inherited his books, records, and stereo?
Will I become Len, as I can already feel myself doing in
little ways, like not letting Hector lick my plate because
Len hated it, and peppering my speech with his expressions? Or will my widowhood gestate some brand-new person with hidden strengths and weaknesses that are a
mysterious composite of me and Len?

I'm far more practically inclined than Len was, particularly with money. (It's probably the Rice businesswoman in
me finally surfacing.) To my surprise, I like punching away
at Len's solar cell calculator, watching the jagged numbers
flash as I figure out whether I can pay off the mortgage and
how much I'll have left to invest in CDs and how much I'll
save by eliminating the commute to New York and whether
I can cut my food expenses if I buy no red meat and subsist
on salads and lentil soups. I like staying within a budget
and playing money-saving games such as passing up an expensive pair of shoes ("Treat yourself, Beck," Len would
have urged, regardless of whether I needed the shoes) or
pumping my own gas or subscribing to magazines instead
of buying them from newstands. I don't even object to the
time-consuming business of preparing my first tax return for
Lester Goldberg. (He had to get an extension this year because of the complications with the estate, but next year I'm
determined to make the April 15 deadline.) Unlike Len,
who hated ordering and cataloging last year's canceled
checks and crumpled receipts—he compared it to babies
playing with their feces!—I like to see the tide of bills and
W-2 forms spreading out over the blue carpet in my study,
to calculate how much I've spent in heat or electricity or
home repairs.

With my friends, I'm becoming more like Len, rather
than less. When Len was alive, I related to Susan and Anna
in much the way I related to him—that is, I asked them for
advice and expected them to listen to my problems. Now I
occasionally slip into Len's role of confidant. I notice this

one evening while I am having dinner with Susan in West-port. We spend the first 20 minutes of the meal talking about Len ("I knew when I first saw you two at Carnegie Hall that you were Len's ideal woman," Susan says generously). But we spend the last hour talking about her and her problems with her latest boyfriend, Paul. Apparently, he is so obsessed with his dead wife that he will not open himself up to Susan. The wife has been dead for two years, but Paul still talks about her constantly and wears her wedding ring on a chain around his neck. Susan doesn't know what to do. She's turning 40 this year and wants to get married. Should she try to be more understanding and hope it will pass? Or should she break with Paul and find someone else?

I have no answers to Susan's dilemma, although I do feel confident, because of my own suffering as a widow, to speak to Paul's obsession with his dead wife. Two years, I tell Susan, does seem like a long time for Paul to continue being so preoccupied with Kaye. But if one has loved another deeply, it's not possible ever to be "finished" with them. If she cares about Paul, she should try to be patient. On the other hand, if Paul is using his grief for Kaye as a pretext for expressing reservations about Susan, that's more serious.

Susan and I continue our conversation in the car driving home. Even though I am tired, I find it a relief to focus on her problems rather than mine. I enjoy the superior feeling that comes when one is giving advice rather than taking it, radiating strength rather than weakness, authority instead of dependency. Now and then, I wonder if I'm saying the right thing or merely mouthing clichés. What would Len say to this problem of holding on to the dead? Would he call it a manifestation of love or neurosis? How does one love another living person while not severing one's connection to the past? But then I hear Len saying that there are no rules, either for loving or grieving; all I can do is listen to Susan as empathically as possible and mirror back her own struggles.

A Time to Mourn

* * *

Today, on Wednesday, April 17, almost four months after Len's death and one year after he was hospitalized at Lenox Hill, I buy my grave. I'm not sure what propels me to pick up the phone and call Mrs. Shipman at the Congregational church in Wilton and arrange to purchase plot #4322 in Hillside Cemetery, situated to the left of Len as you are standing at the foot of the grave, looking up the hill. I suppose it's the desire to link myself in perpetuity to Len, to give him some tangible symbol of our togetherness. I could not carry this off a few months ago because I imagined I would be courting my own end, whereas now, perhaps because I am proving I can survive, death seems no longer such a visceral threat.

But what a curious thing it is to buy one's own grave. To sit in a swivel chair with arms propped on elbows, legs crossed demurely beneath one, and talk, on the telephone, to another living person about whether to have a single stone or two. How startling to write a check for $330.00 and even to make, in keeping with my new businesslike style, the absurd notation along the "memo" line in the lower left hand corner—"1 grave for Rebecca Feldstein." How odd to have the transaction conducted so folksily, Mrs. Shipman telling me I'm "lucky" I called when I did because she's been selling "like crazy" this spring. And my telling her it's not an easy job she has and she does it well and she pointing out, somewhat tentatively, "Well, you get to meet people." And my answering, "Not under the best of circumstances," and then her brief, poignant confession: "What's hardest is that we've lived in this town for so many years and after a while you start to know everyone who's buried there. My son grew up here and went to school here, and I can't tell you how many of his friends are over there."

When Mrs. Shipman and I finish, I get out my journal and jot down this observation: *I understand now what Freud meant when he wrote: 'one thinks about something as one thinks about death . . . one's own death is beyond imagin-*

ing.' I have just written a check for my grave and come face to face with the certain extinction of Rebecca Feldstein, née Rice, and yet all I can focus on is the sweetness of writing this word April, *this number* 17, *and the two digits*, 85, *following the printed* 19——. *April 17, which is no longer a date among others, drab and commonplace, but charged with poetry, an anniversary for rejoicing. April 17, which will be followed, God willing, by May 17 and June 17. What joy to hold these months and days in my hands! Yes, I remember, with a guilty start, that Len will never write April 17 at the top of any check again. Even so, I cannot kill my own glad animal spirits. I, who might be dead, who will be dead, am alive.*

This appears to be the month for family visits. My sister, Harriet, has been urging me to come to New Hampshire and see her new baby girl, born two months ago. I can't put her off any longer, and so I've agreed to take off the last Friday in April and drive up to Hanover to see her.

The visit goes well, better than I expect. Like my father, Harriet is eager to please me. Is it because she feels guilty about disliking Len? Or does she feel sorry for me in my widowhood? Or has the birth of her new daughter brought an outpouring of sisterly affection? I can't tell. But she tries hard to give me "material tokens of affection," her phrase for birthday and Christmas gifts. When I arrive, she has a dinner of roast beef and oven-browned potatoes warming in her big country kitchen. In the guest room, she has laid out three matching towels and a book of poetry beside my bed. She has stocked the refrigerator with my favorite diet soda, and for breakfast on Saturday she serves her incomparable sour cream coffee cake. On Saturday, she and George take me out to dinner.

I, too, am eager to get on with her. I come bearing gifts— two bottles of wine for her and George, a silver baby cup for Cynthia and a "Tropical Barbie" for Mandy. The baby is cute—dimpled and pudgy with a square, mannish face that breaks into a grin when Mandy dangles the baby cup over the playpen railing. Harriet and I talk about the children—how Cynthia is more "laid back" than Mandy was, sleeping through the night and not fussing much. Harriet observes that it may be that she, Harriet, is more "laid back" now, less fretful and more confident of herself as a mother.

"You've really taken to motherhood, haven't you?" I tell her, as I keep her company in the kitchen on Saturday afternoon while she bakes cookies for Mandy's birthday party.

"What do you mean?" she shoots back, not sure whether her younger childless sister is complimenting her or preparing some sarcastic put-down. The lines of her heavy, square face sink into an angry frown, making her look matronly, older than her 35 years.

"I meant it as a compliment, Harr," I soothe, treading gently and feeling the familiar childhood fear of my elder sister, she who possessed the advantages of age, height, bulk, and wit and who could, by word or deed, pummel me into silence. "You just seem in your element baking chocolate chip cookies with Cyncie in her playpen and Mandy finger painting."

"It's not 'all quiet on the western front,' " she says. "Talk to me at four in the morning when Cyncie is screaming and Mandy is up with a fever."

"You wouldn't do things differently if you could have a second chance, would you?"

"No, even if children were returnable, which they're not, I wouldn't give them up."

"Give me up where, Mummy?" Mandy pipes up from the newspapers on the floor, her little freckled face puckered in puzzlement.

"Nowhere, honey. Your Aunt Rebecca and I are having one of our silly philosophical conversations."

"What's 'philosophical,' Mummy?"

"Talking about things that don't have answers. Back to your finger painting, Mand. There's an empty spot on the refrigerator, and it's got 'Mandy's new picture' written all over it. But p-le-a-s-e be careful not to spill paint on the floor, okay?''

Mandy nods happily and plops another fat blob of blue across her painting, which is turning out to be an oozing mélange of brownish purple swirls and squirts.

Harriet cracks two eggs against the edge of the mixing bowl. I reflect on Harriet's dismissing my question about children as "silly and philosophical." How typical of her. I remember the time ten years ago when I drove up from college to visit her. She had already moved to New Hampshire then and was dating George, a local boy who lived in Hanover and owned his own auto body shop in White River Junction. Harriet worked full-time at the same job at which she works part-time now: paralegal for Boyle, Cordes & Brown. We sat up till after midnight drinking. I had been talking about *Nausea*—a book I was reading in an existentialism course—and I was asking her what was the purpose of anyone's life when it ended in death? It was a dark, lugubrious discussion. I remember Harriet getting fidgety—writing notes to her roommates about cleaning the refrigerator and shopping for the party they were throwing next day—till finally she said, "You know, Beck, when you get to be my age (she was all of 24 then), you don't worry about this stuff anymore. It's something you do sitting around shooting the bull in college. In the real world, you think about holding down a job and taking out the garbage. When you're older, you'll understand."

I was older now. I held a job. I was a widow. Did I understand? In a way, yes. I filled out tax returns, consulted with my accountant, and returned calls to my lawyer. And, yes, it was enervating and time-consuming, although I didn't mind some of it, because I was learning to master this "real world" from which I'd been hiding.

But I was still the same person I was then: I had not stopped wondering who I was or how should I fill up my years between birth and death. Looking at Mandy, with a smudge of blue across her freckled cheek, I wonder what my life would have been like if Len and I had had a child. Would I be standing over a mixing bowl wearily spooning dough round and round and removing stray pieces of hair from my face with hands covered with flour? Would changing diapers, making cookies, removing finger paint from the kitchen floor fulfill me or deplete me? Would I write? Would I continue to work at IWN? Would I feel less like a widow because I was a mother?

As Harriet claps across her fresh-waxed linoleum floor and shoves her tray of neatly lined cookies into the oven, I wish I could talk about this with her. I don't. I know what she'll say: I'm better off without children, because they wouldn't have a father and I'd have to support them and my life would be ten times harder than it is now. I also don't mention this child Len and I might have had, because it means bringing up Len, a topic Harriet seems eager to steer clear of.

I realize her silence may have more to do with the fear, which she shares with so many others who are uneasy around the bereaved, of saying something inappropriate rather than with any animosity toward Len. She probably thinks you "get over" a death the way you get over an illness, by getting plenty of rest and diverting yourself from thinking about your condition. By keeping the conversation "light" and talking about everything except Len—my latest IWN profile, Alice's dogs, Harriet's resolve to join Weight Watchers—she imagines she's helping me to forget.

To my surprise, she does inquire about Judi and Mark.

"What do you hear from Len's children?" she asks, winding up the timer for her cookies.

"Not much. I sent them memorial notices and wrote them to say how much their father loved them. I haven't heard back. I expect I won't. Which is fine. Their relationship was with Len, not with me."

"It must have been hard for them, with you being so

close to their age.'' Harriet frowns as she takes Mandy's new masterpiece and lays it out to dry on the stove.

''I suppose it was. I said as much in my letter. I even apologized for not having them at the wedding.''

''You didn't invite them?'' Harriet's voice is incredulous and slightly accusatory.

''I regret it now. But then, well, I guess I was pretty immature and I didn't want to share Len with anyone, particularly with his children.''

''What about Len? Didn't he want them there?''

''He felt badly, but you know Len, whatever I wanted, we did.''

''They must have been deeply hurt.''

''Actually, I think my relationship with them improved during the illness. They were really grateful that I was around. Judi used to say that if it weren't for me, she didn't know who would have taken care of her father.''

''You were a trooper during those months, that's for sure.''

''Wait. Let me get this in writing. My big sister is complimenting me?''

''I've told you before, Beck. We were all impressed with how you handled Len's illness. I didn't think you had it in you.''

''Thanks.''

''What I mean is, before Len got sick, you lived, I don't know, in a fantasy world. You didn't seem capable of dealing with a crisis like that. It made you grow up.''

I'd said as much myself to Dr. Heller, but somehow when my elder sister tells me, I feel condescended to. Should I tell her? I pick out a last, solitary Toll House morsel from the mixing bowl while Harriet scolds Mandy for an eddy of red finger paint leaking off the newspaper. No. It would irritate her. She's feeling magnanimous and I start sniping.

Then, as Harriet rushes to the sink with a sponge and warns Mandy she'll have to take everything to the playroom if she isn't more careful, I am inundated with memories:

Harriet busily repinning my Easter corsage to my spring
coat because I look, as Harriet says, smugly quoting our
grandmother, "like something the cat dragged in." Harriet
instructing me on the fine points of wrapping Christmas
gifts: "Like this," she would demonstrate, measuring and
cutting the paper so there were, at most, two inches at each
end of the box, then crimping, folding, and Scotch-taping
the ends firmly, so there were no unsightly bulges. Harriet,
as a teenager, teasing me about some boy and extracting a
tortured confession out of me (I'd let the boy feel me up at
a party) by slyly announcing that everyone in our school
knew what I was up to. Harriet, years later, walking with
me around Storrs Pond, telling me my feelings for Len were
just a passing crush, assuring me I'd get over him and find
someone more "appropriate."

Of course I resented her. Who wouldn't? But maybe, I
reflect, as Harriet picks up a drowsy Cynthia from her playpen and asks me whether I'd like to hold her, Harriet didn't
intend to belittle me. Maybe she was locked into this role
of elder sister keeping watch over the younger one and would
be for the rest of our lives. Maybe Harriet was rather harmless, in her fussiness and self-importance. Even in criticiz-
ing my choice of Len, she was playing out the role to which
she was best suited: monitoring and clucking, mostly dis-
approvingly, over her baby sister's behavior. Perhaps if I
stopped taking offense, developed a sense of self that was
more secure, less flustered by criticism, I could accept who
I was and who she was. Who knows? My sister and I might
even learn to like each other.

"Careful, now. Support her head. No, not like that, like
this," she says, taking my arm and cradling it firmly under
Cynthia's buttocks. "There, that's better. That's your Aunt
Beck, Cyncie. She's not used to handling little bundles of
trouble like you."

Cynthia rests like a warm loaf of bread in my hand. Harriet smiles and throws her large, muscular arm, still flecked

with flour, across my shoulder. "I'm glad you came, Beck. I'm really glad you came."

My first dream about Len since his death: I am trapped on a mountaintop, trying to get down but I don't know how. I meet a young man who agrees to help me. Together, we thread our way along dangerous rocky ledges to a hut at the farthest promontory of the mountain. Inside, Len, frail and sick, lies in bed with a bandage wrapped around his head. I am happy to see him, and I get in bed with him. The young man says Len was his professor once. I ask Len to help us. In a hoarse whisper, he tells us to fetch the long ladder outside the hut which will reach down the mountain. But we must take care to descend slowly. Once we are on level ground, he says, we will be safe. We find the ladder. But as we begin to creep down the rungs, it teeters dangerously, and we fall backward, tumbling through space, like characters in a cartoon. The student disappears, but I find myself at the bottom unharmed. A desert plain stretches for miles. I begin to walk toward the horizon, taking baby steps.

Dr. Heller's interpretation, which we arrive at after probing the dream's images, is this: I cannot remain any longer with Len, the professor, the wise old man with his books written and his life behind him, waiting for death in a hut atop a mountain. I must get the help of the student, the strong, young, vigorous part of myself. I must also ask Len, the protective, fatherly teacher within me, for guidance. To go may be scary, but not life-threatening since my fall has a safe, childlike feel to it not unlike the tumbles of the cartoon character, Wile E. Coyote, who survives all kinds of trials, rarely getting harmed. Once I am on the ground, I must continue alone, taking the smallest steps. I will get to the horizon, she assures me, if I am patient. She reminds me of the story of the race between the tortoise and the hare.

This is a time, Dr. Heller says, for tortoise steps.

Drowning is not so pitiful
As the attempt to rise.

—Emily Dickinson

May 1985

"I hope you know what you're doing," my co-worker Liza says when she hears I'm quitting. "After my dad died, work was the only thing that kept my mom in one piece."

I explain that I don't intend to stop working, only to stop working at IWN.

"But what are you going to *do* all day?" Liza yelps, as if I were committing myself to a mental institution.

Write.

"You're making a big mistake," she persists. "You're giving up an office, daily routines, people, a dependable income. My mom didn't have to work either, but if she didn't have an excuse to get out of bed in the morning, she would have started drinking or popping Valium. That's how a lot of widows end up, you know."

It's a risk I'll have to take.

Others react differently to my "termination," as the company so euphemistically puts it. Although Frances trots out the nurturing boss routine and asks whether I'll have enough money to put food on the table, I suspect she is glad to get rid of me. A few weeks ago, when I was trying to decide whether to work part-time as an editorial consultant or stop altogether, Frances said, "Fish or cut bait, Rebecca." Harsh words to a woman who had recently lost her husband, but Frances probably considered it good managerial strategy. What else was to be done with this wayward widow who preferred weeping to working, who vanished at noon and didn't return until two or three? Her remark, which made me realize how ill-suited I was to IWN's "lean and mean" corporate culture, propelled me to march into her plush corner office, resignation in hand.

Molly, who will inherit my office and title, confesses that she envies me. She quickly corrects herself and says that naturally she doesn't envy what I've gone through, but she wouldn't mind being able to walk away from these "jokers"—FRP and MDS and all the other "clowns." She sticks a finger in her mouth and laughs.

Jim also envies me but is too polite to say so. Unlike Molly, who could easily quit if she wanted to, since her husband makes over one hundred thousand dollars a year, Jim depends on every penny of his meager salary to pay his mortgage and keep his two children in braces. Jim, who has been writing stories for years with little success, fantasizes taking off on his lunch hour and never coming back. This fantasy is so strong that he rarely leaves 29 Wall Street. When he finds out I'm leaving, he rushes into my office, closes the door, and confides his dream of selling his house, moving south where it's cheaper to live, and writing his brains out. His wife will support him whatever he decides. She doesn't want him to wake up at 50—he is 37 now—tormented by the question, "What if?"

I don't know what to say to him. During my good-bye party in the conference room, he is reserved, even melancholy. Halfway through, he disappears. When I gather up the last of my belongings from my empty office, I find him at one of the word processors revising his latest short story. I knock on the wall of his cubicle. He rises wearily from his chair to say good-bye.

"Maybe we'll meet again on the best-seller list," he jokes.

Jim walks me to the elevator. He tells me to keep in touch. I promise to, but know I won't. In six months, we'll be in different time zones: He will still be here, manacled to the Displaywriter; I will be out there, beyond corporate cubicles and schedules, rejoicing in my freedom. Or ruing it. In either case, our common ground will have vanished.

We shake hands. When the chrome doors of the elevator whir shut, he is gone. I ride in silence, pressed against a dozen other people chatting merrily about weekend plans. When the elevator bumps to a halt and the others hurry away into the bustling streets, I linger behind, walk for the last time past the bald, sour-faced guard with his sign-out book. I won't see him again—or the people on the elevator, or Jim, or my other "friends on the third floor," as their sympathy card said. No more working late at the Displaywriter, no more staff meetings in the conference room, no more exultant exits on Friday afternoon with the weekend looming deliciously before me.

Can it be that I am sad to leave "Moishe's joint"? But why? Jim, Liza, Molly, and I were never close. For two years, we came and went in one another's lives and exchanged nothing more intimate than the periodic gripe about Frances, the admission that we did not intend to spend the rest of our working lives in the corporate communications department of IWN. Other than sharing a table at the Christmas party or eating lunch in the cafeteria, we never socialized. None of my colleagues knew my husband was 32 years older than I. They would never have known, save for a memorial card I placed on their desks with the dates 1922–1984 beneath Len's name.

"Don't make any changes," Frances had said. An old wives' tale, or rather widows' tale, I had thought, skeptical of the stress charts that rate the death of a spouse with a whopping 100 points and a change in work with 36 points. Now, lingering in the marbled, mirrored lobby, I understand why change is frightening. It replicates death. I surrender, at my termination interview, my IWN identification card. I forfeit the blue, serrated-edged paychecks that appear, every other Thursday, in my "IN" box. I renounce credenza and desk blotter, watercooler and copier. I waive my right to the Christmas parties, the farewell gatherings in the conference room. I exile myself from my IWN "family." I prepare to enter into a new phase in which the markings of my past will be as useless as the credit cards in Len's wallet.

But to stay, I remind myself, watching the other employees tripping past me hungry for their real lives again, would be to endure another death. To stay would be to pose as the stranger smiling breezily in the overexposed photo on my IWN ID, this pretty, jaunty creature beneath the block letters of the company logo who looks as if all she worried about was losing a few pounds or buying new shoes, who had not yet heard death speak like an oracle: *Change your life.*

A thin spring rain falls outside. The sky, in dove-gray patches between the skyscrapers, is still light. As I walk up Wall Street, the wet, black stone steeple of Trinity Church gleams like onyx. I think of how many times I have hurried to the subway and never noticed the towering Gothic bell-tower or stained-glass windows, the brass-tipped black gates, the stubs of leaning, ancient gravestones in verdant grass, never considered how the church appears, mythical and fantastic as a black Taj Mahal, at the end of this narrow, greed-dark street.

I quicken my step and begin to swing my briefcase at my side. I toss it up in the air like a tennis ball and run to catch it. I miss and it falls with a thud to the ground. File folders bulging with Xeroxed copies of my profiles spill out all over the sidewalk. I gather them up and begin to replace them in the leather compartments. *Why save them?* I wonder, and before I am quite sure what I am doing, I have stuffed all the folders into a trash basket between the spokes of a broken umbrella.

Then I pick up the briefcase, now light as an envelope, and head home.

I wake at dawn. I listen to the birds. I hear a virtual symphony of them—chirping and humming and trilling and thrumming, now loud, now faint, now in crescendo, now, like the sleepy hoot of the owl, in diminuendo. Bird song mingles with the whistle of the 6:32, rumbling two miles away along the tracks heading south toward Branchville and on to Grand Central. Through the open window comes a May wind, plumping up the curtains and perfuming the room with the scent of blossoming dogwood. Stretching my body diagonally across Len's side of the bed, which is flooded with morning light, and hugging his pillow, I think: *It does get easier. Time and Spring make it easier.*

Alice and I get on better every day. On the first morning of my joblessness, I come downstairs to the dining table set for breakfast with my best china and linen napkins, a vase of daffodils at the center. There are wineglasses full of fresh orange juice, apple cinnamon muffins in a covered basket, bowls of granola topped with sliced bananas.

"I thought we should celebrate your new life!" she says.

Although the table set just so with the orange juice and the fresh fruit evokes poignant memories of breakfast with Len and although I am uneasy with Alice's attempts to insinuate herself into my affections and take Len's place, I remind myself that she has gone to a lot of trouble. It would be mean not to sit down. So I take a chair, not at the head of the table where I used to sit, but in the middle where Gail sat and before her, when he was well, where Len sat. Alice takes my place. These shifts, though minor, feel momentous, as if I were a stroke victim learning to walk again.

"What's the average salary of a free-lance writer?" my accountant, Lester Goldberg, fast talks over the phone with his usual hysteria when I call to tell him I have quit my job and will be paying off my mortgage. "Ten thousand dollars a year. There are dogs in my building that live on more than that."

He launches into a horror story about one of his clients about my age, no, maybe a few years older. After inheriting two hundred grand, she quit her job. Like me, she had been bitten by the writing bug. Moved to Majorca, went through all her money in five years, wrote one novel. Which no one would publish. Came back to New York looking for a job. No one would hire her. The only thing she could get, paid half of what she earned before, was a position editing—I kid you not—porno books.

On the subject of the mortgage Lester is only slightly less apocalyptic. "Why are you in such a hurry to unload it when you can deduct the interest?" I explain I'm paying a 17½ percent interest rate.

"Apply for another loan," he pleads. "They're going down, down, down every day. You could probably lock into a 10 or even a 9½." I tell him that after paying points I wouldn't save that much, and anyway, I want a clear idea of how much money I have left to invest, how much income I can count on. "Okay, okay, you're the boss," he says. Before we hang up, he makes me promise to keep track of all expenses incurred from my writing—"books, paper, pens, Xeroxing, postage, you name it"—since I'll be able to deduct them on next year's taxes. Then he coughs and clears his throat: "It may not be the right time to be bringing this up, but you're not exactly ancient. You could get married again."

I appreciate his concern, I tell him, but marriage is the last thing on my mind right now.

The next day, on the second of May, 126 days after Len's death, I drive to the People's Savings Bank in Bethel and write a check to the branch manager for $23,462.00, the exact amount due on the mortgage, including interest.

The branch manager, a busy young man of about my age with photos of wife and children displayed on his desk, looks up at me and whistles as if I were a finalist in a wet T-shirt contest. "Gee, it's not every day that people come in here and pay off their mortgage," he crows. "Whaddya do for a living?"

I know his question is harmless, but I am angry. Speechless. I'm not about to tell him that I'm paying off the mortgage with my dead husband's pension or that I am a writer who intends to make her living by writing about dying. I demand to know how long it will be before I receive formal notification of payment. "They'll send you a mortgage release notice and the bank's copy of the mortgage," he says, adding an obsequious, "ma'am."

As I drive home, I reflect on the singularity of my widowhood: The branch manager of People's Savings Bank treats me like I've just stepped out of an episode of "Dynasty," Lester thinks I'll be waiting in line at a soup kitchen before I file next year's tax returns, Alice believes I'm on the high road to artistic enlightenment, and Liza, my former co-worker, predicts I'll be drinking myself into oblivion.

But it is easier to fantasize about writing, to ghostwrite across the mind the ineffable lines that touch heaven, than to sit alone in a closed room staring at a blank sheet of paper, straining for sentences to fill it.

I spend hours alone in the closed room doing nothing.

Well, almost nothing. I stack my bills into neater and neater piles on my desk, close or open the curtains to keep out or let in the light, prepare fresh mixtures of "Liquid Paper" correction fluid, measuring out a dropper of thinner and easing the brush stick slowly in and out of the bottle. I dig out the dirt from my nails with a paper clip, comb through my long hair hunting for split ends, and browse through my bookcase. I copy a quote from Len's book, *Choros,* and tape it above my desk: "Searching entails crisis; and crisis, repeatedly provoked and repeatedly resolved, allows self-consciousness to elevate to higher forms." I get more coffee, make half a dozen trips to the bathroom. Twisting and twisting my wedding ring on my finger, I stare out at the grass, growing greener and thicker every day.

In the dazzlingly white, blindingly blank pages of my journal, I write: *Len is becoming more remote. There are times when I forget what he looked like, the white flecks in his blue eyes, the gravelly timbre of his voice, what we talked*

*about on all those walks before the astrocytoma shot its
star-shaped cells across his brain. As time takes me further
from him, further into this year, 1985, that he never dated
on letters or checks, I wonder what 1986 and 1987 will be
like, what I shall feel in five years when, according to the
grief experts, I will have reached the outermost edge of the
time needed to mourn. A time will come when Len will have
been dead longer than I was married to him, longer than I
knew him. Will he become, then, when he is nothing more
than skull and rib cage in the grave, ever more an attenuation of eyes and voice, a distant ancestor of my Len, the
man I can still, with struggle, recollect?*

In my study closet, shut away at the bottom of a toy chest
among old journals and files, is a green and white shipping
box marked "Borum, Pease & Company" containing all
260 pages of my first novel, *The Long Birth.* Beneath the
title page is a brown folder marked "correspondence,"
containing a dozen rejection letters from agents and editors.
Chucking the folder into the wastebasket—it will depress
me to read the rejections again—I carry the box to my desk,
hoping I'll discover something by looking back upon my
younger, literary self.

Leafing past the dedication page with its quote from
Christina Rosetti—FOR LEN ". . . the birthday of my life/
Is come, my love is come to me"—I turn to page 209, the
section in which my heroine, Beth, has recently learned that
her older lover, Eric, whom she met while traveling in Europe and with whom she has been living for two months on
the island of Santorini, is dying of cancer: *Eric's dream is
to finish his book before he dies. Every day, he stations
himself at the table in the living room, his head bent close
to the yellow pad, his fingers moving slowly across the page.
On days when he's too weak to get out of bed, he asks me
to bring his writing materials into the bedroom. Buried
among pillows and blankets, the typewriter balanced on his
lap, he struggles against nausea, dizziness, and fits of*

*coughing to fill the last bound volume of the manuscript.
His eyes shine—like bright rays of sunlight on the ruined
columns of a temple.*

What romanticism! Dying people don't go off to Aegean
islands to finish books and wait, heroically and painlessly,
for death. Gravely ill cancer victims don't have the energy
to hold a pen, let alone type out a hundred pages of meta-
physical tract about artistic creation. Their eyes grow blurry
and unfocused; they don't "shine like bright sunlight on a
ruined temple." And what about my heroine, Beth, toting
typewriters for her older lover, whom she has known for
three months? Was she ever angry, resentful, guilty, fear-
ful? How could she be a mere amanuensis for this established writer 25 years her senior? After Eric dies, Beth
returns to America, resolving to be a poet. Is this likely,
given her watery, undefined character throughout the book—
she had worked in advertising in New York and had quit her
job after her father's suicide to "find herself" in Europe?
Will she develop a self that refracts more than the pale,
ruined light of Eric? Will she become a serious poet? Will
she publish? Will she find another job?

I flip through the yellowing pages, startled at Len's neatly
inserted commas sprinkled like dead insects through the
typescript. Why had I written a novel that so closely prefig-
ured my future? Why had I needed to deal, in a fictional
universe, with an event I would live through four years later?
Had I been so troubled by the age difference and the likelihood that Len would die before me that I needed to prove
I could handle it? Not just handle it, but triumph over it,
for in the last chapter, I depict an enraptured Beth in the
Athens airport writing a sonnet about the soul. Had I sensed
Len's death would be so painful that I needed to poeticize
it? What about the title, *The Long Birth,* and its connection
to my own gestating months of mourning? Was my growth
as an independent woman predicated upon Eric's/Len's
death? And what about Beth meeting Eric, only months af-

ter her father has committed suicide? Was *The Long Birth* about the Oedipal struggle to destroy the father?

My first novel, I'm afraid, has more merit as a psychological document than a literary one. Len would dispute this. But Len's opinion of my writing was skewed by his love for me: "You're better than Edna St. Vincent Millay!" he had enthused after reading my first attempts at writing sonnets, poems that a former writing teacher at Sarah Lawrence termed "too green for publication." Each time I'd get a rejection for *The Long Birth* charging that it contained "no believable characters," "no central problem," "no dramatic tension," Len would mutter, "What do they know? Fool editors in New York! You're too good for them, Beck!"

If Len wasn't dubbing me another Edna St. Vincent Millay, who was I as a writer? My writing teacher had begrudgingly praised my "ear." A novelist in the women's writing group I belonged to before working at IWN said *The Long Birth* "wasn't bad for a first novel," although it needed "a major overhaul." My profiles at IWN had been commended, but they were written to formula. Maybe I was a journalist and a mere business journalist at that. Maybe I didn't have the talent or patience to write "literature" and was deluding myself to think I had anything to say about widowhood, death, or loss. Maybe I was wasting my time listening to the dogs howling at the garbageman and staring at this tiny, perfectly formed question mark Len left behind on p. 105 of *The Long Birth*.

Some mornings, after watching Alice's VW bus disappear through the trees, I leave my pads of fresh paper and computer and slink back to bed. Unplugging the phone, shutting the upstairs hall door and my bedroom door, and closing the curtains, I yank off my jeans, T-shirt, turtleneck, and socks and pitch myself naked across the unmade bed. Then, crouching forward toward the headboard with all my weight resting on my knees and elbows and my rear end in the air, I rub my legs together and squeeze my pelvic muscles tight.

I squeeze tighter and tighter until there is throbbing, burning heat emanating from my pubis and making my nipples swell and my face redden, throbbing until I can stand the tautness no longer and I crumple to the sheets in exhaustion.

After a few minutes, I repeat the little exercise again, this time working myself into a frenzy remembering the night years ago when Len and I went to the strip show in a nightclub in Amsterdam, remembering how I watched the lower lips of the men moisten and curl as they watched the dancer twirling her breasts before them like batons and how afterward in our hotel room when sex went roaring like a circus crowd through my body I made Len fuck me and fuck me, on the bed, on the floor, from the side, and from behind until I came and came, until we collapsed on the bed, giggling.

My hips go still when I recall the last time Len and I tried to have sex. It was a sweltering July afternoon, and our chests were moist with sweat; I massaged Len's penis intermittently for twenty minutes, but he still could not get hard. Afterward, as we lay together in our bathrobes, Len cupped his flaccid testicles and cursed the doctors and the cancer and himself for being such a schlemiel who couldn't satisfy his wife, telling me he wouldn't blame me if I had an affair but begging me not to and then boasting that when the treatments were finished he was going to take off all my clothes and make me dance before him like the Amsterdam stripper and then he was going to tie me to the bed and fuck me until I would beg him to stop.

We never tried anything after that. Len got weaker and weaker until he stopped talking about my having affairs or tying me to the bed. I became so busy worrying about his seizures that I shut that part of myself up, like closing off a room in a house when you can't afford to heat it.

Each evening, Alice wants a progress report on my writing. I tell her I'm thinking about an essay on widowhood, although I'm still in the note-taking stage. Defending my lack of productivity, I explain that Flaubert sometimes wrote only one sentence in an entire day, that Oscar Wilde said he spent the morning putting in a comma and the afternoon taking it out.

These literary allusions are lost on Alice, who says maybe it's still too painful to write about Len's death and I ought to pick another topic. Like what? I ask. A story about Hector and Pucci and LA, she says, her voice trilling with girlish delight, a children's story about how they meet and don't get along and then get to be friends. She could illustrate it. Alice is enthusiastic about this collaborative effort: We'd make money and launch our careers. "It would also be fun and good for you, Rebecca," she says.

Writing a story about Alice's dogs has about as much appeal to me as banging out a press release on group life insurance. But I don't tell her that. I plead ignorance, maintaining that I don't know the first thing about children's books.

She then asks whether I need to be at home to write. Why not take my paper and pens to some exotic part of the world and work there? Like where? I ask. Rent a house in the south of France or go to that Greek island you wrote about in your novel, she proposes. It's not as if you don't have the money, she adds.

"Are you trying to get rid of me?" I joke.

"Of course not. I just hate to see you moping around the house all day."

Mooning about my desk one afternoon, I creep down to the closet in Len's study (I still can't think of it as Alice's) and retrieve the two giant black bound volumes that comprise the 1,012-page manuscript of Len's fourth, unpublished book. If I can't move forward with my own writing career, at least I can further Len's. As I hunt through the file folders searching for the correspondence on *Metamorphosis,* I reflect that this is what widows of famous men do. Yeats's widow, who survived him by many decades, gave countless interviews to scholars and helped publish her late husband's last poems. Picasso's widow, 45 years his junior, arranged exhibitions of the great artist's last works. As I plunk down the weighty volumes on my desk, I remind myself I could do worse than preside over the posthumous reputation of Leonard Charles Feldstein.

But it will not be easy to get this book, a psychological study of human development from birth to death, into print. The manuscript, according to the half-dozen rejection letters from both academic and commercial publishers, is deeply flawed: Not only is it too long, it does not fit into any distinct genre. Quoting extensively from novels and poems to illustrate the 135 themes, the book is neither philosophy nor psychology nor literary criticism. None of Len's books fit into conventional categories, of course; his first and second books were reviewed by journals in philosophy, religious studies, and psychiatry. But this book, the rejection letters contend, breaks all the rules. The response from Fordham University Press, the publisher of Len's previous three volumes, is the most damning: "Feldstein must be mad to think he can do psychology and literary criticism without addressing any of the major movements of the last 50 years in those fields." The external reviewer even takes a swipe at me: "The inclusion of his wife's poems in the book's frontispiece seems utterly gratuitous."

But the cover letter's final paragraph is conciliatory. The press will consider giving the book a second reading, provided it is cut in half. Scanning the manuscript pages, many of which are filled with single-spaced, two-page-long quotes from novels, I am daunted by the prospect of editing the book. But, as I finger the dedication page, "For Rebecca, my beloved wife, with gratitude, with reverence, for who you have been, for who you shall be, with love, passionate, boundless and abiding, for who you are," I know I must try.

I phone Margaret Toulmin, Len's editor at Fordham Press, with whom he had been on excellent terms. Before this letter, that is. She seems pleased to hear from me, sending her condolences and telling me how shocked she was to hear of Leonard's death and how much she'll miss working with him. But when I bring up *Metamorphosis* her voice grows curt. On this subject, she'll offer no consolation.

"You want my honest opinion?" she finally snaps, when I press her about finding someone to edit the book and offer to try my hand at it myself. "I think you ought to just let his reputation stand with *Homo Quaerens, The Dance of Being,* and *Choros.*"

"But it doesn't represent his full oeuvre."

"If this book comes out," she announces with all the drama of a scientist outlining the environmental consequences of nuclear war, "it could seriously damage his reputation." Before I can object, she fires all sorts of questions at me: When did Len finish the book? When did the seizures begin? When was the cancer diagnosed?

"What are you getting at?"

"I wouldn't be surprised if the brain tumor hadn't been, you know, affecting his reasoning when he'd been working on the book. I don't know the facts medically but . . ."

"Margaret, I can't believe you're saying this!" I cry, thankful only that Len isn't alive to hear his own editor attack him. "He finished the book *four* years ago."

"Do me a favor and Leonard a favor and the future of philosophy a favor. Forget *Metamorphosis.*"

I'd like to tell her to go fuck herself. In the interests of Len's posthumous reputation, I politely inform her I'll take the book elsewhere.

Taking a half hour break at mid-morning to ride my bike to the mailbox has become a much-anticipated event in an otherwise unstructured day. I always find something to cheer me—a belated condolence card or a note from the White Institute requesting a snapshot and biography of Len for their newsletter. Today, I receive an item unrelated to Len— a postcard inviting me to a book-signing at a bookstore in

Ridgefield for Mary-Ann Tirone Smith, one of the women in my writing group, whose meetings I haven't attended for two years.

I ought to go, I tell myself, remembering the day—had it been a year and a half ago?—when Mary-Ann called at IWN to announce that Doubleday had bought *The Book of Phoebe*. She was triumphant, especially since her husband, who had been supporting her and their two children on his meager salary as a high school teacher, had been urging her to get a job. For five years she had slaved away from 10 to 3 near the reference desk in the Ridgefield Library, producing first an adventure novel, then a mystery, neither of which she had sold. I didn't think *The Book of Phoebe* was that extraordinary, based on the excerpts Mary-Ann had read in the writing group. But an editor at Doubleday had thought it good enough to advance her five thousand dollars for it. She had reason to be triumphant.

At the book-signing, I feel my usual insecurity around these writer friends, so much further along in their lives and careers. Lilla has had another baby since I saw her, and her nonfiction book about a Welsh village is with a new agent in New York. It was Lilla who called *The Long Birth* "passable as a first novel," but told me to put it away and work on something else. Sarah, a writer of teen romances, praised my novel, but Sarah is generous and praises everything in the group. Sarah sold *Long-Distance Romance* in the interim, and a month ago, under the tutelage of Mary-Ann, she started a work of "serious" fiction. Sally, whom I've never forgiven for tearing *The Long Birth* to shreds over lunch three years ago but who did send a warm condolence note recently, sold a 20-page proposal on a book about memory for twenty thousand dollars. Mary-Ann herself sits at a card table in the center of the store with a stack of books on either side of her, busily signing away.

All are delighted to see me, if awkward about mentioning Len in this festive atmosphere of wine and cheese. They don't seem surprised I've given up my job, but they are concerned about my "writing block." Lilla thinks I shouldn't stay in Redding. She says I should sell my house, put my furniture in storage, and travel for six months. She thinks I don't have enough distance to write about my widowhood. I need time to heal, to fill myself with new sensations and images. If I feel inspired to write—she herself wrote half of a novel in a seaside pension in Nice—fine. If not, I shouldn't worry. Sarah agrees with Lilla that I need distance, both psychologically and physically, but recommends I go to England. Traveling can be stressful, she says, especially given what I've been through. At least I wouldn't have to cope with a foreign language. Sarah offers to give me the names of friends to look up in London and Chipping Camden. Mary-Ann, chattering in snatches as she signs her books, believes writers need time "to lie fallow," though she hastens to add that *she* isn't lying fallow, having just been offered fifty thousand dollars for her next novel.

Depressed and annoyed with myself for being jealous of Mary-Ann, I linger after the party breaks up, gravitating to the travel section. I leaf through guidebooks for Europe—the skinny green Michelin guides for London, the fat, hardbound *Blue Guide* for France. Perhaps my friends are right, I think, coming across *Long Walks in England,* which Len had bought two years ago for a trip we canceled when his cancer was diagnosed. Maybe I'm too embedded in my mourning to write about it. Lilla had quoted a line from Wordsworth about creating poems from "emotion recollected in tranquillity." Perhaps I had too much emotion now and not enough tranquillity. I still could not set foot in the Chinese restaurant where Len and I had always ordered mai tais and the House Special Chicken or the French pastry shop were we'd gone for tea and blueberry tarts. Maybe I needed to put an ocean between me and these landscapes gutted with loss. Maybe, among picturesque, hyphenated towns like Stow-on-the-Wold or Henley-on-Thames, hearing those cheery English voices saying, "Right you are," or pressing my 50p into conductors' hands on double-decker buses in London, I'd forget the typewritten death certificate in its waxy envelope. Forget it so I could find it again, not as a widow but as a writer reflecting upon widowhood.

On Sunday, May 18, lounging in bed with the *Times* spread around me like a fallen tent, I spot a tiny advertisement, not much bigger than an airmail stamp, in the Travel section: *Opportunity of a Lifetime: Combine Travel with learning this summer! Study Shakespeare at Oxford! Live in Christ Church College!* At the bottom of the ad is a line drawing of a skyline of spires and the motto of Oxford University: "Dominus Illuminatio Mea."

Had Len ever been to Oxford? He had talked about our renting a cottage for the summer in the Cotswolds, so he must have seen Oxford. Yes. Now it's coming back. Len had studied at Oxford long ago when he was not much younger than I. He'd gone alone, without Vivian, and had stayed four months. He'd gotten a reader's card for the Bodleian Library and had opened a charge account at Blackwell's Bookshop. The weather had been terrible. He hadn't known a soul and had been lonely. But hadn't he said those four months had been some of the happiest of his life?

Next morning, I dial the 800 number and reach a pleasant secretary with an English accent who talks with me for an hour. As she rambles on cheerily about how the program, sponsored by Florida State University's Department of Continuing Education, offers everything from "Alice in Wonderland" to "Castles and Cottages," I think, Oxford will be perfect. I'll get away from Redding, as everyone is urging, but to a place resonant with memories of Len. I'll be in England, where, as Sarah sensibly points out, I won't have to struggle with a foreign language. I won't have to scavenge for hotels and restaurants every night, because I'll be rooted in one place, staying in a dormitory of Christ Church College and taking my meals in Hall. I'll be busy, attending three-hour seminars every morning in my tutor's sitting room. On weekends, I'll take the scheduled tours to

171

Bath and London. The cost is not prohibitive—one thousand nine hundred dollars for four weeks, excluding air fare. Maybe I'll even write.

When the form arrives, in a midnight-blue brochure with my name and address beneath a white scape of Oxford spires, I fill it out immediately. I fill out everything save for two items: my reason for applying and the name, address, and phone number of the person to be contacted in an emergency. If I told them the truth about why I wanted to study at Oxford—that my husband has been dead for five months and I can't write and my interest in *The Canterbury Tales* is secondary to my need to escape—they would certainly reject me. I end up scribbling something about a passion for the Middle Ages.

But who should be notified if I am struck by a bus in Oxford? Who will be responsible for me now that Len is gone? Flipping through my tiny black leather address book, Len's address book actually, which I retrieved from his wallet and have been using all these months, I turn first to the *P*'s, then to the *C*'s. The Parinis? The Carriers? I find Susan's numbers in New York and Connecticut, Anna and Robert's in New Haven, even Alice's work number in Bethel on the end page, one of the few entries in my own loopy script. All could be counted on if I lay in a coma in an English hospital. But is it fair to burden friends, I ask myself apocalyptically, with such responsibility?

Then I realize the only answer is my own family. I turn to the *R*'s and find, in Len's fine, neat print, the names and addresses of my mother in Florida and Canada, my father in Massachusetts, my sister in New Hampshire. I rule out my mother. I could not guarantee that she would get on a plane and come to my aid in London, especially if it meant having to encounter cold weather or my father. I exclude my sister, because she has her own family to contend with. Which leaves my father, who would fly anywhere in the world on a moment's notice if he were needed, who wants us not to be estranged anymore. And yet, as I type in the address of my grandparents' estate, an address resonant with memories of my childhood, I feel defeated: My husband is gone and I am returned again to the custody of a parent, as if I were 13 rather than 30, as if my brief journey into adulthood had failed.

My routines are temporarily interrupted when my mother stops for a week on her annual migration from Florida to Canada. I never know what to expect with my mother—when she'll come or if she'll come at all. She has a habit of changing her plans. This year is no different. She was due to arrive a month ago, but with one thing and another—fatigue, a head cold, renting her Florida house—she hasn't made it until today. I'm happy to see her, although I know I won't get any work done until she leaves.

On the Monday after she arrives, she pokes her head in my study at 11:30 when she gets up and says, "Had your brekkie, yet, Belchie dog-dog?" I tell her I eat only a muffin when I'm working. She lectures me that this isn't enough to "keep a bird alive." Now that I'm a "woman alone," she says conspiratorily, I've got to take care of myself. Then she says she hopes she's not interrupting anything and settles her large, pink-terryclothed dressing-gowned rear on the sofa, balancing a plate of orange halves on her lap, the first installment of her own "brekkie," which will be followed by Wheatena doused with half-and-half, two hard-boiled eggs, and two pieces of toast, plastered with butter.

"I'm so happy Leonardo left you a little money so you could do a little writing, dearie," she says, rearranging her dish-towel bib and sucking on an orange half. "He always thought you were so talented."

My mother utters "Leonardo" with such genuine affection that I forgive her for barging in on me, forgive her for referring to all my endeavors as "little." I think, *Oh, Mother, dear, fat, orange-sucking Mother, if you talk to me about Len for the next week, if you tell me dozens of anecdotes about him—it doesn't matter how trivial they are or*

173

how many times you repeat them—I will forgive you every-thing: your absence at the funeral, your absence at my wedding, your absence at so much of my childhood.

"The women in our family *were* talented," she contin-ues, as I realize, wearily, that she has no intention of talking about Len but is simply using him as a springboard to dive into the Olympic-sized swimming pool of her favorite topic, the family. "Sweetheart was having shows right up until the day she died, at 95. Mum-Mum wasn't as good a portrait painter as Sweetheart, but Franz Johnston—he was her teacher and one of the Canadian Group of Seven, you know—thought her landscapes were as good as anything he'd done. And you realize one of Newie's lithographs is in the Library of Congress and she's also in *Who's Who in the South*. Not because she's Unc's wife, but on her own ac-count."

"So what happened to you, Mom?" Sarcasm creeps into my voice, but she doesn't notice.

"Well, dearie," she says, pausing to spit out her orange seeds, "I had that poem published in the *Modern Language Journal* while I was at Smith. I wrote it in Spanish, you know. My teacher read it aloud to the class and practically wept he thought it was so good. Then I had Raity and you and I got busy in the community until Ma told me I wasn't spending enough time with my children. I was sick all those years when your father was running around with other women. I did manage to do that still life you have down-stairs. I painted that, let's see, in '74 and '75, so it was around the time of the divorce."

The painting she was referring to hangs above the fire-place in my living room. I was proud of it—its bold, van Gogh–like sunflowers in their dark, rimmed vase against a jet-black background of painted barnboards. My mother liked it, too: She liked the way the flowers were partially cut off at the top, as if they were leaping out of the frame. Although she worried that the black backdrop was morbid, she said no other color would have created such a vivid contrast with the yellow of the sunflowers. She hated most paintings by women—all "watery and airy-fairy and namby-pamby." She liked bright colors, strong, bold shapes, everything solid and sharp-edged.

But it had taken her two years to finish that still life. She hadn't taken up her brushes again. Why? For most of my life, I had asked myself that question. What had my mother done with her talents? Why had she turned her study in the back of our house into a dumping ground for old clothes, into a dog pen for her German shepherd, Sucarno, who "made mistakes" there? Was it because her mother-in-law and husband had "ganged up" on her and destroyed her self-confidence? Was it because my father had been "running around with other women," though he insisted that there had been no one before Jane? In college, I had been convinced that if my mother had been taught to strive for more than a husband and children, she would have succeeded as an artist. But if society were to blame, how could you explain the success of my grandmother, great-aunt, and great-great-grandmother, all of whom had enjoyed even fewer opportunities than my mother? Had Len been right when he said that my mother must have been deprived of nurturing from her own mother and thus had never felt affirmed as a child, never developed the courage and self-confidence necessary to create paintings, let alone weather the failure of her marriage?

"But there's still some life in the old girl yet," she continues, her chubby, girlish face brightening into an innocent smile. "Newie says she'll teach me dynamic symmetry, and I always thought I'd be good at writing a little novel—I'd have to change the names, of course. I know I should drop a few tons. But Leonard told me when I was feeling better, the weight would come off by itself."

"But Mom," I protest, torn between pleasure in hearing her quote Len so sincerely and annoyance at her twisting his advice to serve her own ends, "he wouldn't have approved of your pouring a pint of half-and-half on your cereal. Or thinking you could paint or write without working at it. He would have said you had to discipline yourself. How do you think he got through medical school and graduate school?''

"The poor dear, he probably took ten years off his life getting all those degrees,'' she says, squeezing the last drop of juice from the orange into her spoon. "But you have to feel well, too, dearie. Lots of women wouldn't have survived what I did. You should thank your lucky stars I'm not in the grave with Leonard.''

"Lots of women get divorced, too, Mom,'' I lecture her severely, observing to my surprise that I sound just like my father. "Sure it's hard, but they pull themselves together and go on with their lives. At some point, you've got to let go of the past.''

"Dearie, you don't really understand.''

"Mom, I know you and Dad were making yourselves and everyone else miserable by staying together . . .''

"You don't know all the years your father was running around when I was so sick I couldn't even get out of bed.''

"I remember,'' I say, lowering my voice as I recall those forbidden conversations with my father when we discussed institutionalizing her. "But I also know another person can't make you sick. You choose how you're going to react to something. You choose whether you're going to be miserable—''

"All those years, when I agonized over what I should do: How would I leave my home? Where would I go? What would happen to you and Harriet? Would I have enough to live on? It was a living hell. If I hadn't had Christian Science, I would have been in my grave years ago.''

"But you survived it, Mom. Just like I'm going to survive Len's death.''

"Dear little girl,'' my mother sighs, looking up startled from her dish-towel bib and regarding me with a look of helpless pity, "you've had your own wilderness experience, haven't you? I remember Mum-Mum after Daddy died. It was all she could do to keep from leaping into the grave after him.''

"I've felt that way sometimes.''

"All that kept her going was me and—''

"Mom, I wish every time I tell you something about myself, you wouldn't direct the conversation back to your family.''

"Oh, dearie, I didn't mean any harm. I just thought it would help you to know what someone else's experience was like. For comparison, you know.''

She wipes her wet hands on her bib like a naughty child and regards me fearfully. Her dark eyes dart about the room as if looking for something—a book, a picture, a memento—that will appease me. In my partially opened closet, she finds it—a photo of me in Switzerland frolicking on a wildflower-strewn hillside beneath the Jungfrau.

"Did Leonardo take that?'' she asks, leaping up to rescue the plastic-framed photo that lies on the floor, dusting it off and placing it on my desk.

"You shouldn't keep it in the closet. It's a lovely picture of you. Leonard would be heartbroken to have it stowed away like that. How he adored you. I remember talking to him on the phone after the operation and he said, 'Oh, Maggie, what I hate most is putting Beck through this.' ''

"Did he really say that?''

"Yes, poor thing, he was always more worried about you than himself. He said, 'I'm so glad Beck's got that little job at IWN because it'll take her mind off me.' ''

"I doubt he called it a little job, Mom. And I wish you wouldn't either.''

"Okay, Belchie dearie, no need to raise your voice.''

"The point is, Mom,'' I tell her, realizing I am about to give her the advice she ought to be giving me, "I survived and you did, too. You're sixty years old now and you're probably going to live another twenty or twenty-five years, that is, if you lay off the butter and cream and lose some weight. And you've got to stop obsessing over the past.

You've got to get yourself together to go to a funeral, for God's sakes, and see Dad and not get hysterical over what happened twenty years ago. Don't you think Len would tell you the same thing?''

''He'd tell me to feel well first,'' my mother repeats stubbornly, rising from the sofa with her plate of decimated oranges and announcing that it is nearly 12 o'clock and she'd better get the rest of her ''brekkie'' if we were going to have lunch in Ridgefield by 1.

As she closes the door behind her, I reflect that it may be too late for my mother, too late to give herself the good mothering she never received as a child, too late to reverse the habits of six decades, the thought patterns that had convinced her she was weak, helpless, and dependent, that other people wielded more power over her than she wielded over herself, that she was incapable of giving herself what she really needed—not cream and butter and sugar but their spiritual equivalents, a sense of life's fullness and sweetness.

But I am only 30. For me, there is still time.

Today, on May 26, the day after my mother leaves, I write what might be the first paragraph of my essay.

I am crying as I copy the first sentence from my journal to the yellow-lined legal paper to the green and black screen of my computer terminal. Beneath my tears, there are other sensations, some oddly tranquil. There is the solidity and centuries-deep crustedness of words like *never,* and *know,* and *breath,* and *tears;* there is the order and pattern of grammar to which I must adhere when deciding whether to place a comma here or here; there is the laborer's satisfaction in picking up and working with her tools at last; there is the mystical exultation of closing the distance between Len and me.

For the next seven days, I spend my mornings, afternoons, and even evenings behind the closed door of my study expanding this paragraph into the essay I will submit to a magazine or newspaper for publication.

As I work—hunting for metaphors to capture the invincibility of marriage and the frailty of widowed singleness, looking up words like *hieroglyphic* in the dictionary, copying out the lines of an Emily Dickinson poem I will quote at the end—it sometimes occurs to me that my article may not be accepted. Who, I query myself in these moments of scrutiny when I wish I could summon Len's confidence in me, will be interested in the ravings of a 30-year-old widow? Even though we all die, most people would rather not be reminded of it. I think of the other articles that will be competing with this one, "pieces," as they are called in the trade, on much sunnier topics, like planting tomatoes and naming children. I rehearse the disparaging comments from rejecting editors: "too depressing," "too bleak," or the standard "not right for us." But my words are like cancer cells, dividing and multiplying. They will not be halted. Not even by the radiation of my own self-doubt.

I scribble more notes in my journal, fill my wastebasket with dozens of crumpled balls of paper. The file titled "Len" in the "B" drive of my computer grows. I write of how people say, "Give it time," and how time does bring some relief, permitting me now to notice it is spring, helping me not to despise the luxuriance of grass. Time, too, is responsible for my reading the newspaper again and following the controversy around President Reagan's trip to a cemetery in Germany in which Nazi SS men are buried, an event that proves the dead can rouse the living. And yet time also numbs. Sometimes this numbing is hardest. Sometimes, one welcomes pain because it connects. Tears, I write, are a kind of electrical pulse, carrying the vital charge from the living to the dead and from the dead to the living.

As I work, I grow oblivious of the outer world. My lawyer informs me that Len's ex-wife, Vivian, has hired another lawyer. Am I willing to settle out of court if it comes to that? I am. Len's daughter, Judi, calls to say that she'd like to come up to the house to go through Len's things. My neighbor complains about LA getting into her garbage and reports him to the Redding pet patrol. Alice puts a binder on a house in Litchfield and then backs out. Three real-estate agents write to offer their condolences and a free professional market evaluation of my home. Florida State University enrolls me in "Chaucer and His England" and requests a three-hundred-dollar deposit. Any one of these events would ordinarily throw me, pitch me into worry and brooding and depression. Now, they hardly touch me.

There are certain things I do not write about. I do not reveal my guilt over not being with Len at the moment of his death. I do not talk about the hard moments when he was dying and I wished it would be over. I do not write about assuming the persona of widowhood—how, struggling as I am now to find my place in the world, it defines me, even grounds me. I do not confess how frightened I am of having to let go one day even of this.

I finish the essay on Monday, June 3, at 11 o'clock in the morning. It is a glorious morning. The leaves on the maple trees have grown a full, textured summer green. The blossoms on the dogwood trees are beginning to shed, turning from white to green. The rhododendron bushes on either side of the front door have started to bloom; in another week, there will be a rioting mass of lush, full, pink flowers, flowers coming out everywhere like girls at a debutante ball. The grass is thick, a deep, rain-rich green. Soon, it will have to be mowed. Soon, it will be summer.

But who will read my essay, now that Len is gone?

As I watch the pages—one, two, three, four, five, and six—emerge from the clear glass cover of the Diablo printer, I dial Susan's office in New York. I leave a message on her answering machine, but she won't be able to get back to me until much later. I call the Parinis in Vermont, but hang up when the line starts ringing. They are Len's friends rather than mine, I remind myself. They might resent my calling in the middle of the day. I consider the women in my writing group: Lilla, Sarah, Mary-Ann. But what if they find my essay too raw and intimate? What if they tell me to put it away for a month? I consider reading it to Alice when she comes home, but I remember her copy of Danielle Steele's *Passion's Promise* by her bedside and worry that our taste in literature may differ.

In desperation, I decide to read it to Dr. Heller. I leave a message on her answering machine; she calls back and we make arrangements for a half-hour phone session. Naturally, I'll have to pay her for her time—$32.50—which I resent. But at least I know she'll understand what a feat it was to complete it. I know she won't tell me it's terrible.

That night, sitting on the love seat in my study staring at the photographs of Len on the bookcase and twisting the telephone cord in my hands, I read aloud the stapled together pages of "The Struggle to Say Goodbye." I start to cry when I reach the last paragraph. "It's beautifully written," Dr. Heller says, with much feeling in her voice.

The next day, after making copies at my local library, I send it off into the world in a large manila envelope addressed in my flourishing, felt-penned, calligraphic hand, as if it were bound for the Princess of Wales, rather than Ms. Kathleen Flanagan, Connecticut Editor of *The New York Times*.

A week later, while I am out grocery shopping, Alice takes a phone message for me: "Call K. Flanagan at (212) 556-1234 at *The New York Times*. Anytime until 7 P.M." I am so nervous my fingers feel arthritic as I insert them into the holes of the dialing wheel. She can't be calling to tell me she's accepting it. But then, she surely wouldn't call to tell me she was rejecting it. I seriously consider that she may want to tell me it's garbage and what right do I have to be wasting her time? I remind myself that she is a sensible person in a responsible position and would never do this.

I shudder as the operator puts me through to her, wince as she barks, "Connecticut."

Rebecca Rice

I tell her, in a voice that surprises me with its confidence, my name and explain that I am returning her call.

"We're gonna run your piece." Her voice is throaty, raspy, a caricature of the tough newspaper dame.

"Really?" I wonder if she knows I'm about to drop the phone I'm so excited.

"Yeah," she says. "It's not half bad, considering the junk that piles up on my desk. Whaddya do for a living?"

I mumble something about my profiles for IWN, my fledgling writing career. Then I ask, very shyly, how much I will be paid.

"Seventy-five bucks.

"Look," she says, already bored and eager to get rid of me, "I like what you do. I'll print whatever else you send me. And I'm always on the lookout for new stringers. If you get an itch to do a news story on anything in Connecticut, call me."

I stand cradling the phone with the dial tone bleeping in my ear, still in shock. Alice is rapping at my door, wanting to know what happened.

"They're going to print it."

"That's G-R-E-A-T!" Alice shouts and then bursts through the door and hugs me, LA and Pucci jumping and barking at her heels. LA leaps up on my chest and gives me a slobbery kiss. I pat him distractedly.

"Come on, this deserves a celebration," Alice cries.

"You're right. What do you say to dinner, my treat?"

"All right!"

As I replace the receiver, she says, "Good goin', kid. I have to tell you I wasn't sure you could do it."

182

Bereaved of all, I went abroad—
No less bereaved was I
Upon a New Peninsula—
The Grave preceded me—

—Emily Dickinson

June 1985

In the sixth month of my grieving, I am like a fetus growing longer, heavier, more defined. I am accumulating protective layers of fat cells beneath my skin. Most of my skeleton has hardened, and I already have hard nails forming on my fingers and toes. My eyelids, closed all these months, are opening. My heartbeat is growing louder and my muscles stronger. I am starting to move about. I can punch. I can kick. I can make a fist. I can turn somersaults. If I were born prematurely, I could breathe on my own for 24 hours; I might survive if I were placed in an incubator. But I am still less than half the size of a full-grown human hand. My lungs and digestive system are still too immature to function properly. I need to develop more antibodies. I need to grow heavier, longer, stronger. I am still too fragile to take my place in the world.

For example, I am finding it impossible to make a decision about Oxford. Yes, I have been accepted. I have also sent in the three-hundred-dollar deposit and booked a flight to London. That was before I drove to the supermarket on Sunday morning, June 16, to find my article at the top of the ''Connecticut Opinion'' section of *The New York Times,* beneath Roger Roth's illustration of a woman sweeping up a broken heart. Since the article has appeared, I have received one letter and two phone calls from other widows telling me how moved they were. The women in my writing group have called to congratulate me; even Sally, she who once intimated I should confine my writing to the endorsing of checks, thought it was good. So encouraged have I been that I've already started another article—this one about Alice and how I resent her in the beginning but gradually come to accept and even appreciate her. Alice is working on the illustration that I'll clip to the article when I send it to Kathleen Flanagan, which should be by next week.

Each day, I have been tempted to call the Set Travel Agency in Ridgefield and cancel my Virgin Atlantic flight from Newark to Heathrow, scheduled to leave on June 30. I've considered calling the pleasant secretary at Florida State University to tell her I won't be enrolling in "Chaucer and His England," won't be attending the Oxford program after all. Why would I want to fly to England, or anywhere for that matter, when my life is falling into place here? If I stayed put, I could, in four weeks, complete another two essays. I could work on my outline for a book of essays. I could send Len's manuscript to another publisher.

But everyone, including Dr. Heller, says I'd be foolish to give up Oxford. She points out that I've been under constant stress for the past year, first in coping with Len's illness, then in recovering from his death. A brief vacation can only be therapeutic. Susan says that creating new memories is part of the process of letting go, of permitting the good-byes to become hellos. My father, who has given me fifteen hundred dollars toward the trip, tells me he's proud of my "progress" over these months and hopes I won't back out. Pam Parini believes that reading Chaucer, who is comic and light-hearted, will provide a counterpoint to writing about Len. The women in my writing group predict that Oxford will generate other articles. Alice, who is scandalized by the possibility of my canceling the trip, says, "Come on, Rebecca, you know your husband would want you to go."

True. And Len would be distressed by my forfeiting the $489 plane fare and the $300 deposit. But how is it possible to know what I, independent of Len or anyone else, want? My feelings vacillate from one day to the next. Standing in line at Passport Services in Stamford, waiting among the sandaled, suntanned college kids with *Let's Go Europe!* in their backpacks, I panic. I feel decades older than these kids; I'm afraid of letting my life drift, even for three weeks. Besides, I've never traveled abroad without Len. I'd be safer ensconced in my study writing my essays, building up my uncertain ego rather than subjecting it to the questionable experiment of foreign travel. But the following day, when Lilla is recommending the bell-tower of St. Mary's Church for a panoramic view of Oxford and the Cotswolds, I get excited. *Oh, for heaven's sakes, go,* I urge myself. *It's only for a month, and it will do you good to ferret out new challenges, to fill your head with new images. When you come back, you will be further along in your healing. Your writing can only benefit from such an adventure.*

In the end, I fall back upon Len's method of decision-making: I make two lists in my journal, one titled "In favor of England," the other "Against England." The "in favor ofs," bolstered by quotations from the widows' books—"Every widow I know will go anywhere at the drop of a hat or ticket," says the author of *Beginnings*—narrowly win out, and I decide to go ahead with the trip, hoping I won't regret it.

My preparations for leaving, however, are filled with anxiety. First, there is the ordeal of packing. Given the clothing I'm lugging, you'd think I was going away for a year rather than a month. Summers in England are supposed to be rainy and cold, but I've brought enough boots, sweaters, turtlenecks, and pants to outfit all fifteen members of my Chaucer seminar. I know I'll probably end up grubbing around in my blue jeans and track shoes, but every time I remove anything—the bulky down vest Len and I bought in Switzerland or the floor-length Lantz flannel nightgown I've had since I was a teenager—I envision a dozen situations in which I might need it. I end up stuffing it right back in the same crowded corner of the suitcase.

I worry I am packing the wrong things. Not only am I leaving behind short-sleeved shirts and shorts, but I am bringing only one dressy outfit, a navy-blue-and-black India print skirt and matching long-sleeved blouse, which I'll be wearing on the plane and to a welcoming cocktail party in Christ Church Cathedral Garden. Alice points out there may be other "do's" and wonders why I don't go to Westport and buy myself something "flowery and Englishy and nice." She also notes that almost every item of clothing in my suitcase is dark-colored: black lambswool turtleneck sweater, navy-blue all-wool pants, dark denim skirt. I tell her Georgia O'Keeffe always wore black, that dark colors don't show the dirt and go with everything. I don't tell her I'm more comfortable in these widow's weeds or that I hope to be as inconspicuous as possible.

My two leather-trimmed, soiled-white canvas suitcases bearing the initials *LCF* stitched in gold beneath the handles are filled with mementos. I pack Len's letters to me and his three books, one of which weighs at least five pounds. I take two photographs of him, which I wrap carefully in newspaper and tuck inside the sleeves of a ski sweater. In several pairs of heavy socks, I wrap the marble paperweight pen set with its matching long-stemmed gold pen that he gave me five birthdays ago and upon which is engraved "Rebecca with Love Leonard." I also pack a hand-painted Florentine box that we bought in Fiesole and that he kept on his desk, as well as three polished stones and two shells from Lucy Vincent Beach at Martha's Vineyard, a small stone gargoyle from Notre Dame in Paris, an alabaster tray and liqueur glasses that he brought back from the island of Kos in Greece and from which I sipped amaretto on the night we met.

Mornings at breakfast, Alice and I pore over Len's *World Atlas* and the maps of London, Oxford, and the Cotswolds. We discuss what time my flight will arrive in London, how I will get from Heathrow to Oxford, whether I'll stop in London, how much time I'll have before the course begins. All these logistics elicit every possible fear about traveling abroad: What if I am mugged in London or lose my wallet, like all those foolish people in the American Express ads? What if I become agoraphobic and never venture out of my room? What if I turn around and come home the day after I arrive?

"Don't be such a worrywart," Alice chides. "Besides, you don't know what's going to happen. Maybe you'll meet someone and won't even be traveling alone."

Exactly six months after Len's death, three days before I leave for London, I break my vow never to enter Hillside Cemetery again and ask Susan to meet me there at four o'clock to say good-bye.

The day is cold and rainy, more like the weather awaiting me in England. As I downshift into second gear to mount the steep, winding road into the cemetery, I spot the grave-stone. And yet, even as I locate the small, rounded curve of new Vermont marble off by itself and gleaming white through the shifting fog, the Vermont marble that I ordered two months ago from Bates Brothers Monuments and for which I paid $732.50 including engraving and installation, I pray that the stone isn't his. It belongs to some other dead man, woman, or child locked away beneath the grass in this hill. How can Len, who detested cemeteries and mocked my morbid obsession with them, be here?

Susan is late, as usual. I park my white Tercel, the car that Len always drove to Fordham and that still bears the University sticker in the lower right-hand corner of the windshield, about fifteen feet away from the grave. I step out of the car heavily, carrying the blue delphiniums and white carnations in my arms like a sleeping child. I notice the row of maple trees, now thick-leaved and full-boughed beside the old stone wall in the distance; the clustering moss a deep green beneath the yew and pine trees; the coppery leaves of the Japanese maples shiny with fresh rain. The setting looks much less menacing in summer than in winter, more like a park or the carefully manicured grounds of an estate. In the 19th century, entire families often traveled to cemeteries of a Sunday to picnic and visit their dead. I wonder if there will come a time when I will be at peace enough with my loss to come here and talk to Len, maybe even laugh with him.

That time is not yet. As I creep toward the three-foot-high stone, its top curved like a grandfather clock, as I get close enough to read the three names, LEONARD CHARLES FELDSTEIN, and the lines from Shakespeare beneath them, "But if the while I think on thee, dear friend/ All losses are restored and sorrows end," tears burn like flaming gasoline inside me. I throw my arms around the marble slab and weep into its streaked blue veins of calcium hardness. I weep into the marble, as if it were Len's chest.

Susan comes up behind me, puts her hand upon my shoulder. The ashes of her lover, killed in an automobile crash in Switzerland, are buried twenty yards away. She knows there is nothing she can say now. She must wait with me until the tears run out of my body, until I am still as the graves in this cemetery that have been here for decades.

She takes my bouquet and props it against the stone. One of the petals of the carnations grazes the word "end" in the inscription. I remember what the man at Bates Brothers Monuments told me about Vermont marble, how it is softer and less durable than granite and how, in two or three hundred years, all the letters will be rubbed away, like those teetering dark gravestones in New England cemeteries whose names and dates can no longer be discerned. Long after I am dead and Susan is dead and the other mourners who come to these graves are dead, that word, "end," will blur back into stone.

I follow Susan to a Friendly's on Route 7 across from a Thom McAn shoe store. We sit in our damp clothes drinking hot chocolate and sharing a dish of pistachio-nut ice cream. Susan remarks on how well I'm looking. (I'm not, really; I've gained weight and my face is puffy and I can't get rid of these black, sagging circles under my eyes.) She tells me she's proud of me, publishing my article and taking

190

this trip. She knows Len would be, too. Then she takes a large present, wrapped in cream-colored paper with an enormous red bow, out of her bag, which she explains is a combination birthday and going-away gift. Since my birthday will fall when I am in England, she wants to give me the present now. "Well, come on, open it," she urges. I slice eagerly through the squares of colorless tape along the back, happy Susan hasn't forgotten me. This will be the first birthday in six years I'll celebrate without Len.

The present is an oversized hardcover book on love. Its pages are thick and glossy and illustrated with men and women embracing, kissing, copulating. There are pictures by Chagall, Renoir, Rodin. There are excerpts from D. H. Lawrence novels, poems by Edna St. Vincent Millay and e. e. cummings.

A brief silence. I don't want this book. It's too soon. I don't want to love anyone again. I just want Len back. How can Susan, a therapist and self-proclaimed expert on mourning, be so insensitive?

"I didn't know what to get you," she says, sensing my uneasiness. "I saw this book in New York, at Rizzoli's. I know you can't imagine having love in your life right now, but that will change. It won't be what you had with Len, but it will be good. I can't tell you how or when it'll happen. You just have to trust life."

She hugs me and says she's got to run since she's got a patient at five.

The day before I leave, I decide to buy new luggage. Len's suitcases, though tattered, are perfectly serviceable, but I'm obsessed with carrying my own luggage for this first trip I will be taking alone. Although I had planned to spend the afternoon getting 50 British pounds and color film for my camera, I speed down the Merritt to Bloomingdale's in Stamford and waste precious hours wandering among rows of hanging garment bags, displays of multicolored week-enders and carry-on flight bags.

191

I am paralyzed by the choices. There are collapsible, heavy Cordura nylon bags in blue, brown, and black with white cotton trim by Andiamo, which the saleslady proudly informs me means "let's go" in Italian. There are heavy leather and suede five-piece numbers with brass reinforced trim and pull-out brass wheels by Hartmann, "the top of the line in luggage." There are impact resistant Pullmans by American Tourister in navy and teal; all-cotton, textured tapestry bags by Jordache; tweed-look cheapies by Jaguar; multi-buckled Pierre Cardins in plum and bone.

Exhausted by my indecisiveness, with the store about to close, I grab two of the cheapest Lark-look-a-likes in raspberry nylon, with red leather trim; a flight bag is included in the package sale deal. That night, after I have repacked all my things in the new bags and modeled them before Alice, she says they don't look "me"—they're what a Mary Kay cosmetic rep would take to Miami. And they're flimsy, she points out; they won't last six months, especially if they get banged around on the airport's luggage carousel.

Next morning, with my plane scheduled to depart from Newark at 8:30 P.M., I dump all my clothes in a heap on the kitchen floor, slip the cases into their billowy Bloomingdale's bags, and charge back to the store to exchange them for the more expensive Andiamos. These bags are so durable, with their double zippers and reinforced canvas seams, they'll outlast me, should my plane crash.

Midnight and cruising thirty-two thousand feet above the coast of Maine. Beside me, outside the oval window, a full moon canters through endless hills of night clouds. Soon, we shall begin crossing the Atlantic Ocean. Soon, we shall fly further and further away from the moon and closer and closer to a dusky morning sky and the sun shining so bright against this oval window that I will have to pull my shade against it.

I write to Len. I tell him how I imagine him in the seat beside me studying maps, charting mileages, perking up when the captain announces we're approaching Nova Scotia. I want to take him along on this trip, gaze out the window as he once did, awed before the spectacle of the moon in one corner of the sky and the sun in the other. I write how I am trying to chase away these scenarios of the plane blowing up like the Air India jet that exploded over the Atlantic Ocean killing all 329 people on board. I don't want to die, don't want strangers to find the black vinyl covers of this journal washed up along the beaches of Ireland.

I describe my seatmate, Donald, the retired mailman from New Haven. I narrate the tale of Donald coming to my rescue when I left my purse on the conveyor belt at the security checkpoint in Newark Airport. I was halfway to the Virgin Atlantic check-in counter before I realized I'd lost it, before Donald came panting up behind me carrying it like a wounded animal and saying, "Ma'am, ma'am, is this yours?" Afterward, he followed me to the snack bar, trailed me to the gate, and plopped down in the seat beside me with the excuse that the plane was almost empty anyway and I sure looked like I could use the company.

The things Donald says. Oh, Len, you'd roar if you could hear him. He tells me the story of the rich old woman on his mail route, worth at least 50 million, whose maid brought Donald up to the old lady's bedroom one Christmas where she personally wrote him a check for five hundred dollars. "Used to go to Florida every winter just on those bonuses," he says proudly. I get his opinions on everything from old money to new money—"Them that grew up with it, went to the best schools, they're better"—to the proper attire for women in church, skintight jeans and spiky heels on women over 50 disgracing God and embodying the evil of modern times.

Getting Donald to stop talking requires a major diplomatic intervention, but at last he is slumped beside me snoring into his pillow lozenge, and I am mercifully unmolested with my little bottles of white wine and complimentary packages of honey-roasted peanuts. Maybe I'm drunk, but

I'm almost happy here, six miles above the earth, scratching my missives to Len with my stocking feet tucked beneath me and my journal balanced on my thighs as Len and I ride out of our bodies through the clouds and fly into an English dawn.

But in Oxford, city of "dreaming spires," where he was once so happy, I cannot find Len. Anywhere. I am plunged into a grief so intense it's as if I'm thrown back into the first month of his death again, as if time had never healed me.

I wander into Christ Church Cathedral, into the cloisters of Magdalen College, or into the Botanic Garden, and everywhere, sometimes in the very flagstones beneath my feet, I find graves and tombs and monuments to the dead. I tell myself I should hurry by, should examine the fan-traceried ceilings or the sandstone Reredos or the twelfth-century Norman pillars, but the bones of these dead men will not let me pass. I sit by the Cherwell overlooking Magdalen Bridge and imagine the souls of medieval Jews sighing in the burial ground beneath me. I pause beneath a sunlit dome in a quadrangle of University College and stare at the dead, drowned face of the poet Shelley. Near the choir in Christ Church Cathedral, I stop before the brass plate on the floor announcing the final resting place of Saint Frideswide. In a garden off St. Aldates and along the walls of New College Chapel, I find memorials to the Oxford men killed in World War I and World War II. I study every plaque in the wall, every reclining effigy, every canopied sarcophagus, every bust sculpted after the life or mask cast at the death. I memorize birth dates, death dates, ponder the achievements of priors, bishops, canons, and deans. From every death date I subtract every birth date; I calculate how many years each man had on the earth. Again and again I ask: Did he (or she, although there are few shes) have more or less time than Len?

Mornings, on the way to my Chaucer seminar in Peckwater Quad, I pass through the Cathedral Cloisters, where the paving stones have been ripped up to build a garden and where workmen have discovered two skeletons, which lie exposed in narrow graves. These ghoulish specters are now the province of a team of archaeologists who have placed metric tape across the trenches and fenced off the surrounding area and who scurry about with their trowels and clipboards. My classmates are fascinated by this live archaeological dig and crowd around the off-limits areas, hungry for information. The researchers explain that the skeletons, identifiably female because of their wide hip bones, are thought to be nuns from the priory of Saint Frideswide, flourishing on this site before the founding of Christ Church College. They are both in their early 30s and probably died of the Black Death. (One brazen sophomore from VMI asks whether you can tell if they're virgins.)

These six-hundred-year-old intact skeletons sunk four feet beneath my feet fill me with dread. When I look at their sad, mud-caked eyesockets, I think of Len in his grave, silently shedding the enormous blue eyes that once gazed at me with such love.

Every day I say to myself, "I'm in Oxford! I'm in Oxford!" as if I were reciting a mantra, as if I were Len 30 years ago, but I can evoke only a dutiful listlessness. For me, Oxford is a necropolis. I feign the behavior of student and tourist. I read the prologue to *The Canterbury Tales* in the Bodleian Library. I browse through Blackwell's Bookshop and buy a guide to the Cotswolds. I attend an outdoor production of Shakespeare. I appear for meals in Hall, listen politely as a woman don instructs me about Charles Dodgson, alias Lewis Carroll, a mathematics don at Christ Church whose friendship with Alice Liddell, daughter of a Christ Church dean, inspired *Alice in Wonderland*. My dinner companion directs me to the row of stained-glass windows above the great fireplace where I can find the Dodo Bird, the Queen of Hearts, and all the other creatures of Dodgson's whimsical imagination.

I am unmoved.

All I can think is: Len is history now. He has gone to that crowded charnel house where all the dead of the ages are gathered. He lies in the earth like those nuns with their muddy hips moldering beneath layers of clay and stone. He is with those young men killed in the Ardennes, fallen along the beaches in Normandy. His death is coterminous with Prior Sutton, who died in 1316, and Percy Shelley, who died in 1822. His voice is as inaudible as the voices of John Locke and Charles Dodgson and W. H. Auden. His likeness hangs invisibly among the portraits of all the millions of remembered and unremembered dead.

I keep to myself, though my classmates attempt to draw me out. Most are retired college and high school teachers, and some are quite sweet, sitting down with me in the Junior Common Room and asking where I'm from, inviting me for walks after dinner, alerting me to a Handel concert in Hollywell Music Room. I invent ruses to keep them at bay, always on my way to some destination other than where they're headed. I've never told anyone about Len; it's not the sort of thing I feel comfortable talking about over tea and digestive biscuits in the JCR. One nosy woman from West Orange, New Jersey, a housewife in her late 50s coming to the program with her husband, a retired furniture manufacturer, worms out of me at dinner one night that I have suffered a death in my family. I don't go into detail, but she intuits that I've lost my husband. She proceeds to tell me a long anecdote about her son who died three years ago in an automobile accident and how her daughter-in-law remarried within six months. Everyone in the family criticized the daughter-in-law for remarrying so soon. Everyone but herself, that is. "I told my daughter-in-law what I'm going to tell you: 'You can't spend the rest of your life in sackcloth and ashes.' "

On my fourth day at Oxford, I get lost.

Wandering about the city without my guidebook, I stray far away from Cornmarket and the High and end up down by the railroad station. I realize immediately, from the litter and dingy row houses, that this is a part of Oxford tourists keep away from. Here there are no cozy tea-shops with striped awnings or elegant little wine bars with aquamarine-colored doors. There are only a few fish and chip stands and one or two cheap hotels with letters in their neon signs missing. The streets are empty, save for a few punkish teenagers with shaved heads and filthy jean jackets with skulls and bones on the back.

It is not late, only about 8:30, with another hour of daylight left, but the skinheads slinking about in alleyways make me nervous. I am anxious to get back to the porter's lodge in Tom Tower and Christ Church quadrangle with its little fountain of Mercury tinkling in the dusk and my room three flights up in Meadow, where I can snuggle safely in bed with *The Nun's Priest's Tale*.

I spot a small, slight man coming toward me, in a tweed jacket with a full head of prematurely white hair and a neat, pointed moustache and beard. His face, long-nosed and sharp-featured and melancholy with dark shadows beneath small, sad eyes, bears a slight resemblance to the woodcut of Geoffrey Chaucer on horseback. His appearance, however, hardly registers at that moment; he interests me chiefly because he is no skinhead and will surely know the way back to Christ Church.

I am right. He does know the way. He proceeds to give me precise directions in an accent that sounds more American than English, a detail the tourist in me finds disappointing. Somehow I had hoped he was an Oxonian. Then he tells me he is going that way himself—not true, since he was headed the other way when I accosted him—and will walk me to Tom Tower.

Although I am relieved to be led out of the mean streets of Oxford, I am not accustomed to conversation and feel my shoulders bunch and stiffen beneath my bulky, navy sweater-jacket as we walk. For the first time in months, I am self-conscious about my appearance; I look dowdy as hell in my puffy, ankle-length, denim skirt that could just as well double for a bedspread, my dirty track shoes and crumpled knee-high nylons, my owlish, wire-rimmed glasses that make me look like Leon Trotsky, the wisps of my long hair springing loose from their barrette and dangling about my spindly neck.

We make small talk, trade the usual information about where we're from and what we're doing in Oxford. He is a professor, which doesn't surprise me, and his field is eighteenth-century literature, which also doesn't surprise me given the over-precision of his directions, and he is from some university in the Midwest, Illinois State University or some such far-flung place, and is teaching in that school's summer program at Oriel College.

By the time we get to Cornmarket, I am tempted to tell him I can find my way back. He need go no farther. I don't. And he escorts me dutifully to the great iron-ringed oak doors of Tom Gate.

We pause. Then he says, enunciating his words with that same scholarly precision, "Perhaps you would like to have a beer?"

No. I don't drink beer. I don't go to pubs. It's late. I have reading to do. I think longingly of the photo of Len on my night table, the electric teakettle and box of Balmoral shortbread on the windowsill. No, no, no!

I hear a voice arguing that I can't always be pushing life away; I'll die if I continue to inhabit the narrow sarcophagus my life has become. After some 30 seconds, I hear myself emit a nervous, bird-like, "Why not?"

He asks whether I mind if we stop at his room in Oriel to pick up a sweater. "It's virtually on our way," he points out.

Oh my God, I think, as we hurry out the spiky, gold-leafed, Canterbury gates, *a strange man has picked me up off the street and now he's taking me to his room. What if he tries to rape me, seduce me, even kiss me!* I wrap my sweater tighter around my breasts and hug the high, ivied wall of Oriel College as we walk. He seems oblivious of my anxiety and drones on like a guidebook about Oriel, how it was the college of Cardinal Newman, Matthew Arnold, and Cecil Rhodes and how it got its name from a small, upper-floor bay window protruding from the wall on a stone bracket.

The sight of his room—small, spare, impeccably neat with *Swift: The Man, His Works, and The Age* on his desk, a box of "Black Magic" chocolates on the bureau, and Dorothy Sayers's *Gaudy Night* by his bed—eases my fears somewhat. A man whose darker passions have been sublimated in biographies, chocolates, and mystery novels is not likely to be an ax-murderer. I watch him as he removes a few stray pieces of lint from the gray pullover, as he pulls it, one layered bunch at a time, carefully over his head and down his extended arms, taking care not to muss up his helmet of white hair. He proffers the box of Black Magics in my direction. When I decline, he helps himself to one with his small, nimble hands, taking the paper cup and folding it in half before depositing it in the wastebasket.

He's harmless.

When we settle at an outdoor table at the Turf, tucked away among narrow lanes and overlooking the ancient tower of New College, my drinking companion—I still don't know his name, nor he mine—wipes off our rickety table with a soggy napkin from one of the other tables, apologizing for his "compulsive neatness." I reassure him I never would have noticed had he not mentioned it. By the time our drinks arrive—a pint of foaming bitter for him, a gin and tonic for me—I am remarking on the loveliness of the setting and am barraging him with questions, as if I were interviewing him for an IWN profile.

An interesting life he's had, really: an Irish boyhood in Donegal in a little village by the sea called Rathmullen. (Len would be fascinated by all that.) At 18 he joined a monastery and at 20 was sent to the United States—the monastery was of some kind of missionary order—to Chicago. A few years later, when he had to take his vows of poverty, chastity, and obedience—"I had trouble with the chastity part," he jokes—he left and bummed about for a few years selling encyclopedias and teaching high school. He had no intention of returning to Ireland.

"My uncle wanted to set me up as a chemist in Dublin. That probably drove me into English literature as much as anything else," he observes dryly.

He took his Ph.D. at Northwestern and ended up at Northern Illinois University in De Kalb, where he's been a Hogarth scholar for the past 15 years. He gives me the sketchiest of details about his romantic life: married briefly, now divorced, with one teenage child. I don't ask his age— early 40s, I'd guess.

"But here I've told you my entire life story and I don't know a thing about you," he laughs, ordering another round of drinks.

At first, I stick to the most general data, telling him I'm a free-lance writer and have come to Oxford for a sort of working vacation and that I used to do public relations for a multinational insurance company in Manhattan.

"You don't strike one as the corporate type. I would have pictured you more as an academic."

I thank him for the compliment, although I worry that he's making a backhanded dig at my bedraggled appearance, definitely in the dowdy, female academic mode.

He asks me what I've published. I tell him about my one, lone article in *The New York Times*. He seems impressed, insists I'm too modest, to which I reply, a little sheepishly, that my article was not published nationally but only in a local, suburban edition. Then comes the inevitable next question, which I have almost solicited but nevertheless dread.

"What's the article about?"

By this time, my head is cottony from the gin and tonics and the laughter rising like heavy metal rock from the loud American teenagers at the other tables. Above us, the wind has picked up and is tossing the branches of a few scraggly trees in the courtyard. The moss on the wall of New College is waving ever so slightly before me, merging with the blurry, sad eyes of this stranger leaning across the table.

"It's, ah, about my husband . . . who, um, died of cancer seven months ago."

"Oh, I'm sorry. Maybe you'd rather not talk about it." He touches my elbow lightly across the clean table and then releases it.

"No, no, I think I'd feel better if I could talk about it."

"My mother died a few years ago," he begins. "It's not the same, I suppose, but we were close and I was heartbroken when it happened. Even though she'd been sick for a long time and suffered acutely at the end. . ." I think to myself, *It's not remotely the same; the death of a parent is nothing like the death of a spouse,* but I know he feels awkward and is trying to say the comforting thing.

In that same low, even voice, he asks me what Len died of, how long he was sick, how long we were married, and I begin to narrate the details of the brain cancer, how hard it was to watch a man as gifted as Len literally losing his mind, how difficult it was toward the end, how much harder it is now.

"No one has ever loved me the way he did," I confess to this stranger brooding over his pint of bitter. "I'm lost without him."

"Your face lights up when you speak of him.

"Your life will be very hard," he continues prophetically, "because you won't find anyone like him."

That's what Len used to say himself, I remember sadly, after one of our fights about the age difference: "You'll appreciate me when I'm gone, Beck. Then you'll know what you had." He was right. I sit now across from this melancholy-eyed defrocked Irish monk who keeps mopping up the table and enunciates all his words gravely and who lives in De Kalb, Illinois, of all ridiculous places, and I keep wishing I could blink and this shade would disappear and Len, my luminous, eager-eyed Len, my passionate, exuberant, Jewish Len who pulsed with the wild, gyrating energy of Manhattan, would suddenly fly like Mary Poppins over the moss-tufted wall of New College and plop down beside me.

At 11 the pub closes. We walk back, a little wobbly, along the shadowy, cobbled streets toward Christ Church. Tom Quad is empty and still, lit by a quarter moon scudding through the clouds above the turrets of Tom Tower. Through the closed doors of the cathedral come the muffled sounds of someone practicing Bach on the organ. "Listen," he whispers, and we hurry toward the music and try the doors to get inside. But the doors are locked, and a porter emerges sleepily from the shadows to inform us that the cathedral won't open till eight the next morning. So we content ourselves with standing, hushed and expectant, near the memorials to the men killed in the two world wars. We linger there for five or ten minutes, and the stately, swelling chords spill over us, muting our awkwardness—how will we part? with a handshake? a hug? a kiss?—and gathering us into the music, until we and all the dead, dusty souls haunting Oxford are folded into the chords and there is nothing but Bach playing and playing down the centuries, and Len himself is gathered up in this music, in the thrumming chords along the bass and quick, trilling melody among the high notes and single, sonorous high "C," held and held until the music stops.

As the organist returns to replay a difficult passage along the bass, I find myself thinking that even though I yearn to draw Len out of the music to share this moment, I am lucky to be here now, at Oxford on a damp, moonlit night in early July, with this stranger hugging his thin, gray-sweatered arms to keep warm, this man whom I hadn't known three months ago or even three hours ago and to whom I have entrusted my sorrow. Then, my scholar begins to speak, asking me my name and spelling his for me, "Sean S-h-e-s . . . green, like the color," and asking where he can reach me and do I want to have dinner on Friday? Dinner on Friday? I hear myself piping out flutily, girlishly, a little fearfully, "Yes, well okay," adding that I don't have anything going on Friday, inwardly thinking that this is the understatement of the century, but it will have to be early because I'm leaving the next morning for Bath.

He rests one arm gingerly about my shoulder. He hesitates, looking for some give from my torso, some slight gravitational bend toward him, that will signal he can kiss me. I am suddenly rigid with awkwardness now, and all I can muster is a slight fumbling and brushing against his sweater, which I am close enough now to smell, a woolly, slightly metallic odor of benzine from dry-cleaning. He inches up closer against me, and I descend in a blind, banked bumping toward the flat, narrow channel of his chest. We are embracing now, but it is a tender, tentative, oddly respectful embrace, one that could permit me at any moment to pull away. I don't pull away. It's been such a long time since I've been held.

Then he presses his lips, as lightly as if he were licking his fingers to turn the pages of a book, against my cheeks and whispers, "Strange, strange."

We bid good-bye, and I spin excitedly into the night, my eyes preternaturally bright in the smoky moonlight, my steps light as a ballerina's across the ancient stones.

I can wade Grief—
Whole Pools of it—
I'm used to that—
But the least push of Joy
Breaks up my feet—
And I tip—drunken—

> *—Emily Dickinson*

July 1985

At precisely six o'clock on the evening of Friday, July 5, as "Great Tom" bell strikes the hour, Sean Shesgreen, in cranberry red tie, fresh-slicked hair, and polished shoes, taps softly at the door to my room in Meadow. Still in my bathrobe with my wet hair writhing around my dark, bare skull, I look about as ready for a date as Ophelia preparing to drown herself.

"You're not due for another half hour," I bark, cinching the belt of my bathrobe tighter around my waist and crossing my arms protectively about my chest.

"I was sure, that is, I distinctly remember," he says, his eyes dropping shyly toward his watch, "you had said six." He removes a tiny, red leather calendar from his pocket where, indeed, "6 o'clock" is penned beneath my name and stairwell number.

"Come back at 6:30." I hustle him away, accidentally ramming the door against his shiny shoes.

Sean Shesgreen returns in exactly 30 minutes to find me in my navy-blue-and-black India print skirt and matching long-sleeved blouse with my hair almost dry. In his honor, I have donned white, diamond-patterned, knee-high nylons, sashed my waist with a blue scarf, and adorned my bare throat with the lapus lazuli necklace Len gave me four Christmases ago. I have also exchanged my muddy sneakers for my burgundy-colored heels. Giving myself a final once-over in the mirror above my sink, I'm surprised at how presentable I look, even though I'm still nauseated from the stack of digestive biscuits I wolfed down at afternoon tea and jittery as a teenager at the prospect of going on my first date in seven years. (Will Sean kiss me again? Touch my breasts? Touch other parts of me? What if he sees my filthy underwear?)

Sean Shesgreen takes me to a charming pub called the Trout Inn four miles outside of Oxford. We sit on a terrace at the back of the Thames River overlooking a footbridge across from the lush, tangled overgrowth of wildflowers and gnarled trees on the opposite banks. We take our shoes off and splash our feet in the tingling rapids and watch the shiny, fat fish scatter away from our white toes. We hike about the surrounding grounds, cross the swinging rope footbridge, and follow a winding path that gives onto a grassy plain and the ruins of Godstow Nunnery.

But conversation between us is what Len would call "bad news."

For the entire evening, as I am grilling Sean about his former lovers (I know it's nosy of me, but interviewing is my best defense against anxiety), I am missing Len. I don't tell Sean I'm thinking about Len, how he would have loved the Trout Inn or used our favorite word, "desuetude," to describe the Godstow Nunnery. But it's obvious, from my asking Sean to repeat himself, that I am distracted. The odd part of it is that being with Sean, talking about Ellen and Joan and Pam and Mary, talking and drinking until the dark covers up our faces, all this brings Len more alive than he has been in months. It's as if all three of us are there, sitting in the low wicker chairs on the flagstone terrace before the cool, gurgling river, Len leaning forward, big-eyed and psychiatrist-attentive, as Sean tells about Pam's carrying on an affair with a congressman while urging Sean to make his divorce final and marry her. I can almost see Len nodding sympathetically as Sean speaks, asking Sean why Pam had such power over him, why he couldn't break off with her. I can hear Len telling Sean that some relationships are poisonous and he, Sean, should be grateful he got out.

But sitting beneath hospital-white lights in the Chicago Pizza Joint back in Oxford—we weren't able to get a table at the Trout Inn—I realize this vision of Len is nothing more than a drunken mirage. Len will never sit on the terrace of the Trout Inn, never hear the story of Sean's affair with Pam. I grow quieter and quieter until Sean is asking what's wrong, and I am bursting into tears and telling him how much I miss Len, even after all these months. Poor Sean doesn't know what to do with my tears. He pats my shoulder and says, "You've got a lot to cry about." He asks whether it doesn't get easier with time, and I tell him, still sobbing, that sometimes it's *worse,* because every day there's something else to remind me Len won't come back.

We walk home to Tom Quad in silence. This time there is no fumbled embrace or peck on the cheek, just a limp good-bye and a hurrying away.

Two days later, on a Sunday afternoon, I am lying in bed reading the Wife of Bath's tale. I hear footsteps bounding up the stairs and a soft, tap-tapping on my door. When I don't answer, a white envelope scuds across the floor. Expecting some addendum to the daily circular, the *Mercury,* I am surprised to open the door to the disappearing tee-shirted torso of Sean Shesgreen and the backs of his bare, muscular legs protruding from the briefest of black nylon jogging shorts.

"I was leaving you a note," he says, smiling shyly and rubbing his bare, shapely arms. "I thought you might like to walk along the river to the Isis Tavern some afternoon this week."

"I'd like that," I say, relieved that my behavior at the Chicago Pizza Joint hasn't scared him off. I invite him in and he says he's off to go running. "Like to come?" he asks. "Running?" I repeat incredulously, as if he were proposing that we rob the Ashmolean Museum. He says I ought to get some exercise: " 'Too much study is a weariness of flesh,' " he proclaims with a sly smile.

Fifteen minutes later, in the one pair of Bermuda shorts I brought (which are too tight through the crotch), I am puffing beside Sean Shesgreen down Long Walk in Christ Church Meadow, my heels pounding against the gravel, my buttocks flopping behind me. Now and then he consults his triathlon Timex, explaining we'll do one round at a trot, then step up the pace. I tell him that I'm hopelessly out of shape, but I'll do my best to keep up.

As we run, he explains that he took up running when he turned forty and liked it so much he now runs three or four miles every day and has even entered races back in Illinois. Running, he says, is a wonderful antidote to the tedium of academe as well as therapy for the mild depression he suffers from time to time. I ask him, teasingly, what he has to be depressed about, thinking that I'm the one who's got the corner on that department, and he says just the usual stresses of coping with everyday life—he was depressed after his second book was rejected, and running helped him rework the manuscript until Cornell University Press published it.

"Depression is learned helplessness," he announces, as we turn down the smaller dirt path that meanders along the Cherwell. "Running is a way of taking action. It helps motivate you in other areas. You ought to try it. It would help you through your grief."

I want to tell him that my pain cannot be cured by a few gallops around a track, but then we are rounding up into the Broad Walk, and Merton and Christ Church are rising up from the fields and we're picking up our pace and sweeping past the gated gardens, past the grazing cows, and soon I'm feeling a delicious springiness waving up from the arches of my feet, lightening me.

"I take it Len wasn't athletic?" Sean asks, saying Len's name with such familiarity that I forget my momentary pique at being advised on how to manage my grief.

"Not really. He was your typical Jewish intellectual, hopeless when it came to sports. He regretted that he hadn't learned to ski or play tennis. But sports wasn't a value for him the way it was for me. Learning and studying were more important. When he found out he had brain cancer, he was convinced his body was taking revenge on him for overdeveloping his mind. Who knows, maybe if he'd jogged more he'd still be alive."

"Maybe, maybe not. After all, anyone can get brain cancer—athletes, young people, old people, even kids. It may not be much consolation to you, but he's lucky he lived as long as he did."

"I suppose," I sigh, launching into the story of the young man with the bandaged head in the intensive care unit next to Len. He was 28 years old with the same kind of tumor as Len's. Only it was growing twice as fast. He was always propped up in bed with horn-rimmed glasses trying to focus on the newspaper that his mother would bring every day. The doctors had given him two months.

"You've really been through a lot, haven't you?" Sean says tenderly.

"I guess I have."

"I couldn't have done what you did. Len was a damned lucky man. I trust he knew that?"

"He did."

"Come on, let's sprint the last stretch," Sean says, checking his stopwatch. It's begun to rain and fat, marble-sized drops are pinging against our faces. My legs are aching. I'd prefer to be soaking them in a hot bath. But Sean yells, "Another fifty yards, you can do it!" Then, he's racing ahead of me, rounding up into the Broad Walk, and Merton and Christ Church are rising up again before us and I'm throwing my head into the rain and my muddy Adidas are banging down harder against the gravel path, and I'm sweeping faster, faster, past the grazing cows, past the fence posts shadowed in low-lying mist, and I'm propelling myself with my arms and my breathing is coming so hard it's nearly gagging me. And I'm thinking, with a rush of almost religious gratitude, *At least you're alive! At least you're alive!*

Rebecca Rice

" 'Energy,' " Sean says, as we heave to a stop and he flashes me a sweaty, rain-soaked smile that dissolves the dark shadows around his eyes, " 'is eternal delight.' "

When Sean Shesgreen asks me to have dinner with him that night, I say yes. I find him quite intriguing with his fierce opinions on depression and exercise. He's completely different from Len, no question. His mind is pragmatic rather than speculative. He's got no patience with metaphysics or mysticism. He's rooted in the physical, sensual world in a way Len never was. Unlike Len, Sean is didactic, although he's probably right about my exercising more. But I like him, especially when he quotes Blake and flashes that mocking Irish smile. As I race around my room, hunting for clean underwear (if he sees my underwear tonight, at least it will have had a good dousing in Woolite), throwing on my wrinkled navy-and-black flowered skirt and daubing my lips with coral lip gloss and clattering down the steps to meet him at Meadow Gate, I realize I'm looking forward to my second date with this strange man I met on an Oxford street.

That evening, in the Emperor Wine Bar, we talk about our childhoods. Sean tells me about his alcoholic Irish father who never worked a day in his life and who abandoned his wife and children when Sean was three. Sean remembers visiting his father every week in the pub and how he would often be drunk before noon. Sean says that he has been haunted by his father's wasted life. A rebellious boy and poor student, Sean was warned he would turn out like his father. I tell him about my parents' bitter divorce and my mother's being so depressed she couldn't get out of bed. I confide that I also grew up hearing how much I resembled my mother and that I, too, have been obsessed with her failures. I explain how Len's love helped me believe in myself, but it has still been difficult for me to get started in my own career as a writer.

As we share our confidences, I am conscious of a familiar lightness and ease waving through my body, not unlike what

212

I used to feel when Len and I talked closely. I can trust this man, Sean Shesgreen. Like me, he has suffered. You can read it so clearly in those deep lines singed into his forehead and in his large, brown melancholy eyes ringed with their black circles. And yet, I reflect, leaning closer as we sip our Irish coffees, his face has not been coarsened by suffering. His features—the perfectly proportioned nose, the high cheekbones—are fine and contain that aristocratic, almost feminine delicateness favored by English portrait painters like Sir Joshua Reynolds. Sean's face has this unusual combination of sensitivity and strength, naïveté and wisdom. Len, who enjoyed studying faces, would have liked Sean's face.

The last customers leave, and we are thrown out. The exercise and wine have made me light-headed. As we are bidding good-bye outside Christ Church Cathedral—this time, to our disappointment, there is no organ playing—I ask Sean, in a dreamy, wavering voice, if he would like to walk in Christ Church Meadow.

But Meadow Gate was locked hours ago. We pause in the archway of the gate-lodge, our eyes shrouded in the darkness. He says he ought to be going before Tom Gate closes, too. I murmur yes, but hope he won't leave yet. Do I ask him up to my room? For coffee? A digestive biscuit? Then what? I barely know him. Do I want to sleep with him? To lie beside him in my narrow bed, to feel his hands touching my face, my hair, undoing my blouse? Oh Lord, it's been a lifetime since I've felt these things.

We stand there subdued in the silence, swimming around and around each other like fish, coming centimeter by centimeter closer to one another until our mouths begin to search for, graze, then fasten down upon one another, and my languid, water-logged body is sinking backward, diving down into his, and his shapely arms are wrapping around my back, and his tongue is in my mouth waving in a wide circle against my teeth, and his hands are sliding down my back and he is taking my buttocks in his palms and pulling up my long rayon skirt and sweeping me closer until we are stumbling, like one hydra-headed beast, up against the dank wall and I feel his strong, roiling legs leaning their hardness against me, and I know that I am going to let him stay with me tonight, know that all I want is to be wanted, to kiss and be kissed, to feel my body rise like a wave toward his, to close my eyes and wrap my arms around his neck and feel him moving inside me, to put an end to these long months of sobbing and dying.

I awake to the tiny sapphires in my wedding ring glinting like dead bird's eyes against the dark skin of Sean's back. Shame washes over me like morning sickness. Len has not been dead seven months. Already I have betrayed him. Couldn't I have waited a year like those women in East Africa who, on the first anniversary of their husband's death, gather at the graveside to cut their mourning cords and marry a second husband? I disengage my arm from Sean's back and twist and twist the ring on my finger, remembering how much Len loved our wedding rings and how he never took his off. Toward the end when he could no longer write his name and could barely speak, he would lie in bed turning and turning the ring on his finger, as if those pin-sized stones set in their houses of filigreed gold arches were all that soldered his spirit to brightness and blueness, as if the ring had the power of canceling that final moment when his fingers would no longer be able to touch. Now Len is buried with his ring, and those six blue stones refract his dissolving hands. Now my womb is filled with the semen of this other man, whose taut-muscled, sleeping flesh spreads out over my bed. The stones in my ring have witnessed another loss.

But what good is this guilt, I ask myself, stroking the infant-soft skin of Sean's back and admiring the way the morning light sheds through the half-open red curtains and falls upon his slender, compact runner's body—his shapely calves, his muscular thighs, his dark, curly pubic hairs. What a miracle that Sean is alive and not dead! When Sean wakes and nuzzles his nakedness against me, smiling and murmuring a sleepy good morning and wondering whether I'd like a backrub, I know I must let my guilt go. Catching Len's boyish smile from the color photographs across the room on the desk, I wonder if Len isn't, at this very moment, rejoicing in my good fortune. Wherever he is. Then, I turn over on my stomach and close my eyes while Sean strokes, with his soft scholar's hands, each of my toes.

After Sean and I part, I stroll toward Cornmarket in search of a new pair of jogging shorts. I take the long way round, walking down quiet Magpie Lane, in love with the sound of my heels clicking along the uneven cobbles. Oxford seems no longer a necropolis, but a radiant Byzantium, a magical Xanadu, the city Len saw when he studied here 30 years ago. I listen to the cacophony of church bells ringing out the noon hour. I follow crowds of Japanese tourists taking pictures of one another beside the Roman heads of the Sheldonian Theatre. I watch streams of French, German, and American teenagers toting their bulging backpacks and lining up in front of Barclay's Bank for British pounds. I observe fat-cheeked, elderly English ladies window-shopping at Marks and Spencer's. I wave to the tourists crowding the decks of the open double-decker buses headed for Blenheim Palace.

I feel 20 years old again.

Sean and I are together every day, touring the colleges, picnicking in the Botanic Garden, running along the Isis. We exchange gifts: I give him a box of Black Magic chocolates and he presents me with a bright green Oxford tee-shirt (claiming, as Alice did, that I have too many dark clothes). He comes to lunch with me in Hall, talking animatedly to my classmates on everything from the summertime weather in Ireland to the virtues of living near Chicago. We attend a dramatization of *The Canterbury Tales* in the Oxford Union and join my tutor afterward in her room in Peckwater Quad for port. I bring him to the cocktail party

in the Cathedral Garden, where we taste the English con-
coction "Pims" and meet a tutor from St. Hilda's College
who praises Sean's book on Hogarth.

At the Bodleian Library, he shows me the engravings of
eighteenth-century street vendors that he is writing about.
His face becomes radiant and childlike as he bends over the
Morocco-leather volume, pointing out the lovely features of
the match vendor and the strawberry seller, carefully turning the old, water-marked French paper to "Colly Molly
Puffe," the tiny, hunchbacked pastry seller; "Madam Cres-
well," the hag-faced whore-turned-madam; and, poorest of
them of all, the nameless, crippled iron-monger dragging
his steel boot behind him. In loud, excited whispers, Sean
explains how these wretched people often slept three to a
bed, how they contracted diseases and were jailed for va-
grancy or debt, and yet maintained their dignity, which you
could see in the pin-seller's patched skirts and the rope
dancer's proud carriage. So much does Sean forget himself
in fleshing out these characters whose cries once filled London's streets that we're ejected from the reading room because he's making such a racket.

As he blushes and apologizes like a schoolboy to the fierce
librarian, I think, *He really isn't so different from Len, after
all. He cares for these downtrodden vagabonds in the same
way Len cared for ideas.*

Sean and I spend hours in tea-rooms and pubs talking.
We talk seamlessly, effortlessly, the way Len and I did. I
find myself remembering anecdotes about Len, not just
about his illness but when he was well. I tell Sean how
irreverent Len could be. I remember when we went to an
art opening in SoHo where a woman friend, the wife of a
wealthy Pepsi-Cola executive, was exhibiting her paintings.
The opening was very soigné—lots of pretentious people
swaggering about in expensive clothes and trying to sound
hip. Len was his usual ill-at-ease self, hovering around the
food, stuffing himself with cheese and crackers until he got

tipsy from the wine, which he normally didn't touch. Walking back to the car, he met two homeless men, introduced himself, and told them about the opening. It was free, he said; they could eat some passable brie and crackers and stare at some art. Len led them up the street toward the gallery, telling them they had as much right to be there as these rich Wall Street types, in fact more right, because begging was more honorable than stealing. There was a scene as the Pepsi-Cola executive blocked their entrance, upon which Len called him a "soda jerk," before I dragged Len home.

Sean loves this story and tells tales of his own rebelliousness—the time he was arrested at the MLA convention for putting up a poster that said, "The Tigers Of Wrath Are More Powerful Than The Horses Of Instruction"—incendiary words in 1968. The hotel police called the cops. Sean and two colleagues were dragged away in a paddy wagon, booked for destruction of private property, and thrown in the Tombs. The other prisoners thought Sean and his colleagues, dressed in suits and ties, were undercover cops. "I thought we'd be raped and killed," Sean laughs. Released on bail five hours later, Sean missed four job interviews. Later, FBI agents came to Northwestern University, where he was a graduate student, to interview the chairman and two of Sean's professors about the incident.

"You and Len would have gotten on famously," I laugh.

I haven't done much writing at Oxford. Between my adventures with Sean Shesgreen and my Chaucer assignments, I haven't had time. Remembering what the women in my writing group said about lying fallow, I try not to berate myself for my silence. But when I begin my 10-page paper on the vision of death in *The Canterbury Tales,* I decide to approach the project as if it were one of my essays, hoping I can rewrite it or incorporate certain passages into a subsequent essay when I return to Connecticut.

Once I begin, I become absorbed by the paper, staying

up late at night in my room in Meadow, filling up three by five notecards with quotes from the Knight's and Pardoner's tales. I like reflecting upon another culture, so far removed from my own, whose attitudes toward death are so unlike mine. In Chaucer's time, when most people did not live past 40, death was a far more common event than it is today: Men died in battle, women in childbirth, to say nothing of the hordes who were carried off by the Black Death, which first raged through England and Europe in 1348, when Chaucer would have been about eight years old. Unlike twentieth-century America, where death is secreted in hospitals and rarely mentioned in polite company, death was everywhere in medieval England. In Chaucer's day, carts loaded with corpses headed for burial in the churchyard were as numerous as carts traveling to market.

Chaucer's characters are forced to accept death. In the Knight's tale, King Aegeus talks about the "transitory" nature of this world, where fortunes change, from "woe to joy and back to woe again." He explains that just as every man who ever died must first have lived, so every man who lives is destined to die. Aegeus' son Theseus argues that death is as natural and inevitable as the falling of oak trees or the wearing away of stones on a highway or the drying up of rivers. All people must come to an end as well—young and old, king and page, in bed or at sea. Those who grumble over the inevitable are rebels and fools. Prolonged mourning is pointless, offering consolation neither to the soul of the dead nor to the living. In the end, the survivor must "leave woe and be merry" and thank God for his grace.

Will I be able to accept Len's passing with such philosophic detachment? I wonder, as I finish typing my paper at midnight in the office behind the Junior Common Room. Then it comes to me, walking drowsily with aching fingers through a dark Christ Church courtyard to meet Sean, who is sleeping in my bed back in Meadow: part of me already has.

A Time to Mourn

* * *

Today, at lunch, I fall into conversation with the inquisitive housewife from New Jersey, she who had instructed me, two weeks ago, to "give up the sackcloth and ashes." She tells me, *sotto voce,* that she was sitting behind me last night in the Oxford Union with my "handsome friend from Oriel" and almost didn't recognize me. She can't get over the change in me since our talk at the beginning of the course. I've "blossomed." I look "absolutely radiant." I'm no longer "hiding my sexuality." (The nerve of her!) She's not the only one who has noticed, either; she mentions two or three elderly ladies, who've been charting my transformation as well. My gossipy friend reminds me of what she told her daughter-in-law: "Never feel guilty for happiness."

Do I feel guilty about Sean? In the beginning, yes. Now? No. I feel only this intense joy in being alive again. I *have* changed in these past weeks. Not just physically—the cerise bloom on my cheeks, the earrings and necklace I wear every day, and a new jauntiness in my walk and even the loss of a few pounds because I'm too excited to finish meals. But emotionally, too. My anger seems used up now. I feel like a person who, having been bedridden for weeks, is up again and able to move about. Every sensation is unutterably precious: the way Sean says the Irish-sounding "airly" for "early" when we are reading poetry by the Isis; the rain-washed, early evening light falling across Peckwater Quad; steam rising from wet umbrellas in a crowded tea-room; Sean's handsome, aristocratic profile against a cloud-brimming Constable sky; his strong, bare thighs scratched here and there with brambles as we rest, after running, in the long grass by the Cherwell.

I meet Sean's Irish sister, Anne, today. She has come down from Castlebar in the west of Ireland, and the three of us spend the day together. Sean, with Anne on one arm and me on the other, gives us a tour of Oxford, then buys us drinks at the cellar pub in University College, followed by dinner at the Old Parsonage Hotel on the Banbury Road.

Anne is small, dark and fine-boned like her brother. Even at 40, she is still a beauty. At first, she is aloof. She lets Sean do most of the talking, while she narrows those dark Celtic eyes upon me and holds that pert, shapely nose of hers ever so slightly aloft. Sean warned me that she can be quite the snob when she is of a mind, and I suppose she is deciding whether I am good enough for her brother. Apparently, I pass the test. As the evening wears on, she becomes more and more voluble, entertaining Sean and me with gossipy stories about her neighbors in Castlebar, the woman who goes off to a hotel in Dublin once a month to carry on a discreet affair with a businessman from Manchester. It may be her thick Irish accent, which makes everything she says come out like a poem by Billy Butler Yeats—"Ah, Becky, when Eye was a slip of a garl, Eye could turn a fein mahn's head, I could"—but I'm enchanted by her. I have to stop myself from saying Len would have been enchanted, too.

The three of us get on "like a house on fire," as Anne would say. Anne compliments me by telling Sean that I remind her, with my long hair, of "Mammy when she was young." But I am flabbergasted when she says, after having imbibed too many "wee jars," that when Sean and I get married, we'll have to go to the Ring of Kerry on our honeymoon.

But what of my affair with Sean Shesgreen? Will it end in marriage as Anne has so drunkenly predicted? Or will it last only as long as these bucolic Oxford days, dying a natural death when I surrender the key to my room in Meadow and we fly back to our real lives, I to my desk in Connecticut, Sean to his university in Illinois?

Sean has asked me to come to Ireland with him for a week before returning to America. At first I say yes, and Sean and I make plans. He draws maps of Ireland on napkins in restaurants, and we talk about visiting Rathmullen and the house he grew up in on the shores of Lough Swilly. We discuss renting a car and driving into the Yeats country, then south to Dublin to see his other sister, Mona, who lives in Howth, 20 minutes north of the city. I have never been to Ireland, and I am excited, asking Sean if his Irish accent will come back and feeling dazzled with my good fortune, first meeting Sean on an Oxford Street, then being swept off to his native land, as if I'm the real-life heroine in one of Sarah's romantic novels.

An hour later, I am full of ambivalence at the prospect of this trip. I've known Sean for exactly 19 days. Len has not been dead a year. I'm not ready for such a whirlwind romance that may lead who knows where. Besides, Sean is 14 years older than I am. After Len, I always thought I would find a man my own age, who wouldn't leave me a widow again. Do I want someone who will parent me, see to it that I get enough exercise and wear colorful clothes? Sean's life is, like Len's, shaped and finished—he has a teenage daughter, a burgeoning career—whereas mine is still gestating. At 30, I am a beginner in everything—in finding my voice as a writer, in handling my money, in discovering reasons to live. I should suffer through my struggles. Alone. Without help from him or any man.

The next day, I am heartbroken at the prospect of not going to Ireland and am calling Virgin Atlantic for the third time in 24 hours. I remind myself of how happy Sean and I have been over these weeks. Why should I deprive myself of more time with him? He's not that much older. Fourteen years is not 32 years. Sean is in far better physical condition than I am. Did I not say to him, "Compared to Len, you're a virtual child," when we talked about the age difference? Maybe I wouldn't want a man my own age. How would he relate to my widowhood? Sometimes Sean seems barely mature enough to understand it. Maybe I need a man to take care of me, especially now when I am vulnerable. And what's so virtuous about more suffering?

Poor Sean. What is he to make of my feelings for him, which fluctuate like English summer weather, where rain and sun war with one another, sometimes from quarter hour to quarter hour? How is he to react to my changing my mind for the third time about Ireland, declaring that I cannot take more time away from my writing? What is he to think about this sad, mad widow he picked up on the streets of Oxford?

The weekend before the course ends, Sean and I rent a car and drive to the Cotswolds to a small hotel in the hamlet of Upper Slaughter. The Lords of the Manor is a refurbished stone parsonage set on the edge of the village, overlooking a small meadow where horses and cows graze. In the far distance, there are vistas of sloping fields, dotted with hedgerows. Len would have loved the Lords of the Manor— its friezes on the ceilings and huge stone fireplaces festooned with coats of arms; the chintz-covered sofas and matching drapes in the drawing room; each of the cheery guest rooms outfitted with an electric kettle and teacups on a tray-table by the bed.

I am happy in the Cotswolds. We take walks through the tiny villages of Upper and Lower Slaughter, passing the squat Norman churches and the honey-colored limestone cottages with their auburn chimneys. We follow the footpaths through the fields and lean against the grassy ditches bordering the roads. Before dinner, we take sherry in the drawing room, chatting with some of the other guests, including a booming American couple from Texas who inform us, as we slip in from the terrace through the French doors, that we must be "artists." The man, who is connected with a bogus-sounding university in Texas, *knows;* he can "see it in our eyes." We titter, amused and flattered. And even though I'm sad when I remember that people used to say the same things to Len and me—that is, after they'd gotten over the shock of our age difference—still, I'm secretly pleased. I like being with Sean. I like being part of a couple again.

Dinner is an elegant affair, with appetizers, two different wines, a grapefruit sorbet between courses, and a delicious boeuf à la something with a green peppercorn and mustard sauce. Sean's epicurism charms me. When he raises his wineglass to say, "Here's to the Slaughters," I laugh heartily.

After dinner, we walk along the narrow dark road toward the village of Lower Swell. The air is heavy with the smell of cow manure, and the silence is ancient, unplowed by passing car or highway thrumming in the distance. On either side of us, the dark fields bank and crest above us like waves. In the sky, a three-quarter moon grazes among the clouds. Sean links his arm through mine and begins to warble, very softly, "In Dublin fair city, where the girls are so pretty. . . ." As he sings, cocking and swaying his head, his flat, middle-western twang giving way to the melodious Irish lilt of his past, especially when he gets to "singing cockles and mussels, ah-liefve, ah-liefve-oh," I begin to warble along with him. When he gets to the part about Molly Malone's dying from fever, I think that Len must somewhere, somehow, be with me now, in the mist rising up from the fields or the inky, billowing trees or the moon scudding through the clouds. If I didn't believe this, could I really go on singing and singing?

That night, Sean is impotent.

We are lying in the big oak double bed with the floral comforter bunched at our toes, and I am on my knees bending over his uncircumcised penis, caressing it, stroking it, rubbing its shaft loosely between my thumb and forefinger. But still it lies there, huddled inside its burrow of skin like a frightened mouse. I renew my caressing with a determined vigor, thinking that maybe I'm doing the wrong thing—in all the six years Len and I were together, there were only two or three occasions (one after the craniotomy) when he couldn't get an erection. Sean jokes that his "member is misbehaving" and blames "the drink." He says we'll have to try again in the morning.

"Maybe you're afraid of me," I say. "You think I'll reject you."

"Possibly," he admits. Then he asks me to stop.

We lie quietly in each other's arms, and he finally says he hasn't really recovered from his break with Ellen, the woman he was to have married three months ago.

"You're not the only one who is grieving," he says, his voice breaking, as if he were about to cry.

I stroke the soft, dark skin of his back and ask him what went wrong. Why didn't it work?

"I thought I was in love with her," he begins. "We picked out wedding rings, even looked at houses. She said she wanted to spend the rest of her life with me. We talked of getting old together. But after we announced our engagement at Christmas. . . ."

Christmas, I think reflexively, was when Len died.

" . . . her depressions got worse. She would weep for hours over the phone. She was seeing an analyst four times a week, but it didn't help. I listened to her problems endlessly. I went to the library and read everything I could about clinical depression. I suggested she try running. But she couldn't let go of her unhappiness. We began to fight constantly. One night she announced she was going out with someone else.

"That was the last time I saw her."

The bed creaks beneath us as Sean twists away from me. Then, as if they are coming from far away, the hallway or the next room, I hear a few breathless sniffles, what I recognize so well as the beginning of tears. Sean crying? Not possible. I tug at his shoulder and roll him toward me and see that his eyes are bloodshot. His cheeks are raw with tears. He really is crying, and I am full of disbelief, because I imagined that he was too tough to break down. And then, maybe because tears are contagious and there are still so many left within me, I throw my arms around his quivering shoulders and caress his thick hair and cry, too.

* * *

The night before we are to leave Oxford—Sean to fly to Dublin, I back to America—I realize that my period is a week late. At first, I think it must be the transatlantic travel altering the rhythms of my menstrual cycle. So certain am I of this possibility that I consider not even mentioning it to Sean. But as I begin to reconstruct a timetable of the days we had sex, I realize that first time we slept together fell on the fourteenth day of my cycle. If I had been *trying* to get pregnant, I could not have picked a more fertile time.

"Were you?" Sean accuses me, as we sit over our farewell dinner at the Cherwell Boathouse.

"Was I what?"

"Trying to get pregnant."

"Of course not. The last thing I expected was that I would meet someone, much less sleep with him."

"Why didn't you say anything? You must not have been altogether unmindful of the day."

Altogether unmindful, I think mockingly. Why can't he get rid of that insufferable pedantry?

"I wanted you too much to say anything," I finally admit.

The waiter refills our glasses with water.

"What are we going to do?" Sean says, more gently and taking my hand.

"I'll have to get an abortion, I suppose."

"That would be hard for you after all you've been through. I wouldn't want you to go through it alone."

An abortion. Another death. Another loss. The canceling of a real embryo, not a metaphorical one, that would have spent nine months in my body, that would have sprouted legs and arms and lungs and a brain. An actual baby whose heartbeat I might have heard, whose kicks I might have felt against my belly. A boy or girl whose progress through infancy and childhood I might have watched, a daughter or son, who would have been like me and yet possessed her own mysterious dance of being. A child who would have helped me bury my grief for Len, a child who would, in all likelihood, bury me.

But this baby isn't Len's baby, I remind myself. Nor does it belong entirely to me. Half of its chromosomes, which will determine its scx, height, blood type, and temperament, belong to this white-haired, sad-eyed Irishman seated across from me who looks so despondent, who seems to have aged 10 years in 10 minutes. Only last week I imagined marrying him and moving to De Kalb and even having a child, but I didn't expect any of these fantasies to come true. At least not immediately. Woe to those who get what they ask for! I'm touched that he's giving me the phone number of his sister Mona and telling me when I can reach him and pleading with me to come to Ireland, especially if I am pregnant. He is kind, generous, and sensitive; he'd probably be a good husband and father. I know he would be a good father, because he raised his teenage daughter, Deirdre, by himself. But do I know his other virtues well enough to spend the rest of my life with him?

I could have the child myself. Plenty of unmarried women do these days. But am I prepared to be a single parent? To bear the child alone, to raise it alone, to be responsible for clothing it, feeding it, taking it to the doctor, and sending it to college? Children are supposed to cost somewhere between $100,000 and $150,000 to raise to adulthood. I can barely support myself. How would I have enough for a child? And what about my fledgling writing career? When would I have time to write a book, or even a five-page essay, with a baby crying and demanding to be nursed and no one to help me look after it? Besides, I'm a widow. My belly would begin to swell even before the first anniversary of Len's death. What about the other metaphorical fetus inside me, this self that is in the middle of its last trimester and waiting to spring forth from the tomb of Len's death, from the womb of my widowhood?

"Fifty pence for your thoughts, woman," Sean says, introducing a more jovial note into our silence.

"Oh, I don't know. I'm thinking that it's life that's hard, not death. Death just happens, and whether you're the one who is dying or the survivor, you have no choice but to accept it. But here we are now, two living people having to make an impossible choice, whose consequences will affect us, you, me, the child, forever. It's terrifying. It almost makes you envy the dead because they don't have choices anymore. They can't make mistakes."

"Now look, no point in getting morbid. Let's approach it one step at a time," Sean says sensibly. "First of all, we don't know if you are pregnant, right?"

"Right."

"Until we do, we can't know what our options are."

I nod, taking a hefty swig of water—if I am pregnant, I shouldn't be drinking wine—relieved for my overwrought imagination to be quieted by Sean's practicality.

"Too bad we can't get hold of one of those home tests. But the pharmacies must be closed. You're catching the eight o'clock bus to Heathrow tomorrow, so that means we've no choice but to wait until you get back to America. If I tried you on Thursday from Ireland at 11 at night, it would be 5 in Connecticut. Do you think you'd know by then?"

"I-I think so," I whisper, stuttering at the prospect of this answer, "positive" or "negative" that will alter my life.

The next morning, we rise early and Sean helps me carry my luggage to the bus stop on the High Street. He presents me with a shopping bag of assorted going away presents: a copy of his last book on Hogarth, two packages of Balmoral shortbread, and a box of Cadbury's chocolates. I'm touched by his thoughtfulness and tell him I could get used to being taken such good care of. He says he's concerned about me and wishes there were more he could do. I promise to call if I get my period before I take the pregnancy test.

When the bus arrives, Sean gives my bags to the driver. "I guess this is it," he announces, and we throw our arms around each other. We hold one another for a long time

227

until the bus driver revs his engine and I am the last passenger who hasn't gotten on. "Better hurry or you'll have no choice but to come to Ireland," Sean jokes. We kiss one final time, and I mount the steps, turning back to wave and feeling a slight queasiness, as if I'm about to cry. Then the bus pulls out down the deserted High Street, past Queens College, leaving behind the small, waving figure of Sean Shesgreen with his fine, sensitive face. And I am filled with sadness and confusion because I will miss him, and because I never thought it would be possible to miss anyone but Len.

*As imperceptibly as Grief
The Summer lapsed away—
Too imperceptible at last
To seem like Perfidy—*

—Emily Dickinson

The Final Months

I enter the last trimester of the first year of Len's death. I look back on my former self in those first months of grieving—the embryo of my widowhood raging within me, my psyche sick and bewildered by the changes thrust upon it— and I cannot believe I have evolved so far so fast. How could I have known on those bleak February days when my only goal was to get through the winter that in six months I would be flying back to America from England writing a drunken letter to Sean Shesgreen? ("When I close my eyes, I see us among foggy quadrangles, towering stained glass windows, tables in low-ceilinged, stone-walled pubs and moons through clouds over Christ Church Cathedral. . . .") How could I have known, when I was nauseated with longing for Len and hating the world because it would not give him back, that my bitterness could not last forever, that it too was subject to time and decay? How could I have known that on a drowsy August morning with its promises of temperatures in the 90s and memories of driving Len to New York for a CAT scan, a nurse would be stabbing a needle into my arm to take blood for a pregnancy test?

The test results, I learn from the nurse who phones back on Thursday, August 1, at 4:15—the hour of Len's death, but it is a measure of how far I have come in my grieving that I don't immediately make the connection—are negative. I am relieved. So relieved that my very ears seem to exhale with the release of tension. I bike to Topstone Pond for a

quick swim before Sean calls at five. Plunging into the tepid
water—it's been in the 90s for weeks now, and the upper
layer is warm as bathwater—I swim out as far as I can to
the ropes of plastic buoys beyond the wooden rafts. Floating
on my back and feeling the afternoon sun flush against my
face, I think back to that night in Meadow and consider
what I've needed to deny during this episode of my pregnancy scare: In my inability to say no to sex with Sean, I
wanted unconsciously to be pregnant, to bear the child Len
and I never had. And yet I never took such chances with
Len, I remind myself. I used my diaphragm scrupulously,
and we never even had a pregnancy scare. Is it possible, I
wonder, paddling into shore and remembering how Len
would always stand beside that large rock holding my towel
open for me, that Len and I weren't meant to have a child?
Not only because of his age but because I wasn't ready to
be a mother? Is it possible that in these eight months since
Len's death I've been learning to mother myself and that
one day I'll be ready to have a real child, perhaps with
Sean?

Sean, calling me punctually as he had promised from his
Uncle Manus's in Rathmullen, Ireland, is surprised to learn
that the test was negative, for he says he was "already reconciled" to my being pregnant and had decided he would
urge me not to make any decisions until he could come to
New York. He had even convinced himself it might be good
for Deirdre, his daughter, to have a brother or sister. His
voice, despite the echoes, static, and delays as it bounces
off satellites and whistles through the receiver, is warm and
resonant, oddly reassuring. We both feel happy and relieved
and talk for a long time. Sean says he misses me and wishes
he'd been able to convince me to join him, because he knows
I would have loved Ireland, loved meeting his uncle, a retired solicitor who is close to 80 and full of stories. He puts
his sister Mona on to say hello. She has a thick Irish brogue
like Anne and sounds tipsy. She invites me to "come to
Dublin, with or without this bad brother of mine." Sean

gets back on. I worry about the cost of the phone call, and he says, a little drunk himself, "It's only money." Before we hang up, I am asking him whether he might stop in New York anyway, on his way back to Chicago, because I would like to see him again. This pregnancy scare, I explain, has made me feel close to him, maybe even a little in love with him.

"In love with me?" he asks, his words sailing back to me in giddy astonishment.

"Yes, I mean, I think so," I stumble. "I know I've been giving you pretty confusing signals, but I've been thinking about you a lot since I've been back, and, well, I want to be with you."

Alice listens to the saga of Sean over our breakfasts together. At first, I am reluctant to talk about him. I fear she may be unsympathetic and conclude I couldn't have loved Len if I am so swiftly replacing him. I underestimate her. She tells me she's never seen me looking so well and wants to hear all the details of Sean's and my legendary meeting on an Oxford street. "It's almost as if your husband was kind of leading you there," she observes dreamily. She also informs me, before I take the pregnancy test, that if I want to have the child she'll help me take care of it! I'm afraid I burst out laughing at her offer, given so earnestly; somehow a ménage of young widow, spinsterish tenant, three dogs, and a baby strikes me as too ridiculous even for a TV sit-com. When she finds out I'm not pregnant, she is disappointed but says she's not giving up on me.

On the seventh of August, so hot that my rubber-soled sandals adhere to the steamy blacktop of the parking lot at Kennedy Airport, I am waiting at the TWA International Terminal for Aer Lingus Flight #324 from Shannon. As the hordes of flush-faced passengers thump through the swinging doors, wheeling their luggage carts and searching out expectant faces, I panic: What if I don't recognize Sean Shesgreen? I peer into every male face as it parades up the incline, ruling out this one or that one because the complexion is too florid, the cheeks too plump, the hair too dark. If I were waiting for Len, ah, if I were waiting for Len, I would spot him before he even came through the doors—big-eyed, grinning, and disheveled with his mismatched socks and shirttails coming out, he would be waving and blowing kisses and causing such a commotion that all eyes would be upon us. But Len is late, I reflect ironically. Len is later than this flight from Shannon. He is days late, months late. I could wait for him for the rest of my life, and he would not come.

In the last heat of straggling passengers, I spot a slight frowning man with a full head of peppery white hair, impeccable, if a bit harried, in white dress shirt, pressed gray trousers, and lugging a Cadbury's Chocolates shopping bag. I hoist one uncertain arm in the air. When he sees it, sees me, he begins to smile. The shadows fly away from his eyes, and he hurries toward me. We are embracing. As he is thrusting his tongue in my mouth, I am wondering whether I really am in love with him. I don't know, can't know. But it doesn't matter. Because this moment of feeling his hands undoing the buttons of my shirtdress and his fingers pulling up my skirt against my warm thighs as we kiss again and again in the car is all.

Susan and Anna approve. Alice does, too. The day after he arrives, we have a small dinner party, my first since Len's death. Alice makes calligraphy place-cards, and Sean cooks a feast of asparagus vinaigrette, spinach lasagna, and puréed turnips and carrots with ginger. I get out my best Wedgwood china and the hyacinth-blue tablecloth, last used at the funeral. We are seven, including Anna's husband, Robert, and the baby, Clare. We crowd about the table, our faces ruddy with wine and candlelight. Sean is gentlemanly and charming, and the talk sails effortlessly from Oxford to cookery to the dearth of psychiatrists in Ireland—''When an Irishman has a problem, he goes to the pub,'' Sean remarks dryly.

In the kitchen, Susan whispers, ''He's lovely and so handsome!'' Anna gushes, ''He's a poet! Just the sort of man I hoped you'd find!'' Alice says I should hurry up and have that baby.

There is one awkward moment. Sean is pouring his Robert Mondavi Chardonnay, and everyone is making toasts and I am remembering the last dinner party at this table, three weeks before Len died. Anna and Robert were there with the baby, who was just a month old, as well as a priest from Fordham, a kindly, soft-spoken man in his 70s. Len slumped in his wheelchair at the end of the table, too weak to talk, barely able to swallow a few forkfuls of the pumpkin stew that Gail made. He smiled as we talked of winter and Christmas, his enormous eyes glassy and unblinking above his beard, long and thick as an Old Testament patriarch's. After dinner, the priest said mass and talked about Len's being at the end of his life and the baby's being at the beginning of hers. We passed around the communion chalice, and I helped Len take a sip and Anna helped Clare. Anna and I cried. But Len continued to smile.

''To Len, who is with us tonight,'' I am suddenly blurting out, as Sean is praising the wine's exquisite nose, ''whose love has made me everything I am.'' There is silence. Susan glares at me. Sean, gripping his wineglass in mid-air, looks startled. Only Anna and Robert murmur, nod, and take the requisite sip.

''Bringing Len up like that is hurtful to Sean. How can the two of you build a relationship if Len is between you?'' Susan chastises me later, admitting that she may be overly sensitive because of her problems with her widower boyfriend, Paul, he who continues to wear his dead wife's ring around his neck, even after two years. If I'm serious about Sean, Susan says, it's not fair to him to continue wearing my wedding ring. I should put it in some special place where I can take it out and be with it when I need to be. Alone.

I call Sean ''Len'' today.

Sean and I have spent all morning in bed, not even getting

up for breakfast, which Alice brings up for us on a tray and leaves outside the door. We sit naked on the bed buttering our toast. The late summer sun comes through the skylight warming our warm bodies, lazy and easy after sex. We are talking about how relieved we are that I'm not pregnant because we can take our time and see what happens. And I am saying, "Maybe I'll swallow my pride and come to De Kalb," and he is saying, "Oh, you must, and I want you to meet Deirdre and Steve. But in the meantime, what about that tour of the house you promised me?" I remind him of our promise to take Alice to lunch, but add that we should have time for everything, even for a walk in the North Salem fields (where Len and I loved to walk, but I keep that to myself) and dinner in Westport. And I am thinking, despite a passing melancholy as I remember my wedding ring sunk in its velvet box, *This is what it was like in the beginning with Len, when everything was new and the simplest acts were full of adventure, and life gave and gave. . . .*

The phone rings. I run downstairs to answer it, since the phone in my study has migrated to Alice's room. It's Susan wanting to arrange Sunday brunch before I take Sean to the airport. I bellow up the stairs, "Le-e-n, is 12:30 okay?" I immediately realize my error and feel my stomach bolt. And not because I have offended Sean, who wastes no time in telling me he wishes I'd get his name straight, but because I have violated my memory of Len, who is, was, not in the least like Sean. I aggravate the situation by telling Sean he should be complimented I would call him Len.

"I don't compare you to Ellen, do I?" he snaps.

Driving to the airport, I apologize to Sean, explaining that the last thing I want is to use my grief as a weapon to wound him. Such acting out serves no one—not Len, not Sean, not me. I tell Sean that I hope it will be possible for me to let my feelings for him and my memories of Len, which are, after all, two separate things and need not be confused, live side by side. I don't want to be one of those widows who make their lives a shrine to the memory of their dead husband. I tell Sean about Susan's problems with her widower boyfriend, Paul: I don't want to put anyone through that. I won't be able to stop loving Len, but that doesn't mean I can't let those feelings settle into a safe, private place where they don't threaten Sean. I ask Sean to be patient. It hasn't been a year yet. It will take time. Sean says he wasn't hurt by my calling him Len—anyone could make that kind of slip—but when I said he should be complimented to be called Len, that stung. It's as if I can't accept him for who he really is. Not true, I insist.

When I accidentally pull into the "Long Term" instead of the "Short Term" parking lot at Newark Airport, Sean jokes that maybe *this* mistake bodes well for our relationship, maybe we're headed for "the long haul."

"The possibility is not without its appeal," I laugh.

"No double negative," he teases.

"Right. How's this? I'd like to have a long-term relationship with you."

"I'd like to have a long-term relationship with you, too."

The day after Sean flies back to Chicago, I find in my mailbox a suspiciously familiar large envelope with no return address, a patchwork of crookedly affixed stamps, and my name and box number scribbled in my all-too-recognizable loopy, girlish script. My heart sinks, for I have received these dreaded S.A.S.E.'s, these suicide letter-bombs before. I don't even have to open it to know it contains the copy of the article I sent to *The New York Times* before I left for Oxford. But what infuriates me is that Kathleen Flanagan, who had promised to print whatever I wrote, doesn't even tell me why she's rejecting it. I receive a form letter addressed to "Dear Contributor," bemoaning the hundreds of submissions she receives and wishing me "good luck in placing it elsewhere."

I am not crushed. This is what writing is about, I tell myself, to be accepted one month and rejected the next. I can't take it personally and must get it in the mail again.

I'm surprised and pleased to be lecturing myself so wisely and sensibly, administering the sort of advice Len might have given me. As I print out cover letters to Karen Larsen, at *Redbook,* and Janet Chan, at *Glamour,* I realize this rejection could even be a blessing. These magazines pay far more than the *Times,* and maybe I'll make some money.

I assume Ms. Flanagan rejected the second piece because she didn't want another article on widowhood. For this next essay perhaps I should write about something else. But I can't abandon my list of ideas to be collected into some future book about mourning. There is the essay I'd like to write about inheriting money, the guilt and responsibility I feel knowing that my freedom has been bought by Len's death. There is the idea I had about death and memory, how in order to go on one must forget and yet how one must also remember, because not to remember is to kill the dead a second time. I want to write something about changing attitudes toward death in history, where I incorporate the ideas in my Chaucer paper. These essays are waiting in my head and heart, sleeping chunks of brainstone to be quarried and sculpted into shape. But I need to be published again, to build my career as a writer. I cannot afford to lose this editor, even if she is rude and unpredictable, even if she rejects my next article.

What to write? Some journalistic piece about an event or person in Connecticut, as she had suggested? A story on the woman who sells muffins in the train station? The new rape crisis center in South Norwalk? But these topics feel so remote. I need to pick something I care about, something that "keeps you up at night," as Eliza, a new member in my writing group, put it. If not Len, then what? I flip through my journal to the letter I had scribbled to Sean on the plane coming back from Oxford. I read: *I can't get over the thought that I may be carrying a human child, my child, your child, inside me. . . ."*

That's it, the pregnancy scare. *But what about my readers?* I think guiltily, remembering the five or six letters I have received from other widows telling me how moved they were by "The Struggle to Say Goodbye." They'll think I'm a fraud. One month I'm writing about how I can't throw away Len's old tax returns because they are like precious artifacts from a lost civilization, the next about getting knocked up. But to write honestly is to take risks, as Len himself said many times, even the risk that people will reject you.

I check out books on pregnancy from my local library. (How strange that only four months ago I was carrying out books on death.) At seven weeks, when most abortions are performed, the fetus already has a human face with eyes, ears, nose, lips, and tongue; it possesses a brain and the never-to-be-duplicated palm prints that form a tiny "M" on its hand. Len was once such a fetus. I was once such a fetus. Sean, too. What if we had been vacuumed out of our mother's wombs? But this kind of argument could be read as a manifesto for the "right to lifers." I must avoid polemic, stay close to my feelings, close to the terror of having the child and not having the child, the grave responsibility of permitting an unwanted child to be born, and the pain of being haunted for the rest of my life by this tiny ghost that could not become flesh.

The loneliness of the writing life! All morning and all afternoon in the house, like an invalid, like a shut-in. I often go the whole day seeing no one except Alice, the garbageman, and the dogs. I don't mind it when I am sitting up alert before the companionable green cursor on my computer, my fingers working away at the clicking black keys, my mind lost in the fireworks of words blazing or being swallowed by the starry dark night of the screen. But when nothing's coming, when I can't find that drugged forgetting and I remember that the random rustle on the stair is not Len bringing me more coffee, not Len wanting to read this page he's working on, not Len leaving me a note, written in mock Jamesian style proposing, should I so desire it, that we enter into amorous and perhaps copulative relations at three o'clock . . . then, the loneliness is unbearable and I feel I'll go mad.

In these morgue hours, I wonder what I am doing in this house, where every square foot echoes with the steps that will never fall here again. My life has vanished, and my remaining is as foolish as the English lingering in India after the demise of the British raj, as dangerous as the White Russians clinging to their dachas after the Bolshevik Revolution. Len has fled. I should, too. Lest I be hunted down by those vigilante mobs—the most vicious are those holed up in my own psyche—who know too well I am obsolete, a relic from the ancien régime who should have been eliminated.

I ought to get out, sell the house, move. I hurl myself into action, as if I were forced to leave the country in 24 hours. I phone my neighbor, a real estate agent, and arrange for the house to be appraised. I drive into New York and spend the afternoon looking at co-ops, appalled at the closets you can "steal" for $150,000. With maintenance costs and the expense of living in Manhattan, there's no way I could get by on fourteen hundred dollars a month. I phone another agent in Westchester. I look at three two-bedroom condos in my price range, one boasting a view of the Hudson. But the prospect of living alone with Hector among all those sleepy suburban streets with their closed-curtained windows and deserted sidewalks depresses me.

Meanwhile, the value of my house has skyrocketed. According to my neighbor, who has already made me an offer, it's worth $189,900—$60,000 more than what Len and I paid for it. Alice, who has been looking at houses for months, says, "Get a second opinion. It's got to be worth more." I call Century 21, who sold us the house four years ago. The market is hot, hot, hot, they cry, even now in September when buyers begin to fall off. They recommend I list the house at $229,900. I tell them about my neighbor's offer of $189,900. "You'd be giving it away," they scoff.

Who would have predicted that this rather ordinary ten-year-old, eight-room Cape Cod house of sixteen-hundred square feet, with its small kitchen, unfinished basement and one-car garage would have appreciated by almost one hundred thousand dollars! Len would be flabbergasted. He always suspected that this "petit bijou," as he called it, would go "up, up, up." But he'd be outraged if he knew that our neighbor, whose kids took communion at his funeral, was trying to screw me out of forty thousand dollars! I ought to tell her she can take her offer and stuff it!

"Do it, Rebecca," Alice eggs me on. "Don't be a wimp!"

Into this mania of buying and selling comes Sean on the telephone at nine every other evening. How I've come to depend on those long-ringed hummings rousing me from my lists and calculations and Alice singing upstairs, "R-E-B-E-C-C-A? It's S-E-A-N," and me yelling down to her "I've G-O-T it," and shutting the door and curling up on the couch with the phone in my lap and giving myself up, like a teenager, to an orgy of talk. The hours we log on the phone! Last night, a marathon of two and a half hours with me narrating the tale of my neighbor's machinations and Sean observing that it's a great story and I ought to write about it. Oh, writing, I complain. I finished the article on pregnancy—

"Which you promised to send me."

"Right. I'll put it in the mail tomorrow. But now I'm finding it impossible to get started on anything. I want to move, but I haven't the foggiest idea where. Susan thinks I should take an apartment in New York, but New York will break me financially. I'd have to get a job."

"Look, maybe this is a crazy idea, but why don't you think about coming to De Kalb? We'll fix up a garret for you somewhere, or get you an office in the university. De Kalb isn't exactly the most stimulating place on earth. But it's cheap and there's nothing else to do but write. You won't waste your time dodging roaches and muggers in Manhattan. And you won't be lonely because you'll have me in bed with you at night.''

"That," I purr happily, "would be nice. But what about Alice? The house? My connection, such as it is, with the *Times?"*

"Alice will relish having the house to herself. And why tell anyone you're in Illinois? As long as you own the Redding place, I would think you could still write for the Connecticut section."

"This isn't the first time I've thought about this, you know. Back in Oxford, I fantasized moving out to live with you, but it seemed bizarre then. I worried that I'd be giving up some last phase of my mourning, dropping myself in your lap and expecting you to finish healing me. I worried about getting involved with an older man again."

"You talk like I'm in my dotage. I'm forty-four years old!"

"I just worried I'd fall into the same pattern with you as I did with Len—letting you take care of me, getting too dependent."

"I'm not Len! And where is it written you have to be miserable? Or lose your independence?"

"You're right," I concede. "There's no intrinsic reason why I should slip into the old patterns. Although, in Illinois, I won't have Dr. Heller to keep me on the straight and narrow."

"You could see someone here," Sean says, pointing out, as he has before, that De Kalb is as far from Chicago as Redding is from New York.

"Okay, so let's say I move to De Kalb," I continue, liking the idea more and more but feeling duty-bound to raise all possible objections, "and it doesn't work between us. Let's say you hate the way I cook or wash dishes or clean the toilet. You've been leading the life of the happy, fussy bachelor for a long time."

"Fussy, yes. Happy, no. Look, the worst thing that can

happen is that in two months I'll help you move back to Connecticut.''

''What I like about you is your utter lack of sentimentality.''

As we talk, my eyes meet a broken wood-framed color photo of Len and one of his former girl friends that I found recently in some old boxes in the cellar. It was taken ten years before we met. Len has his arm around this young woman with her immense bust and teased blond mane, and he's grinning sheepishly and squeezing her within an inch or two of her breast, and she is laughing, coquettish and sexy as Marilyn Monroe. It didn't last. She left him for a sex therapist who made piles of money and bought her a house with a tennis court in Westchester. But for the brief millisecond it took to snap this picture Len was ecstatic. Then I think: *Len was not afraid to take risks. I shouldn't be either.*

One rainy morning in mid-September before I leave for Illinois, I decide to give away Len's clothes. I'm not sure what possesses me, after all these months, to call the Salvation Army and get directions to the nearest drop-off center in South Norwalk, to drive down to the liquor store at Ancona's and load the car up with boxes. But once my mind is intent upon the task, I act with a ruthless efficiency.

I get rid of everything—shoes, coats, ties, socks. Even Len's Harris tweed jacket that he wore all through our trip to Europe together and that the Parinis had wanted him to be buried in is folded among the short-sleeved polo shirts and tangled ropes of colored ties. If I let myself, I could crawl into the musty dark of these clothes and press my face against their sweatless, masculine dankness and weep. Every sleeve I touch washes me with memories. Here is the bone-colored gabardine suit that Len wore to our wedding. I loved this suit on him because it brought out the blue in his eyes. Here are the green-striped Adidas I bought him when he complained that he didn't own a pair of sneakers. Here is

243

the sapphire-blue Irish knit sweater, identical to my cardigan model, which he wore so much the elbows had to be patched. How can I give this away? This sweater *is* Len— Len tying it around his waist as he walked along the beach, Len pushing up its sleeves as he paid bills at his desk, Len spilling droppings of oatmeal on it in the last months of life. Then I notice that the ribbing around the collar is frayed, chewed away by mice. I crush it down against the other sweaters and close down the flaps of the Johnny Walker box, relieved for the excuse not to keep it.

As I load the boxes in the car, heaving them into the trunk and squeezing them together on the backseat, I remember those words of Yeats we had read at our wedding about an old man being nothing but "a tattered coat upon a stick, unless soul clap its hands and sing." Without Len's soul, these clothes are just tattered things, nothing more.

In the blistering rain, I make the 40-minute drive to South Norwalk, getting lost twice in the city's slums before I find the squat, bunker-like structure of the Salvation Army. It's closed. I drive to the back and park in front of the immense fatigue-green dumpsters. They are jammed with debris. I empty out my boxes and stuff the dry-cleaned suits and folded sports shirts helter-skelter between broken chairs and ripped books.

I drive away, leaving the empty boxes dark and limp in the rain.

It is a relief to say good-bye to Connecticut, to pack up my computer, books, files, and the bound volumes of Len's manuscript, to load the U-Haul roof carrier and every square inch of my Toyota, allowing a patch of free space in the back for visibility and just enough in the front for Sean, whom I'll pick up tomorrow at Newark Airport, and for Hector, who will have to squat between Sean's legs. Of course, this is only the first stage of my leave-taking. I haven't put the house on the market, sold my furniture, or donated any of Len's five thousand books to the Mark Twain

Library. I'm going to Illinois for a trial three months. If the relationship fails, I can still come back to Len's reproduction of Adam touching the hand of God above the stereo and the bag of wedding cards in the third, creaky drawer of the filing cabinet.

Alice will stay on in the house, and I'll phone her once a week to make sure the pipes haven't burst or the septic tank hasn't backed up. I feel irresponsible to be skipping out, but Alice assures me that she and the dogs will take good care of the place. In some ways, the house has already shifted ownership to her in these last months. When I was in Oxford, she hung two of her paintings in the dining room, moved the sofa away from the window, and started stacking old newspapers beside the fireplace. She bought an expensive rocker for her room and stuck my old armchair with its paisley throw in the hallway. In the kitchen, she stored her tea and cookies in "my" cupboard to the left of the stove rather than in "her" cupboard to the right of the stove. Although at first I was disturbed by the Alicification of 99 Chestnut Woods Road, now I welcome it, since I can leave without regret.

My friendships with Susan and Anna are strong enough to survive the move; we will call, we will write, and Susan has said she'll try to get to Chicago next month for a family therapy conference. The women in my writing group are hoping I'll return for periodic visits. My relationship with Linda and Jean-Guy in Canada will not be affected; it's as easy to fly to Ottawa from Chicago as it is from New York. I will stay in contact with the Parinis in Vermont, although they phone less often these days. As for Len's colleagues, students, and former patients, most have stopped making vague promises about "connecting" with me in New York. I don't resent them for it. They are older than I, some by a whole generation. Their attachment was to Len, not to me. Now that he is gone and I am presumably "over" my grief, there is nothing to sustain the connection.

My family is supportive of my new relationship with Sean,

particularly when I promise to bring him to Pittsfield for Thanksgiving. My father, who never thought I'd meet anyone in Oxford, wonders whether Sean is "a tweedy fellow" and says I'll have to send copies of Sean's books to put up beside Len's. About my move to Illinois he is less enthusiastic: "What in God's name are you going to do in De Kalb," he barks, "contemplate your navel in a cornfield?" It is a tribute to my improved relationship with him that I laugh instead of rage at this remark. My sister, who fears I may have found a younger version of Len, an absentminded professor type who will disappear into the bathroom with a book at family gatherings, is worried I will leap into marriage. "She's not going to marry him, is she?" Harriet anxiously queries my mother over the telephone. My mother, on the other hand, is overjoyed I have met Sean. She talks about how it's all right for her, a woman in her 60s, to be without a man, but it's not good for me. "You shouldn't be alone by the fireplace in your childbearing years, dearie," she says.

I won't call Len's children to tell them I am leaving, although I will leave Sean's phone number with Alice, should they need to reach me. There's no point in mentioning Sean. They wouldn't understand and would probably say something hurtful, such as I couldn't have loved their father very much. Neither of them answered the letters I wrote them in February. Perhaps they are angry about the money or have gotten swept up in the bitterness of their mother's lawsuit against the estate. Now that their father is gone, maybe they would prefer that I too faded out of their lives. The last time I heard from Mark was on Father's Day when he called to ask for directions to the cemetery. I asked him if he wanted me to meet him at the grave, and he said no, he wanted to be alone. I last spoke with Judi four months ago when she came up to the house to go through Len's things. She took a few paintings that had hung in her childhood home in New York and a half dozen cartons of books, including *The Collected Works of Sigmund Freud*, since she said she was considering becoming a therapist. She wanted the *Encyclopaedia Britannica,* but I told her I needed it for my writing. It was petty of me not to give her the volumes; after all, I could have bought myself another set.

In my new will, which I signed in my lawyer's office last week, I left each of them about thirty thousand dollars or what they would have received had Len's pension and life insurance monies been split more equitably. I suppose it was my way of atoning for having inherited so much money and in having been a less-than-ideal stepmother.

How I love to ride on long trips in the car, to sit with my foot resting like a sleeping cat on the accelerator and a Styrofoam cup of coffee with a hole ripped through its plastic lid in my free hand, to watch the houses and fences and fields whir by, pick out the big green-and-white signs welcoming me to each new state, my heart stirred by the promise that here in Pennsylvania I have a "friend," here in Indiana I can "wander" like some happy, barefoot child. Speeding along the highway, suspended between one exit and another, coasting down steep mountainous grades or riding along the plains into a purple sky, I can almost believe that Len is not dead but has simply gone, like me, upon another adventure.

The main street of De Kalb, Illinois, with its drab two-story brick storefronts, abandoned warehouses, and rusty traintracks coming from nowhere and going into nowhere, is so ugly it might have been cut out of a painting by Edward Hopper. And yet, three weeks into my experiment in this mid-western ghost town of "Barb City," former barbed-wire capital of the world, I feel an unaccountable freedom, perhaps because every experience, even of drabness and vacuity, is new and framed in a vivid, even gaudy aestheticism. There are no memories here. In the vast sky, all around me from one end of the horizon to the other like an immense billboard advertising the existence of God, I cannot find Len's dead face.

But the living Len, the spirit over my shoulder, the voice talking in my head, Cowardly Lion and Tin Man to my Dorothy on her way to Oz, is with me. At the Junction, a local eatery where you can get a breakfast special called "The Trail Blazer," I can almost hear him sputtering with laughter at the 21 different kinds of barbed wire—the S-barb and the split-diamond barb and the saw-tooth barb—displayed by the cash register beneath a yellowing advertisement for "Dr. Cox's Barbed Wire Liniment—Money Refunded If Wounds Do Not Heal Without Blemish."

When I tour the Ellwood House, a Victorian mansion all done up in brick with white pillars and wraparound porches in the center of town, I hear Len whispering that this barbed-wire bloke must have been a first-class crook to have amassed so much cash. When I walk along the Kishwaukee Kiwanis trail, which runs along the tiny Kishwaukee River near the university, my bemused comment to Sean—"The Loire it's not!"—is exactly what Len would have said. The first time I spot the eight bleached white, ten-storied flat-roofed dorms stuck up against the sky one after the other like extraterrestrial warriors in some inter-galactic space parade, my moan of disbelief is Len's. But when I drive out with Sean past K Mart and Wal-Mart and Farm & Fleet to the ocean of cornfields and bean fields and winter wheat fields, my soul is uplifted, as Len's would have been. Here, amidst all this infinity of country, one's gaze broken only by grain elevators and lone prairie farmhouses that huddle, like hoboes, against the big thundering or heat-blazing skies, I hear Len saying that it gives you a primeval feeling, as if you were back in the ice age, the glaciers warming and thawing until giving way to the first life forms.

Thirteen thirty-one North Thirteenth Street, 50 feet from the Jewel supermarket and Lehan's Drugs, is modest, oh so modest, as Len would say, and quite a comedown from the comparative splendor of 99 Chestnut Woods Road, with its two acres. When Sean and I first drive down Thirteenth Street with its jerry-built bungalows and postage-stamp lawns, I gasp with all the horror of a Connecticut suburbanite riding through Harlem. When we pull into the double driveway that Sean shares with the neighboring house, an itty-bitty, 50s-style ranch with aluminum siding, and Sean pipes happily, "We're home," I hear Len saying, "No way."

I am relieved when Sean parks the car closer to the rambling 1890s farmhouse, with its spacious front porch on the other side of the driveway. Inside, the house is surprisingly homey: original oak floors and moldings, leaded glass windows, Oriental rugs from Beijing, and on the walls eighteenth-century engravings. The furniture is garage-sale eclectic, some of it elegant, like the walnut sideboard in the dining room, some of it tacky, like the brown-and-white checked couch in the living room. The house exudes a scholarly bohemianism, wherein each object, whether it's an elephant-folio volume of Hogarth engravings or black marble bookends depicting *The Thinker* by Rodin, has been lovingly placed. Even in the bathroom, a marble sculpture of a reclining nude perches on the porcelain sink.

"If there is any cultural life in De Kalb, it's at 1331," says Steve Kern, Sean's friend who teaches in the history department and stays over two nights a week in the spare bedroom. Steve, a brilliant, fast-talking Jew who has lived in New York and Boston and who is always mooning for "the East," is saying this partly to keep me in De Kalb, since he imagines that the superior charms of Connecticut will lure me back at any moment. In fact, Sean's house, a mecca for some of the more intriguing types who've found themselves thrown down in "Barb City," could just as easily be on 13th Street in Greenwich Village as in De Kalb, Illinois. There is Patricia Bonnet, a Belgian graduate student from Brussels who lives in the attic and who is carrying on an epistolary affair with an American who is teaching in Nicaragua. Whenever she gets an airmail letter from this man, we all gather around the kitchen table to read it aloud, both for its evocations of life in Managua and to help Patricia, who is in the middle of divorcing her Flemish husband of 10 years, decide whether her lover's intentions are honorable. There is Sean's friend Sam Kinser, a Renaissance historian who specializes in the history of carnival and who lives in Oak Park but maintains a commuting marriage with a Frenchwoman who lives in Paris. There is Deirdre Shesgreen, Sean's lovely, shy daughter who is in her last year at De Kalb High and who detassels corn in the summer and works as a checker at the Jewel after school and who hangs out, on a Friday night, with her giggly teenaged friends, listening to the Violent Femmes.

"Age quod agis, do what you do," Sean says to me, somewhat severely when he is eager to get to work and I would just as soon have another cup of the dark French Roast coffee that he grinds each morning and that I take with a half cup of steamed milk. I'm not suggesting we fritter the whole morning away, only that we prolong, for five or ten minutes more, this moment of closeness in the kitchen talking about Steve or Patricia or Sam's wife, Helene, beneath the wall above the stove papered with wine labels and a poster of Angela Davis, bearing the words, "She Fights to Win and So Do We."

But Sean is adamant about getting to his desk, even on mornings when he doesn't teach. I ask him, somewhat flirtatiously, how he could prefer *Occupational Costume in England from the 11th Century to 1914* to gazing at my face across the breakfast table. "You'll turn into a paper clip," I joke, resisting the urge to tell him Len would always put his work aside if I wanted him to. As we are hurrying along the concrete walkway past the grove of crab apple trees toward the skinny, brick skyscraper of Zulauf Hall, I implore him at least to stop at my office on the seventh floor before going to his on the tenth.

We say good-bye in the elevator. Although I am petulant,

my mood grows more sanguine when I turn my key in the door of Room #712, which belongs to one of Sean's friends who is on leave and which I'll have all to myself for the next three months. As I switch on the overhead lights, flick on my computer, and slip my floppies into the disc drives, I realize I'm lucky Sean takes my writing seriously and won't be tempted to waste half the day schmoozing. Because I must write, must work. Otherwise, what am I? A lost widow in a backwater town with too much time and money on her hands.

I spend eight and nine hours a day in that office on the seventh floor of Zulauf, its rectangular window overlooking the Field House parking lot, big as two football fields, which ends in a mall of shops, housing Kampus Korner and The White Hen Pantry. In the distance I see the Star Wars dorms and beyond scraps of houses and trees lost, like tiny rowboats, in the curry-colored sea of October fields. A peculiar place to find myself thrown down in, I often think, hearing the thump, thumping of NIUers barreling down the halls, or meeting some scowling professor in the women's room who stares at me suspiciously as I dry my hands on the retractable towel. Such a setting might give some people writer's block. For me, just the opposite. In one month, I've written a travel article on Oxford, an essay on inheriting money, and now I'm beginning a longer piece titled ''Widowhood at 30,'' commissioned by *Glamour* magazine.

Although I've already signed the contract, I'm wary about doing this article and wonder whether I can write in the *Glamour* mode, especially about something so unglamorous as death. The editor, Janet Chan, wants me to focus on such issues as sex and dating again, and she advised me to study past issues of the magazine to get an idea of their style. As I leaf through a stack of 1983 issues in the NIU library, I cannot imagine my words among articles like ''5 Wrong Reasons to Choose a Man,'' ''Body Confidence: How to Get It, How to Use It,'' and ads for ''Cover Girl'' lipstick. But I'd be a fool to renege on the contract. After all, how

many beginning writers have editors chasing them all over
the country to sign them up for one article? If *Glamour* buys
it, I'll make two thousand dollars. Even if they reject it, I'll
receive a "kill fee" (appalling term, under the circum-
stances, but Janet Chan uttered it without irony) of four
hundred dollars.

My main obstacle will be to keep the article under two
thousand words. I want to narrate everything: how we were
planning a trip to Marjorca to celebrate my thirtieth birthday
when Len first experienced those ten-second lapses of consciousness and how it was as if someone had lifted the needle from the record of our talk and the music stopped. Then,
just as suddenly, the needle went down again and the music
continued, as if there had been no silence. I want to write
about how, in the beginning, we were going to fight. Two
hundred fifty rads of cobalt five days a week for a month.
A three-week recuperative vacation at Martha's Vineyard.
Vitamins. Rest. Special diets. Music. Humor. Laughter.
Poetry. "Do not go gentle into that good night." Cancer
was no longer a death sentence. The tumor could, the doctors said, lie dormant for two to five years. At 61, Len was
still young. He had more books to write, cities he longed
to see, days and years he was still hungry for.

I want to describe the loneliness of those days when Len
got worse and we rented the house in Chilmark and I drove
him every afternoon to the places he loved—to the Gay Head
Cliffs where we had once watched the sunsets, to Menemsha
where we had walked along the docks by the lobster boats,
to Lambert's Cove where the sand was seashell white—and
he was so groggy from the Dilantin he slumped in the front
seat beneath his terrycloth cap and sunglasses, too weak to
get out of the car. I must write about how I sometimes hated
him for ramming so much pain up against my 30-year-old
face whose lines I counted in the mirror each night, and yet
there were moments, watching him listening, with a far-
away stare, to the B-Minor Mass on the couch in Redding,
or when I would just say his name and that slow, sad smile

would float out of the whirlwind of his beard, and I knew that he was taking me deeper and closer into life than I had ever been before, that I was as close as I would ever get to God.

Note for section on sex and dating again: The oversexed widow is a bit hackneyed, dating back to Shakespeare and Chaucer's Wife of Bath with her legendary ''colt's tooth,'' widowed not once but five times. And yet, there may be some truth in the cliché. I am filled with an almost predatory sexual hunger these days, wanting Sean sometimes two and three times a day in all kinds of improbable places—in the kitchen, in the car, occasionally even in Sean's office at the university. It's not simply because I have gone so long without it. Or because Sean and I are becoming more sexually compatible. Or because of the infamous ticking of my biological clock. I am more passionate than I've ever been in my life because sex is the most radical and total way one can escape death. Lying beside a naked Sean, closing my eyes while he is kissing my breast or taking my clitoris in his mouth, the unbearable images of Len that still haunt me from time to time—Len two hours dead, Len in the satin-lined casket in the grave—dissolve like foam. When I am intent on taking pleasure or giving it, my mind and body focused on nothing except the building rhythms of erotic release—release from the body through the body with the body—I feel I shall implode with immortality. I cannot think of death. Len's death. My death. Sean's death. Death dies and dies and dies.

Building a new relationship (I'll have to skip the dating, because I never did that) may be more difficult, however. You're drawn to the new person because he possesses qualities that remind you of your dead husband: I am drawn to Sean because he is older and paternal, because he is an academic and writes books and is successful in his career and encourages me in mine. But he can never be Len. When I realize I cannot graft Sean onto my memories of Len, there is anger and resentment. For instance, Sean is far more stubborn than Len. This point is made clear during Sean's and my first major fight, which centers upon a poetry reading, of all ridiculous things.

I am eager to go to the reading and expect Sean to accompany me, since the poet is a local celebrity. Sean says he doesn't like to go out in the evenings, especially after a full day of teaching. The bookstore where the reading will be held is only ten minutes away; I point out that the reading can't last more than an hour. Sean is adamant. He wants to stay home. I am disappointed and angry and inwardly leap to the inevitable, destructive comparisons: Len would have gone with me, even if he were exhausted. I keep these observations to myself, until Sean starts telephoning about an ad for a used lawnmower, which, as it turns out, he must see that evening, upon which he informs me that he will drive me to the reading himself, stopping to look at the lawnmower on the way. That does me in. "You're too tired to go to a poetry reading but suddenly peppy when it comes to buying a Turbo Vent Jacobsen." I call him selfish, willful, a philistine and a fraud, knowing I am behaving like a three-year-old but unable to stop myself. We don't speak in the car, nor when I return that evening. Only the intervention of a third party—Sean's friend Steve Kern, who finds the entire episode comic—convinces us to "live and let live."

There are other times when I find, to my guilty surprise, that I am getting things from Sean that I did not get from Len. Sean's very unwillingness to "do my bidding" forces me to define more clearly who I am and what I want, something I did not do with Len, whose wishes and opinions rarely differed from mine. There is clearly no danger of my losing my identity to Sean; our bracing conflict assures that we remain two distinct, if disagreeing, selves. As much as I am exasperated by Sean's hard-headedness, I occasionally find it an instructive contrast to my own idealism, which Len never challenged. Sean won't shrink from telling me when my writing needs work. After he says that certain paragraphs in my latest essay are "overly sentimental," I rewrite and improve them. He also helps me to see my relationship with Len more clearly: He points out that Len must have felt tremendous sexual insecurity with me, in terror that I would leave him for a younger man. (This is true—Len would become wildly jealous if I even talked to another man at a party.) Sean thinks that Len's "worship" of me, worship that was intensified by my youth, good looks, and even my well-to-do New England background, was tinctured with fear. My relationship with Len, Sean charges, has spoiled me. I can't expect him or any man closer to my own age to love me so uncritically. "What you had with Len was a fairy tale," Sean is fond of saying. "I'm the real world."

Keeping faith with the dead and yet not distorting or sanctifying them—this is also the "work" of mourning. Sean leads me out of the underworld of grieving, where the air is motionless and I risk suffocation and solipsism. I return to the world to argue about poetry readings and lawnmowers, realism and idealism, power and dependency. I am back, without even realizing it, in life, in the vital push and shove of ideas, which is, after all, where I started from, where I was when Len was alive.

November 7, 1985: The anniversary of my wedding. The fourth if Len had lived. I receive telephone calls at my office from my family. Harriet phones first thing in the morning after she gets Mandy off to school. She says she didn't think sending a card would be appropriate (typical of Harriet to worry about what's appropriate), but she wanted me to know she had not forgotten the day and was thinking of me. I thank her for calling and confide that I wanted to observe my anniversary in some way but wasn't sure how. Her call helps. She says it's been a tough year for me, but it sounds like things are getting better. She asks how my writing is going, and I tell her about the "Widowhood at 30" article.

"Imagine my little sister writing for *Glamour*," she laughs. "Does this mean you're going to improve your sartorial splendor?" Definitely not, I joke. As we talk, trading good-humored sisterly jibes, I think: Harriet will probably always consider my marriage to Len an aberration, may even consider me an aberration, but I don't need to feel embittered toward her. I can tell her how much it means to me that she has remembered my wedding anniversary. In time, fewer and fewer people in my life will know the significance of November 7, 1981. But Harriet will remember. When she says, "Love you lots, Beck," I can reply, "I love you, too, Harr." And mean it.

My mother calls later in the morning to say she knows I'm probably feeling a little sad about "Leonardo." But "he blessed us all, dearie. I'll never forget how he helped me with my difficulties. We were lucky to have him among us for the time we did." I can't help but chuckle at the Biblical phrasing about "having him among us"—it makes Len sound like Moses or the "risen Christ," as my father put it. And yet, I'm grateful for my mother's affection for Len. Her genuine appreciation of him means far more to me than her not attending the wedding or the funeral. Her love for him even compensates for her shortcomings as a mother. For the rest of her life, I know I can count on her to speak of Len with affection and thus mirror back to me not only Len but my best self loving Len.

My father, whom I can count on not to canonize Len, calls after lunch to say that he too has not forgotten the day, then launches into a discussion of Len's fourth book and wonders what I'm doing, if anything, about getting it published. I explain that I'm waiting to hear from another editor on it, but that it may have to be cut down. A former student of Len's has written that he'd like to edit Len's unpublished writings, and I may just turn the book over to him, especially since I'm getting busier with my own writing. My father says that he occasionally dips into Len's books but complains that they're "too damned wordy. Why didn't Leonard ever learn to write a simple, declarative sentence?'' We've had this conversation before. I explain to my father that his quarrel is with philosophy rather than with Len's writing. ''You'd have the same reaction to Hegel or Heidegger,'' I point out. Then he tells me that at least my writing—he's referring to my first essay in the *Times,* which I sent him a few months ago—is clear and simple, if a bit on the grim side. I thank him and joke that optimism has never been my forté, inwardly praising myself for being less sensitive to his criticisms. He asks how life is ''in the land of barbed wire.'' When I jokingly assure him that I haven't turned into an S-barb, we discuss plans for Thanksgiving, and he says he's looking forward to meeting Sean.

My phone calls take up a good part of the day, after which I wander around the office on the seventh floor of Zulauf, wanting to create some private anniversary ceremony and yet unsure precisely what. I close the curtains against a setting sun blazing like a nuclear fireball across the plains and take out my wedding ring from its velvet gray box in my desk drawer. I haul out, from a cubbyhole behind the printer, a Marks and Spencer's shopping bag filled with ''Len'' memorabilia—the blue leather photo album that I had started to put together before he died, the folder of Len's letters to me that has accompanied me everywhere these past months, the blue-and-gold hand-crocheted coasters with the letters *L* and *R* that one of Len's patients gave him, a few miscellaneous stones and shells from Martha's Vineyard, a grainy, black-and-white photograph of Len as a boy that I had retouched and reframed a few months before he died. I arrange all these items, altar-like, on my desk, the boy Len in the center looking somber and shy as he poses, in tweed coat and knickers, in an armchair holding an open book, his adult counterpart a few inches away, secured in the ''wedding'' section beneath the laminated pages of my photo album, looking far more exuberant, if rumpled with age, in his white gabardine suit with his arm secured around the waist of his long-haired bride, she who smiles gaily in her

dusty rose Victorian gown and yet whose expression is like
that of the boy Len—diffident and uncertain. Then, I take
out my journal, a new one with a cerulean blue cover that
I bought last week in the campus bookstore.

*Dear Len—Four years ago, on a bright, windy November
day, I married you. In some ways, it was crazy, quixotic.
You were 32 years older, more than a generation removed
from me, and no one in our mutual families approved—your
children, my father, my sister. Even my mother, who adored
you and loves to quote you, said today that it was a shame
you were "so old" for me. You were. But even if I could
have seen the future on that clear, ocean-whipped day when
we posed for Harriet's camera beside the ivy-covered, brick
church on Water Street in Edgartown, even if I had known
that we would never celebrate our fourth wedding anniversary and you would be dying of a brain tumor before our
third, I still would have married you. In that brief time, you
gave more affirmation and affection than any human being
could possibly hope for. A sense of joy in life that was tonic
for my tendency toward depression. (How odd that you, so
much older, were far more hopeful than I, who was, after
all, young, with my life ahead of me. Does it have to do
with the changes we experience as we move closer to death,
the way we must mobilize all our mental and physical en-
ergies to stay alive, rendering despair a kind of indul-
gence?) And you gave me your love, a love that was big
enough to include not only me but art, poetry, music, travel,
people, and ideas—even your devotion to "the beast," Hector.*

*You gave me much in our brief time together, my Len. But
now, almost ten months after your death, I know that you
have given me as much in your death. I think you'd like the
person I've become. You'd probably find it amusing that I'm
writing this article for Glamour on Widowhood at 30. It's
not what you had in mind when you said, "Write a poem,
Beck." But I would tell you that I hope to make my living
as a writer, and I would show you the signed contract in*

which Condé Nast offers to pay me the fat sum of two thou-
sand dollars upon acceptance of my two thousand-word ar-
ticle, and I know you would be won over. Not only because
I'm making something of my talents as a writer but because
I've been able to order the chaos of my grieving into an
object outside myself, not perhaps into "art" yet, but maybe
into a preliminary "pencil sketch" that will herald a larger,
more serious work. I remember your telling me the story of
that patient who would call you in the wee hours of the
morning, threatening to swallow all the Valium in her med-
icine cabinet. She never made an actual attempt, and one
day you suggested that she try making a study of suicide,
recording not only her own thoughts but reading case his-
tories and studying suicide in different cultures. She stopped
seeing you after this, and you never knew whether she fol-
lowed your advice. But during these last months your advice
to her has haunted me. I'm sure that if you were alive, you
would rejoice in my writing about widowhood.

Losing you has made me stronger, Len. Not in the months
immediately after your death, when I wept every day and
felt isolated and angry at everyone—my family, my co-
workers at IWN, even Susan for giving me a birthday pres-
ent. Sometimes I was even angry at you for getting brain
cancer and ruining my easy, little life. I use my mother's
word "little" here deliberately, because I was, in truth,
"littler" before your death, squashed like a bug when one
of the women in my writing group trashed my novel or when
we didn't get invited to some dinner party and I was con-
vinced it was because of our age difference or when my
father would make one of his stupid jokes about my being a
grandmother. It's hard to explain, Len, but the experience
of placing your heavy, dead hands upon my head has been
a kind of baptism. The woman writing you this letter is a
different person from the girl you married. She is bolder,
more willing to take risks—whether it's the risk of giving up
her job or moving a thousand miles away to live with Sean.
She gets along better with her family—has forgiven them for
not approving of you, has stopped railing against them for

failing to fulfill her own impossible expectations of what a mother, father, and sister should be. She recognizes that no one but herself is responsible for what does or doesn't become of her, no one but herself can determine whether the adversity of your death will weaken or strengthen her.

It could have been different. Crisis breaks as many as it builds up. My life could have miscarried. I could have followed you into death, like Cynthia Koestler or Dora Carrington. I could have lived, but grown more bitter and isolated, turning to alcohol or pills or food. I might have retreated to bed like my mother during her "difficulties" or ended up on the back wards of some mental hospital nodding on lithium. I'm still not sure how I escaped such a fate: it has to do not only with my love for you, which would make such giving up a betrayal of you, but with other factors as well: my genetic heritage, which, for all my fears of weakness, has made me as tough a character as my father; my youth, which has helped me recover faster than I might if I were older; the money you left, which has given me the freedom to write and travel, even the fluke of meeting Sean in Oxford's Jericho ghetto.

You would like Sean. Tonight, if you came to dinner, which he cooks on Tuesdays and Thursdays so I can stay late at the office to write, you would enjoy lamb chops with a zinfandel sauce, roasted red peppers, with a dry white wine, followed by a strawberry tart and chocolate truffles. The food would be delicious, the table elegant, the conversation lively. Sean would show you around his house, and you would admire, as I did, the elephant-folio of Hogarth prints, the rugs from Beijing, the silver candelabra from Georgian Dublin. Sean would "draw you out" the way you like, asking you questions about doing therapy. You might talk about whether therapy helps people, and you would win Sean's confidence by saying you believe it does, but probably no more than a good relationship or work that you love. You might discuss me: Sean would tell you, jokingly, that he wished you hadn't adored me so much and behaved like such a "saint," because it has made coming after you dif-

ficult. You would laugh and tell him how you used to say I would appreciate you when you were gone and you're secretly pleased because your prophecy has come true. Still, you would agree, as Sean offers you another lamb chop, fills your glass with wine, entreats you to have another truffle, that it's wrong to compare a living man with a dead one, to create this impossible triangle with you, the invisible husband, in the middle. You would promise to discuss the problem next time you appeared to me in a dream.

You would stay late at Sean's because you'd be having a good time. Patricia Bonnet would come back on her bicycle from her evening class on Emily Dickinson, and she would sit at the table eating a slice of strawberry tart, and she would tell you about her plans to teach English in a girls' boarding school in Edinburgh next year. Deirdre would return from working as a checker at the Jewel, and you might tell her your funny story about being fired from the A & P when you were a teenager for stacking the canned vegetables in bizarre patterns. At midnight, you would rise reluctantly from the table and tell Deirdre and Patricia Bonnet you enjoyed meeting them. Then you would take Sean's hand and say how grateful you are that I wasn't alone on my wedding anniversary, how happy you are that I have found him and made an end to mourning.

Love—is anterior to Life—
Posterior—to Death—
Initial of Creation, and
The Exponent of Earth—

—Emily Dickinson

December 27, 1985

"What's it like to have lived so long?" I once asked Len shortly after we met when I was still, at 23, so young and so awed by this wise old man who had consented to be my lover, and I imagined I could take all his years and swallow them whole because then I'd understand life, then I would be wise.

I remember that day as if I had just pulled its still-warm image from a Polaroid camera. It was one of those bright, windy Saturdays in mid-March, one of the first days when you could go without a coat and people were sunning themselves along park benches and florists were displaying the first daffodils and forsythia along the sidewalks. Len and I had been tramping all over the city like characters in his favorite movie, *Children of Paradise,* which we'd just seen at the Carnegie Hall Cinema. We'd wandered up Broadway, past the mimes in front of Lincoln Center, past the patchwork of street vendors hawking their radios and watches along the sidewalks. We'd stopped at the corner of 72nd to buy fresh-squeezed papaya juice from an outdoor cart, and since we had two more hours until I would go home to Brian, the man I would leave to marry Len, we kept walking, ending up at Riverside Park, where we stopped to lean against the rusty filigreed iron railing and watch the barges steaming up the Hudson.

Len had a gift for storytelling, and I had a gift for listening. That day, I pressed him for stories that took place before I was born. He told me about the crash of '29 and how

265

his father lost all his money and the bank repossessed the family's home. He talked about his break with his best friend, Irving, who became a communist in the 40s. He remembered his year as an intern at St. Elizabeth's Hospital in Washington, D.C., after the war, where he was almost fired because he refused to assist at a lobotomy. He talked about seeing Ezra Pound, who was then a patient at St. Elizabeth's, reading in a lawn chair on the grounds.

"What funny questions you ask." He had laughed when I'd asked him what it was like to have so many memories. We stood listening to the water slapping against the oily, wooden piles, while he thought. The wind caught his unkempt, thinning hair and stood it on end, and his blue eyes were so dilated that he looked as if he were on LSD. He wasn't. This was just his way of being in the world, looking rumpled and crazy, a little "meshuga."

"It's not that different from when you're young," he had said, in a rush of words as he often did. "After a while, the years blend together, and it just feels," and here he drew a deep breath and fixed upon me that eager, childlike smile that had beguiled so many women before me, "like one long day."

One long day. It was more a poet's answer than a philosopher's, conjuring up those timeless metaphors of morning's youth and manhood's noon and night's old age. But what made me remember it, even more than the image, was the way he had said it. With such feeling. As if he had been blessed to have been given all those mornings and midnights, blessed to have had the energy to be first doctor, then philosopher, then psychiatrist, to have married, to have had children, divorced, written books, had affairs, lived in Europe, hiked in the Grand Canyon, and taught in Switzerland. Blessed to have witnessed six decades of the century's history, to have remembered people selling apples on the streets of New York in the depression and heard Hitler's speeches over the radio in World War II and lived on the Left Bank in Paris in the 50s and demonstrated against the

Vietnam War in the 60s. All these experiences and so many others I would never know Len had jammed into the one long day of his life. And even though Len's face, skin slackening and sand-blasted, revealed how hard that long day had been, he was, as he took my arm and we marched up the Hudson, still exuberant. He was almost as young as I was.

On this sub-zero degree afternoon of December 27, 1985, the first anniversary of Len's death, as I pull my ski mask down over my face and follow my loping shadow across the snowswept plains, I am still shocked that the long day of Len's life is over, that there will be for him no more windy March afternoons, no more Decembers. It is still hard to understand that I will pass through the second and the third, perhaps even the thirtieth and the fortieth anniversary of his death without ever taking his arm or hearing him laugh. And yet, as I watch the blue-ringed sun descend into layers of frigid mist on the horizon, I know that his passing into "death's dateless night" is a mystery my day-bound, summer-and-winter-bound imagination will never comprehend. Perhaps the dead, traveling at twice the speed of light and dancing on the edge of a universe curved back on itself, know why time takes us fast or slow through our lives, where we go when the birthdays stop. Perhaps Len, away these 365 days and wise with the knowledge of stars, knows. Maybe, in 30 or 40 years, when my pulse stops and a stranger shuts me up in this snowy earth, I will see Len again and be wise, too.

Until then, I will turn back toward the warmth of Sean's kitchen and follow the path of telephone poles past the tin-can buildings of the De Kalb Forge and the squat little bungalows of Thirteenth Street coughing smoke out of their chimneys. I will consider, as I watch the householders drawing their curtains against the frosted dark, how much there is to be done in the long day of my life. Books I want to write. A man I hope to marry. Children I yearn to bear. Countries I plan to visit. A new century I expect to see. I know I cannot survive my remaining decades without bearing more loss. My marriage may fail. My books may be rejected. My children may turn against me. Soon, my body will begin its slow decline. My face will wrinkle, my eyesight will blur; the eggs in my ovaries will pass away. I will grow old, and age will bring more death—deaths of my mother and father, of friends, perhaps of a husband again.

All I can hope for is that I will, like Len, love these days more passionately as they pass. Love the smell of pot roast in Sean's kitchen and the glass of full-bodied burgundy and our plans for a winter vacation in Mexico. Love the sounds of my mother's and father's and sister's voices as they call to say they are thinking of me on the first anniversary of Len's death. Love the haunted hours of this freezing December night as I press my face against Sean's chest and listen gratefully for his breaths. Love my memories of Len marching up the Hudson with me on his arm.